Narrating China's Governance

People's Daily, Department of Commentary

Narrating China's Governance

Stories in Xi Jinping's Speeches

Translated by
Jing Luo

人民出版社 **Springer** Open

People's Daily,
Department of Commentary
Beijing, China

ISBN 978-981-32-9177-5   ISBN 978-981-32-9178-2   (eBook)
https://doi.org/10.1007/978-981-32-9178-2

Jointly published with People's Publishing House
The print edition is not for sale in China Mainland. Customers from China Mainland please
order the print book from: People's Publishing House.

This Springer imprint is published by the registered company Springer Nature Singapore
Pte Ltd.
The registered company address is: 152 Beach Road, #21-01/04 Gateway East, Singapore
189721, Singapore

PREFACE: ELABORATING ON THE GOVERNANCE OF CHINA BY TELLING STORIES

A brief review of the world's history suggests that famous statesmen and thinkers have the common characteristic of being apt at telling stories. It is a tradition and a notable ability of the leaders of the Communist Party of China (CPC) to tell stories. At the closing ceremony of the Seventh National Congress of the CPC held in Yan'an, Chairman Mao Zedong narrated the story of "the foolish old man who removed the mountains" before the Party representatives. The story is that every day a foolish old man incessantly tried to dig up the mountains. Moved by his persever-ance, God sent a celestial being to earth to remove the two mountains from in front of his house. Through this story, Chairman Mao made clear that the CPC would even move the emotions of "God" as long as it benefited the revolution. For the Chairman, this "God" represented all Chinese civilians, with the "two mountains" being imperialism and feudalism.

Secretary-General Xi Jinping is a master of telling stories. He is skilled at conveying profound meanings and affecting others through his story-telling, and such skill can be seen in his speeches to congress, talks dur-ing investigations, addresses during state visits, and articles published in newspapers. His stories are concrete and vivid, understandable and pro-found, and they glow with "Chinese wisdom" and "Chinese strength". To some extent, they reflect the profound humanistic consciousness and philosophic thought that distinctly characterize his style of leadership.

It is said that one story is better than a dozen arguments. At seminars with youth representatives on China's Youth Days in 2013 and 2014,

Xi Jinping encouraged young people to make the best use of their time and study as much as possible by citing anecdotes from his own life about reading. When he lived and worked in Shaanxi Province as an "educated youth", he never stopped reading, even while herding sheep on mountain slopes or hoeing the fields. The recounting of his experiences of reading is much more vivid and affecting than the narration of historical figures' feats of arduous study.

The *People's Daily* once published an article titled *The Flavor of the Faith*, which narrates the anecdote of when Chen Wangdao was translating *The Communist Manifesto*. His concentration was so strong that he mistook the ink for brown sugar and unconsciously ate it. This story embodied the sweet flavor of the communists' spirit and faith. To inspire the Party members and officials to maintain their ideals and keep their faith, Xi Jinping has repeatedly told this touching story of the Party's history.

In his speech at the Meeting Commemorating the 50th Anniversary of the Establishment of China-France Diplomatic Relations delivered on March 27, 2014, Xi Jinping said, "Napoleon Bonaparte once compared China to a 'sleeping lion' and observed that 'when she wakes she will shake the world'. Today, China, the lion, has awakened, but it is a peaceful, amicable and civilized lion." Such contradictory but meaningful narration cleverly rebutted the "Chinese threat theory" and communicated to the world the value of the Chinese dream.

A Chinese saying goes, "Telling a good story will help you yield twice the result with half the effort." China's excellent traditional culture is interspersed with colorful stories and anecdotes. We cannot read them only from the perspectives of various ancient Chinese schools of thought, but rather, we should read them through the lens of popular legends. Everlasting and unfading over time, these stories and anecdotes affect the ideas and lives of generations. Story has a magic power to quickly establish an emotional connection between the narrator and the audience and to create an ideological resonance between them. Abstract conceptions can never match the ability of narrative details to convey conviction. However, with regard to narration, even the most consummate narrative techniques can never match the capacity of real sentiment to move audiences.

The ancient Chinese proposed that "writing is a means of conveying truth." Regardless of whether he is at home or abroad, the stories and anecdotes told by Xi Jinping are his means of communicating the Chinese "way" of sharing historic culture, the Chinese "way" of approaching reform and development, and the Chinese "way" of participating in world governance and building a community of fate with the other countries of the world. He likes to guide audiences toward the "way" by explaining the profound in simple terms and enlightening them as to the "way" by giving them systematic guidance. At home, he communicates the Party's policies so that they penetrate audiences' minds and hearts through down-to-earth expressions to build consensus on reform and development. Abroad, he puts forth effort to establish new concepts, domains, and expressions that are understood by both China and the rest of the world, so that China's development advantages and comprehensive strengths can be converted into advantages of international speech. This is why Xi's stories are fascinating and thought provoking.

Xi expounds upon the Chinese "way" of sharing historic culture by telling stories. It is an important ruling style of Xi Jinping to seek out notable stories in the treasure trove of historical material. As he has commented, "For any country in the world, the past always holds the key to the present, and the present is always rooted in the past. Only when we know where a country has come from can we possibly understand why the country is what it is today, and only then can we realize in which direction it is heading." He often makes the past serve the present by quoting ancient fables, fairy tales, and historical events to explain the present and reality in a clever way, in hopes that people will learn from them and acquire wisdom and knowledge to enhance self-cultivation and doing well in their work. For instance, in his night talk at Yingtai with then-US President Barack Obama, Xi described the history of Yingtai: "Yingtai witnessed many historic events. The Qing Emperor Kangxi made the policies there to pacify civil strife and recover Taiwan from the Ming loyalists. Emperor Guangxu, who had launched the Hundred Days of Reform when the dynasty began to fall into decay, was imprisoned by Empress Dowager Cixi after his modernizing reform failed." Hearing this story, Obama sighed with emotion, "China and the US share that aspect of history-that reform nearly always encounters resistance and demands courage to push forward." Xi concluded, "Knowing the modern history of China is of great importance to understanding the Chinese people's ideals today and their path toward development."

Xi expounds upon the Chinese "way" of reform and development by telling stories. Since the 18th National Congress of the CPC, the central leadership with Xi Jinping as general secretary has formed new concepts, new ideas, and new strategies for the governance of China. President Xi Jinping's series of important speeches is a highly concentrated expression of new concepts, new ideas, and new strategies. In his speeches, he is skillful at building consensus as well as clearing up confusion and reassuring misgivings by telling stories, citing instances, and presenting facts. In doing so, he makes abstract theories and abstruse principles easy to understand. With his anecdote of swimming in Xiamen, Fujian Province, in the 1980s, he once exemplified that to cross the "river" of reform, we should know well the nature of water, and we should employ both the methods of strengthening top-level design and crossing the river stone by stone and understanding this steady approach as an important means of promoting reform. He also related "his memory of Liangjiahe in northern Shaanxi Province" to express his affection toward grassroots activists and his wish that we remain true to our original aspirations in reform and development: "We rely on the people of the CPC for our survival. We must bear in mind the purpose of serving the people wholeheartedly. We should always remember that we are the servants of the people and take the people's fundamental interests to heart."

Xi explains the Chinese "way" of great power diplomacy by telling stories. He employs a warm, down-to-earth tone, succinct without a loss of profundity. These are the characteristics of Xi's speeches on international occasions. He has already built a weighty "brand" on the platform of international politics with a fresh style of speech and a unique charm. The concepts of the Chinese Dream, cooperation and mutual benefits, sound values of justice and benefit, Asian security, the community of common destiny, and the path of peaceful development convey a powerful diplomacy with Chinese characteristics, made easy to understand, remember, communicate, and accept as Xi has blended them into the stories he has told in his speeches. In the speech delivered at the State Great Khural of Mongolia on August 22, 2014, Xi Jinping stated, "China wishes to provide Mongolia and other neighboring countries with both opportunities and space for common development. All countries are welcome to get on board the express train of China's development and hitch a lift. As the saying goes, 'If you want to go fast, go alone; if you want to go far, go together.'" "Hitch a lift" was originally an expression used by some countries to mock and discredit China. Yet this derogatory expression was cleverly transformed by Xi Jinping into an expression that not only refutes the misrepresented "China responsibility theory" but also conveys China's diplomatic concept of cooperation and mutual benefit.

A philosopher once said, "The people who are good at telling stories will win the support of the audience, and then they will win the right of speech." Both history and reality tell us that only if a statesman has a deep understanding of the history and culture of his country, insight into the trends of world civilization and the ability to tell his people and foreign friends in an understandable way about his concept of governing his country and such concept is understood and recognized by the people can he serve his country as a good ship's captain and steer his country to victory after sailing through stormy seas.

The further into the past one looks, the farther forward one is likely to see. Theory is gray, but stories are colorful. As a saying goes, "Once the roots are established, the Way will grow therefrom." What inspired us to compile this book, *Narrating China's Governance: Stories in Xi Jinping's Speeches*, was that we hope to show readers a way of learning the art of consensus and help them understand how to manage state affairs, to tell the stories of China more compellingly, and to write new stories of China together.

Beijing, China   Yang Zhenwu
                                                                          President of the *People's Daily*

INTRODUCTION

UNDERSTANDING CHINA THROUGH XI JINPING'S NARRATIVE ON GOVERNANCE

Stories provide the logic underwriting the narrator's arguments, concepts, thinking, and foresight including his persona and establishes a channel of communion with his audience leaving an indelible impression is if s/he is the master storyteller or narrator. The Storytellers was an important school of thought during Han Dynasty in China, which was classified under the category of "Masters and Philosophers" along with the likes of Taoists, Confucians, Legalists, Mohists, etc. The novellas or short stories section in the *Complete Library in Four Sections* (Sikuquanshu), a compilation running into over 36,000 volumes ordered by Emperor Qianlong in 1773, includes 123 books ranging from Han to Sui Dynasty of which the *New Account of Tales of the World* (Shishuoxinyu) is the most famous collection. Though the book includes miscellaneous stories including those of supernatural, but what is the most striking feature of the book is the style of the narration and commentaries which make an instant connect with the reader.

In the same vein, *Narrating China's Governance: Stories in Xi Jinping's Speeches* strikes an instant chord with the narratee and compels the latter to seek more information which to a large extent has been provided in the accompanied commentaries at the end of each story. With genuine creativity, Xi Jinping engages his audience in a sort of conversation, where moods and sentiments of the narrator are mirrored in the narratee with elements of refreshing surprises. Notwithstanding, Xi Jinping's educational background of chemical engineering, he eloquently and passionately takes us through the entire journey of Chinese civilization from ancient to contemporary times. The tapestry that has been woven tells us the beauty and grandeur of China's landscape; the words of wisdom from sagacious personages like Confucius, Mencius, and others; literary spectacles of the giants like Si Maqian, Li Bai, Du Fu, Bai Juyi, etc.; valor, heroism, and patriotism of Yue Fei and many unsung heroes of the Chinese revolution, pain, and agony caused by the destruction, barbarity, and humiliation of a century; the heroic struggle of the people in the revolution led by Mao Zedong; the trials and tribulations of the Cultural Revolution, miracle of the four decades of reforms initiated by Deng Xiaoping; and stories about the Chinese dream, rejuvenation of the Chinese nation, the Silk Road Spirit offering the new global good—the Belt and Road initiative and much more has been narrated with passion and profundity. Xi Jinping has shunned formalism and has advocated short and crisp writing, no wonder he refers to Mao Zedong's epitaph dedicated to the Monument to the People's Heroes which summaries the entire modern history of China in just 14 characters! It is for the same reason that he appreciates the Government Work Report drafted by Deng Xiaoping in 1975, which for the first time advocated the "Four Modernizations" for China.

Although *Narrating China's Governance: Stories in Xi Jinping's Speeches* is divided into only two sections, namely, domestic affairs and foreign affairs; however, besides covering the facets mentioned above, could be further classified into stories about Xi's people-oriented thought, anti-corruption crusade, and poverty alleviation; stories about China's traditional value system and cultural soft power; the miracle of the reforms and rejuvenation of the Chinese nation; the Belt and Road initiative and the idea of common development, common prosperity, and common security in the region and beyond; people to people and cultural exchanges; socialism with Chinese characteristics as the development path of China, etc.

First and foremost, the "people-oriented thought" remains at the core of Xi Jinping's governance of China, essentially the reinforcement of China ancient philosophical thought. The Chinese dream, the goal of "two centenaries", his tirade against the "tigers and flies", reinforcing the "mass line" as a fundamental of the Party, providing the best public services and goods to the people of China and beyond in the form of state-of-the-art infrastructure including the high-speed rails, the length of which was more than doubled during his first term in office, as well as promoting close people-to-people relations as far as China's relations with foreign countries are concerned. Anti-corruption campaign has been an ongoing crusade aimed at providing the people a clean government with good governance. "Governance lies in reassuring the people; reassuring the people lies in observing their suffering." "Dispelling the suffering of the people is like treating your own severe illness." These two ancient adages form a microcosm of Xi's people-oriented thought (p. 59).

Xi has elucidated his point by using anecdotes and telling stories of the ancient incorruptible and upright officials. While on investigation tours in the interiors of China, he has cited the examples of clean and righteous officials to drive home his point. For example, while in Lankao, Henan province, he narrates the story of Zhang Boxing (1652–1725) of Lankao who had told the people that "Though a thread of silk or a grain of rice is tiny, it concerns my reputation. Though a cent or a dime is negligible, it is derived from the hard-earned wealth of the people." With the anecdotes of Zhu Geliang (181–234) and Sima Guang (1019–1086) as regards their honesty and diligence, Xi Jinping exemplified the political attainments that the Party officials must have. By using the tragedy of "Farewell My Concubine" as a metaphor, he also cautioned Party officials and members that a poor work style will cause the Party to lose the support of the masses and push the Party and country to end in tragedy (p. 30). He also cites the downfall of the flourishing Tang Dynasty (618–907) to emphasize that corruption is a cancer of society and to remind the whole Party to take history as a mirror, to learn the historical lessons, and to fight unswervingly against corruption.

In 2018, when I listened to President Xi Jinping's New Year message, the line that struck me most was "Can I get a big broad shelter a thousand, ten thousand spans wide, huge roof that all the world's poor people can share with smiling faces?" This I thought was the most powerful message conveyed to the domestic as well as international audience while revealing his own conscientiousness toward the sufferings of the people. Xi Jinping has expressed his resolve to eradicate poverty by 2020 so as a moderately prosperous society in all aspect is established when China celebrates the first Centenary in 2021, i.e., the hundred years of the establishment of the Communist Party of China. Invoking "To be the first in the country to worry about the affairs of the state and the last in the country to enjoy oneself" quote from the famous Chinese reformer Fan Zhongyan (989–1052), Xi narrates heart-wrenching stories as to how some of the Party officials such as Jiao Yulu turned around the fortune of poverty-stricken Lankao by planting paulownia for windbreaks and sand fixation, and in turn converting paulownia as a major industry in Lankao with an annual output value of RMB 6 billion yuan by 2014 (p. 86). In the same vein, when he was in Ningde, an extremely poor region in Fujian, Xi Jinping traveled through all the nine counties under Ningde and fully pulled it out of poverty. When he left the post from Ningde, 94% of the poverty-stricken households in the region had had their problems of food and clothing solved (p. 105).

Xi Jinping has attached importance to extensive field investigations through which an individual is identified with the masses on the one hand and he gets to know about the empirical realities on the other. It is in this context that he has referred to the Xunwu County investigation in Jiangxi by Mao Zedong in 1930. It was an extensive 185-page investigation whereby Mao got to know about the bewildering social, political, and economic complexities of the rural Jiangxi. It is the same context where he tells stories about "learning and thinking" invoking adages from Confucius (551 BC–479 BC) and Xun Zi (?–238 BC). According to Xun Zi, "if you do not climb a high mountain, you will be unaware of the height of the sky. If you do not look down into a deep gorge, you will be unaware of the thickness of the earth." Therefore, Xi Jinping's commitment to practicality and achievability is demonstrated by his field investigations before and after assuming the supreme leadership of the Party. For example, in December 2012, just after assuming office, he braved the snow and severe cold blizzards and traveled through the narrow and bumpy roads to get to the depth of Taihang Mountain, one of the poorest areas of China (p. 217). The same is true when he served as County Party Secretary of Zhengding, Hebei, as he toured all the villages under Zhengding, going on foot or riding his bicycle. While serving in Fuzhou and Ningde, he traveled to all townships under them.

Second, as China continues to advance economically and endeavors toward realizing the two centenaries, Xi Jinping sees the stimuli in China's traditional value system and cultural soft power and the dialogs between the civilizations. It is for this reason that he dumps the "clash of civilizations" theory of Huntington and approves the paradigm of "learning from civilizations." According to him, it is the civilizational interaction that has enriched cultures and civilizations and enhanced understanding between the people and nations. Undoubtedly, the inter-civilizational exchange is fundamental to the community of shared future. It was the unhindered circulation of ideas, technology, objects, and people that enriched these civilizations. Whether it was the birth of Chinese Buddhism or the dissemination of western regions' astronomy, literature, music, languages into China, or technologies such as sugar making, paper manufacturing, steel smelting, silk, porcelain, tea, etc. traveling from China to the world enriched the knowledge systems across the world beyond doubt. Moreover, this happened owing to the unimpeded flow of the people.

Xi Jinping reveals that during the golden period of the Chinese civilization, i.e., the Tang Dynasty, of all its foreign ministers 29 were foreigners, while the number of foreigners serving as officials were as many as 3,000. There is a detailed analysis of Tang's prosperity and openness in the *Study in History* by Wang Guowei which states, "In the South China Sea, there are merchant ships from the Arab Empire. In Chang'an, there are Zoroastrian temples built by Persians. Foreigners flock here like they are returning home because the Tang Dynasty is in the middle of its heyday" (p. 171). Therefore, it is of little surprise that Xi has been invoking the Spirit of the Chinese culture as well as the 'Silk Road Spirit' which he says favors peace and cooperation, openness and inclusiveness, mutual learning and mutual benefits. He tells us the story of Kasyapa Matanga and Dharmaraksa, two eminent monks from India, arriving in Luoyang, China in 67 AD where they translated the *Sutra of Forty-two Chapters*, the first ever Chinese translation of Buddhist scriptures. Xi also tells us stories of the white horse carrying Buddhist scriptures to China and scholar-monk Xuanzang's pilgrimage to the west, and the great Chinese navigator Zheng He's seven voyages into the Indian Ocean who irrespective of having a brute force never seized an inch of foreign land. The unearthing of the 20 pieces of Roman and West Asian colored glaze from the underground palace of Famen Temple Pagoda in 1987, tells the same story of unimpeded civilizational exchange (p. 314). Therefore, as rightly said by Xi Jinping, "civilizations have become richer and more colorful through exchanges and mutual learning."

Third, through Xi's stories, we travel through the entire period of Chinese modern history and then on to the miracle of Chinese reforms. If the ancient history of China was of civilizational glory and dialog, the modern history of China (1840–1949) has been termed as a century of humiliation and lost opportunities. This was the time, when China was humiliated, its sovereignty infringed upon, and its people bullied by foreigners to quote from one of Xi Jinping's speeches from the *Governance of China* (p. 189), a clear reference to China's defeat in the Opium Wars (1840, 1856), Sino-French War (1875), the Sino-Japanese War (1895), and the War of Resistance Against Japanese Aggression (1931–1945). Largely this is the period when China was forced to sign humiliating unequal treaties and lost precious opportunities to rise as a power (pp. 169, 191). For example, between 1842 and 1895, Japan and Russia could modernize but not China; between 1912 and 1945 though China established a republic but could not modernize, this was the period when late entrants like Turkey did turn over their economy. Another lost opportunity was during the late 1950s and the period of the Cultural Revolution (1966–1976), the period when the labor-intensive industries moved from developed countries to developing countries, China lost but Korea, Singapore, and Chinese Taipei developed rapidly. Chinese, however, do believe in their own saying that "the crop that is sown late ripe early," for it took the UK and US almost 150 years to realize the modernization; Germany, France, and other European countries on the contrary did it in 70 years; with this logic, China could realize its modernization even faster. I myself have been a student of China studies since 1986 and a witness to the earth-shaking changes since 1991 when I visited China for the first time. I have been mystified by the developments in China, and have no definite answers as my understanding remains inconclusive and incomprehensive, albeit I am not in the category of those who characterized the reforms in China as the westernization, and predicted the disintegration of China, or China moving toward the western democracy. The following figures answer some of the questions partially.

After 40 years of reforms and opening up, China's per capita GDP reached over 9000 US dollars in 2018 from the meager 384 US dollars in 1978. As revealed by Xi Jinping in his speech marking the 40th anniversary of reforms and opening up on December 18, 2018, the share of China's GDP in the global GDP has risen from 1.8% at the beginning of reform and opening up to 15.2%, and its contribution to world economic growth has exceeded 30% over the years. The total import and export volume of China's goods has increased from 20.6 billion US dollars to more than 4 trillion US dollars. In the last 40 years, 740 million people have been alleviated from the poverty, and the urbanization has reached 55.26%. Today China boasts of 22,000 km of Hi-Speed railways (largest in the world), 123,000 km of expressways nonexistent prior to the reforms. China didn't have a single private enterprise prior to the reforms, at present there are over 20 million!

In *Narrating China's Governance,* Xi Jinping demystifies some of these figures by telling the stories of some of the unsung heroes who have been behind such an astounding success. For example, Xi tells the story of Zheng Chunlin who irrespective of being differently abled raised minks and provided employment to dozens of families in the 1980s in Zhengding County, Hebei (pp.155–57). Millions of migrant laborers were equal partners in this success story. With the restructuring of the Chinese economy gradually taking shape during recent times, Xi Jinping narrates how innovation and supply-side structural reforms are taking place in China. He tells us how smart terminal products produced in Chongqing, especially laptops accounted for one-third of global laptop production in 2014. The BOE Technology Group Co., Ltd., the Chongqing company to which Xi Jinping paid an inspection visit, has become world's leading suppliers of the semiconductor display technologies, products, and services, with a marketing and service system covering Europe, the US, Asia, and other major regions (p. 163). Nonetheless, the miracle of the reforms has been accompanied by great damage to the ecological environment, here again, Xi cites examples of world's top eight pollution incidents that killed thousands of people (p. 207). Therefore, building a sound ecosystem remains an important element of Xi Jinping's governance stories, which is demonstrated by his APEC Blue story.

This has been possible, for the Chinese people according to Xi Jinping has chosen the present path, theory, and system in the course of historical explorations. Adhering to the notion of Chinese thought of continuity, Xi sees the development of socialism as a continuous phenomenon that has been advanced by all his predecessors irrespective of differences in guiding principles, thinking, and policies during the revolution, development, reforms, etc. phases. The path which is economic development remains the main priority guided by the theory developed by first to his generation of the Chinese leadership, and guaranteed by such a political and economic system that is rule based. The system has been successful in guaranteeing unity, diversity, social cohesion, and peaceful development; therefore, rather than abandoning the system, it would be further improved, and perfected albeit requiring discipline from the party and government officials.

Fourth, in section two, dedicated to China's foreign affairs, Xi Jinping narrates thought-provoking tales of friendship, people-to-people bonds, common development, and prosperity. The stories about people who stood by China during the times of war and barbarity rekindles the touching memories of Norman Bethune from Canada, Dwarkanath Kotnis from India, Jean Bussiere from France, Michael Lindsay from Great Britain, Hans Schippe from Germany, Bernhard Arp Sindberg from Denmark, etc., who tirelessly and selflessly helped Chinese people when in the abyss of sufferings during the War of Resistance Against Japanese Aggression. John Magee, an American who regarded China as his "home", was in Nanjing, and secretly filmed the Japanese atrocities inflicted on Chinese people by the Japanese during the Nanjing Massacre of 1938. The story of "The Flying General" Tang Duo, the lone Chinese pilot who fought with the Luftwaffe in the Soviet Union, Poland, and Germany, and Air Marshal Aleksej Sergejevič Blagoveščenski's fighter plane company composed of Chinese and Soviet pilots destroying 36 of the Japanese fighters during Wuhan air raids are equally thrilling.

Xi Jinping affectionately telling these stories while feeling indebted toward these foreign friends also reminds us that peace is not easily come by, and it must be resolutely defended. Other stories, be it the stories of Pablo Neruda and Jose Venturelli of Chile or Antonio Fernandez Arce and Guillermo Da Ino Ribatto of Peru or the Peruvian gold inlaid with Chinese jade used in the gold medals for the 2008 Olympic Games, or the "Love of Africa" group in Zimbabwe doing a brilliant job in ameliorating the condition of Zimbabwean orphans, or Xi's special meeting with the Manorma Kotnis, sister of Doctor Dwarkanath Kotnis in 2014, etc. speak volume about the universal brotherhood and the internationalist spirit of these people. The tale of an Arabian restaurant in Yiwu City opened by Muhamad from Jordan or the story of Valentina and Ruslan from Khzakistan reveals how people have integrating their own dreams with the Chinese dream of happiness and success. According to Xi Jinping, the Chinese dream is never closed or isolated, but it is interlinked with dreams of people around the world (p. 259). Chinese football team under Milutinovic qualifying for its first appearance at the World Cup, and Mexico under Ma Jin sweeping all eight gold medals for diving events at the 2011 Pan-American Games demonstrates that mutual cooperation can do wonders and that developing together is much better than developing by oneself (p. 267). This is what exactly he means by the Silk Road Spirit which is all about peace, cooperation, openness, inclusiveness, mutual learning, and mutual benefit.

Finally, I have found *Narrating China's Governance: Stories in Xi Jinping's Speeches* extremely thought provoking, vivid and lifelike, simple but profound reflecting the historical and present realities of China, reflecting a strong sense of continuity and connectedness, be it the Chinese society, Communist Party of China, or China's relations with its neighbors and major powers. It remains a must read not only for the domestic but especially the foreign readers who wish to know more about the Chinese leader, his governance of China, and the course China may be taking in future.

B. R. Deepak, Ph.D.
Professor and Chairperson
Center of Chinese and Southeast
Asian Studies
Jawaharlal Nehru University
New Delhi, India

CONTENTS

PART I

About Domestic Affairs

CHAPTER 1

Stories of Incorrupt Government: "The Corruption and Unjustness of Officials Give Birth to the Decline of Governance"

REFUSING GOLD WITH THE FOUR KNOWS

There is a famous story in Chinese history. Yang Zhen, an official of the Eastern Han Dynasty, was transferred from the Prefectural Governor of Jingzhou to the Prefecture Chief of Donglai. On his way to Donglai to assume office, when he traveled to Changyi, Wang Mi, the County Governor of Changyi, who had been recommended by him when he was the Prefectural Governor of Jingzhou, heard of his arrival and visited him empty-handed during the day. However, that night, to repay him for his recommendation and help, Wang intended to make Yang a present of ten catties of gold, saying, "It's late at night now, so no one will know." Yang responded, "The heaven knows, the earth knows, you know, and I know. How could you say nobody knows?" Wang felt ashamed to hear that. As an official, Yang was honest and upright. In reply to the advice of his friends and elders to purchase properties for his scions, he always said, "I'll bequeath the title 'descendant of an incorruptible official' to them. It's a rich legacy, isn't it?" This is truly the consciousness of incorruption.

– Speech at the Seventh Plenary Session of the 18th CPC Central Commission for Discipline Inspection (January 6, 2017).

© People's Publishing House 2020
People's Daily, Department of Commentary,
Narrating China's Governance,
https://doi.org/10.1007/978-981-32-9178-2_1

Commentary

China has had many stories of incorruptible officials since ancient times. For example, Yang Xu hung the fish that his subordinates presented to him outside as a refusal of bribes, Zihan treasured the morality of incorruption, Kong Fen said no to embezzling money when he was an official in an economically developed area, and Bao Zheng did not take even an inkstone as he left office. Similarly, Yang Zhen's stories of "refusing gold with the four knows" and "bequeathing the reputation for incorruptibility to descendants" have endured.

Yang Zhen, whose courtesy name was Boqi, was born in Huayin, Shaanxi Province. He was a famous scholar in the Eastern Han Dynasty. Entering the political stratum at the age of 50 and eventually reaching a position among the Three Counselors of State, he kept himself free from corruption and bribery throughout his official career. The deed of "refusing gold with the four knows" was originally recorded in the *Book of the Later Han-Biography of Yang Zhen*. It was also written in the *Biography of Yang Zhen* that, "Yang Zhen was so impartial and incorrupt that he always refused private visits. His children and grandchildren often ate vegetables and went out on foot. An elder among his old friends proposed that he should start some businesses for his descendants. However, he retorted, 'I'll bequeath the title 'descendant of an incorruptible official' to them. It's a rich legacy, isn't it?'"

Because of the story "Refusing Gold with the Four Knows", the later generations often called him "Four Knows Yang", "Prefecture Chief Four Knows" or "Mr. Four Knows", and the Yang Ancestral Hall and Four Knows Hall were preserved in the government compound of Laizhou until the Ming Dynasty. Hu Ceng, a poet of the Tang Dynasty, praised Yang in the *Poem on History- The Land West of Hanguguan*, "Yang Zhen was dead and buried in the land west of Hanguguan, where it is bleak and desolate. However, he left the good reputation of 'the four knows' in the world, which will last forever."

Yang not only exercised self-control to protect himself from immorality but he also had the courage to criticize abuses in officialdom, even daring to speak out against the imperial family. Geng Bao, an uncle on the maternal side of Emperor An of Han, Yan Xian, the brother of the empress and some other kinsmen of the emperor had recommended their relatives or friends to him for official positions. Knowing the candidates' lack of conscience and ability, he always gave them a flat refusal.

Such superior moral quality and family tradition are the noble heritage of his descendants. According to historical records, Yang's family remained incorruptible and maintained the family tradition of rectitude for four generations. His son, Yang Bing, lived secluded in a village and made a career of teaching until the age of 40, when he went out of the village and started his official career. Adopting his father's style, "Yang Bing was celebrated for incorruptibility, shutting the door in the face of a former subordinate who proposed to offer him a large bribe." Yang Bing's son, Yang Ci, a grand commandant, as well as Yang Qi and Yang Biao, the great grandsons of Yang Zhen, all followed the family tradition of rectitude. Yang Zhen's incorruptible deed of "bequeathing the reputation of incorruptibility to one's descendants" has been retold throughout the ages.

At the Seventh Plenary Session of the 18th CPC Central Commission for Discipline Inspection, Xi Jinping emphasized that, "The leaders and officials of the Party must value consciousness and must be conscious. Consciousness and consciousness-raising will guide us to the right side of conduct." He recounted Yang Zhen's stories of "refusing gold with the four knows" and "bequeathing the reputation for incorruptibility to descendants" to illustrate the importance of consciousness for a person to gain a foothold in society, start his career, expound his ideas in writing, and cultivate morality. Only a conscious person can distinguish right from wrong and encourage healthy trends while dispelling perverse ones. Consciousness is the "touchstone" of one's ideological attainment. In the face of contradictions between publicness and privateness, righteousness and self-interest, right and wrong, good and evil, as well as pain and pleasure, that which directs one's choices is consciousness.

Pertinent Dictums and Deep Truths

Mei Cheng, a scholar of the Western Han Dynasty, told a thought-provoking story in the *Seven Elicitations*. The prince of Chu fell ill. Wu Ke diagnosed his illness as malaise and gave him a prescription of learning and exploring "pertinent dictums and deep truths", aimed at healing him with morality. Gradually, the prince's face lit up, and, all of a sudden, the illness disappeared. Comprehensively strengthening Party discipline requires both a temporary solution and a permanent cure. A temporary solution refers to applying drastic remedies to repel an unhealthy atmosphere and punishing crimes with stringent laws, and a permanent cure calls for us to cultivate our culture and to maintain the foundation of government.

– Speech at the Seventh Plenary Session of the 18th CPC Central Commission for Discipline Inspection (January 6, 2017).

Commentary

The *Seven Elicitations* is an allegorical literary work produced by Mei Cheng, a master in Fu (a literary form in ancient China). The work presents a fictitious story: the prince of Chu was sick, and Wu Ke went to visit him. They engaged in a discussion from shallow to deep on the basis of the state and cause of the prince's illness. The discussion consisted of seven elicitations and answers, with each question and answer conveying a connotation.

Wu believed that the reason why the prince fell ill was that he provided for himself and lived comfortably to an excessive extent. He took a horse-drawn carriage wherever he went, ate greasy food, and lived in a dwelling where a constant temperature was maintained. In the palace, there were plenty of maids to wait on him. Consequently, he was dispirited and became riddled with ailments. This was not a physical problem but one of spiritual degeneration, for which medicine and acupuncture were of no avail. The illness could only "be expelled by pertinent dictums and deep truths."

Accordingly, Wu introduced the pleasures of music, fine food, a riding carriage, travel, hunting, and contemplating the great ocean waves, enlightening the prince as to changes in lifestyle, and the prince's face gradually lit up. Finally, Wu proposed to introduce "the most senior and resourceful scholars with prestige and wisdom" to the prince and invite them to explore the principles of state government and self-cultivation with the prince by "discussing subtle truths and distinguishing right from wrong." Hearing that, the prince suddenly stood up by leaning on the table, and the illness disappeared completely.

Through a conversation between fictitious characters, the *Seven Elicitations* exhorts nobles not to abandon themselves to a life of debauchery, creature comforts and enjoyments. The seven pleasures, in fact, imply the dialectical relationship between material and spirit. If a person indulges in pleasures and debauchery and lacks spiritual pursuit and moral self-discipline, a variety of pathogenic bacterium will multiply in his body, as in the story of the prince of Chu, "whose spirits were low, and he seemed to suffer from various diseases." Therefore, only if we make up for a deficiency in mental nutrition can we gain substantive health. Chairman Mao also appreciated the *Seven Elicitations*. At the Lushan Conference, he instructed subordinates to print and distribute the article to all participants, and he even wrote a long commentary on it.

In a figurative style, and with imposing writing techniques as well as a profound meaning, the *Seven Elicitations* can be regarded as the forerunner of the long Fu of the Han Dynasty, having a great influence on the literature of later ages. In *Dragon-Carving and the Literary Mind*, Liu Xie wrote "As the first poem in the genre of 'Seven', the *Seven Elicitations* by Mei Cheng is rich and variegated as rolling clouds and forceful as gusty winds." Followed and studied by later generations, this literary form developed into the genre of "Seven", such as the *Seven Stimulations* by Fu Yi, the *Seven Debaters* by Zhang Heng, the *Seven Expositions* by Wang Can, the *Seven Edifications* by Cao Zhi, the *Seven Attestations* by Lu Ji, and the *Seven Orders* by Zhang Xie.

Xi Jinping seeks to stress, through the story of the *Seven Elicitations*, that only by improving cultivation and strengthening faith can we maintain the foundation of government. As the saying goes, "A firm foundation will stabilize the country, while an unstable one may endanger it." Xi often emphasizes "reinforcing the root and cultivating the vitality." "Root" refers to the foundation or heart. Only a firm root can absorb nutrients and grow into a plant with luxuriant foliage. "Vitality" refers to vigor or spirit. Only with abundant vigor can we resist evil influences and maintain exuberant vitality. Securing the foundation requires us as a nation to fortify our ideals and faith and improve our accomplishments in the spirit of the Party.

No "House of Cards" in Anti-corruption

As the struggle against corruption continues to deepen, a number of notable tendencies in public opinion are emerging in our society. Some emerging opinions have even received considerable support. For example, some of these views include the ideas that anti-corruption has nothing to do with the interests of the masses; anti-corruption leads to acts of nonfeasance by officials; anti-corruption hinders economic development; anti-corruption is all about power struggles; and anti-corruption should be slowed down. Under these circumstances, we must differentiate and analyze such vague views and incorrect remarks and guide the tendencies of public opinion to refute erroneous statements, defuse negative emotions, and eliminate prejudices and misunderstandings. To create a good atmosphere of public opinion to improve Party conduct, build a clean government, and fight corruption in a meaningful way, we should make clear that the anti-corruption actions of the CPC are not the work of elites who look up to certain people and look down on others, nor are they the product of a "House of Cards" that is rife with scrambles for power and profit, nor an "unfinished building" with a beginning but no end.

> – Speech at the Sixth Plenary Session of the 18th CPC Central Commission for Discipline Inspection (January 12, 2016).

Commentary

House of Cards is an American political TV series, which tells the story of a cold-blooded American congressman and his wife who is as power-hungry as he is, ruthlessly fighting for power and money in the American political arena.

Francis Underwood, the hero of the TV series, is a wily politico with almost no bottom line. To defeat the incoming Secretary of State, he sends his subordinate to drink and take drugs with the witness to blackmail the witness into giving false testimony. To trap the Minister of Education, he betrays the venerable former minister and pretends to be a sympathetic colleague. He even coerces his subordinates into loyalty to him with the skeletons in their closets, and he goes to all lengths to retaliate against them once they become disloyal. The show's style of critical realism has won it much acclaim and many fans.

Premiering on February 1, 2013, the first season of *House of Cards* received much attention from politicians and people in many countries as soon as it was released as it unfolds dangerous games of power-for-money, power-for-power, and power-for-sex deals among American politicians in an extremely realistic manner. Both former US President Obama and former British Prime Minister Cameron have openly said they have watched it. The American presidential election in 2016 was full of ups and downs, which can be regarded as a realistic version of *House of Cards*. With the confirmation of the production of the fifth season, this TV series will continue to showcase the black-ops and contemptible intrigue of Western politics.

Michael Dobbs, the author of the novel, *House of Cards*, is a British politician. He entered politics in 1975, successively serving as the Government Special Adviser and Chief of Staff of Mrs. Thatcher's government, and he eventually retired as the Vice Chairman of the Conservative Party. What makes his novels of officialdom realistic and marvelous is his real-life experience in Western political circles. The foreign media has said of the novel, "This blood-and-thunder tale, lifelike and thoroughly cynical, certainly carries the ring of authenticity."

At the Sixth Plenary Session of the 18th CPC Central Commission for Discipline Inspection, Xi Jinping emphasized that the anti-corruption actions of the CPC are not the product of elites who look up to certain people and look down on others, nor of a "House of Cards" that is rife with scrambles for power and profit, nor are they the product of an "unfinished building" with a beginning but no end. This is a convincing retort against the vague views and incorrect remarks such as "anti-corruption has nothing to do with the interests of the masses" and "anti-corruption is all about a power struggle," embodying the firm determination of the Central Committee of the CPC headed by Comrade Xi Jinping to fight against corruption with an iron hand.

This was not the first time that Xi used "House of Cards" as metaphor. When he made a state visit to the US in September 2015, a reporter asked, "Does anti-corruption in China involve a power struggle?" Xi replied, "We vigorously investigate corruption cases and insist on cracking down on both tigers and flies to comply with the people's requests. There is no 'house of cards', and this has nothing to do with a power struggle." President Xi, who is good at telling stories, astutely answered the sensitive question using a cultural symbol of the US, winning widespread praise from both audiences and the American media. The claim of "no 'house of cards'" suggests that the CPC is firm in rectifying its working style and fighting against corruption.

The Hard-Earned Wealth of the People

There was a famous, honest, and upright official in Lankao named Zhang Boxing, who served successively as the Governor of Fujian, Governor of Jiangsu, and Minister of Rites. To decline presents from all parties, he pointedly wrote the *Official Denunciation of Giving Presents*, saying, "Though a thread of silk or a grain of rice is tiny, it concerns my reputation. Though a cent or a dime is negligible, it is derived from the hard-earned wealth of the people. If I treat the people with more lenience, then they will receive more grace. Even if I take a bribe of only one penny, then my moral quality is not worth a red cent. How can we regard this as a conventional practice of social intercourse? An ill-gotten gain, if any, would break the principle of incorruption. If you say it is not misgotten, then where does it come from?" In my opinion, this can also serve as a mirror for us.

— Speech at the Enlarged Meeting of the Standing Committee of the Lankao County Party Committee of Henan Province (March 18, 2014).

Commentary

With regard to the incorruptible officials in the Qing Dynasty, in addition to Yu Chenglong, who is known to all, another who we must mention is Zhang Boxing. Zhang Boxing was born in Lankao, Henan Province, in 1652 and died in 1725, having served successively as the Governor of Fujian and the Governor of Jiangsu, eventually reaching the position of Minister of Rites. Emperor Kangxi once commented on him as follows: "Boxing is an official of rectitude and integrity. This is known to all." Emperor Kangxi further stated that "there is no one in the world more honest or upright than Boxing."

When Zhang was the Governor of Fujian, he specifically wrote the Official Denunciation of Giving Presents and posted it over the gates of his residence and yamen (the local government office in ancient China) to decline the presents arriving in quick succession. Concise and comprehensive, this official denunciation set out that, "Though a thread of silk or a grain of rice is tiny, it concerns my reputation. Though a cent or a dime is negligible, it is derived from the hard-earned wealth of the people. If I treat the people with more lenience, then they will receive more grace. Even if I take a bribe of only one penny, then my moral quality is not worth a red cent. How can we regard this as a conventional practice of social intercourse? An ill-gotten gain, if any, would break the principle of incorruption. If you say it is not misgotten, then where does it come from?" Reading the official denunciation, the gift-givers felt snubbed and left quietly. This denunciation was subsequently read widely, and it became "an iron law" of political integrity.

In the year of famine, Zhang "allocated and transported money and food from his hometown and arranged for the sewing of cotton-padded clothes to save the people from hunger and cold." He even gave a command to open the province-owned grain depot for disaster relief, for which he was accused of arbitrariness, to which he asked in reply, in stern and just words, "The grain depot or human life, which is more important?" How could the people refrain from respecting and supporting such an upright and kind official? When he left the office of the Governor of Jiangsu, Yangzhou, people intended to give him fruits and vegetables as farewell presents; however, he graciously declined. "When you were in office, you got nothing from us except a cup of water. Now, you are outgoing, don't decline our good will!" sobbed the people. Having no alternative, Zhang took a green vegetable and two pieces of bean curd, which conveyed the meaning of "clean hands."

Lankao is designated by Xi Jinping as a contact point of the second round of the Program of Mass Line Education and Practice. At the Enlarged Meeting of the Standing Committee of the Lankao County Party Committee, Xi related the deeds of Zhang, illustrating that scrupulous abidance to the principle of integrity in small matters is the first line of defense against corruption and the foundation for a positive work ethic. Xi quoted the *Official Denunciation of Giving Presents* in full to remind all Party members of the profound philosophy that quantitative change will lead to qualitative change because "most corrupt officials take the road of corruption and degeneration starting with self-indulgence in small matters."

"This can also serve as a mirror for us," Xi asserted in this article. This embodiment of the self-disciplined consciousness of strictness in the prevention of abuse of power, and honesty in the performance of official duties, reflects that the culture of clean government in ancient times and historical experiences and lessons in combating corruption and upholding integrity provide a rich basis for today's anti-corruption education. On many occasions, Xi has told stories of ancient incorruptible officials and quoted mottoes about clean government. Under his auspices, the Political Bureau of the Central Committee of CPC has even conducted a collective study in the practices of anti-corruption and the building of clean government in Chinese history.

Farewell My Concubine

Our Party gained the support of the overwhelming majority of the Chinese people as the dominant political force in China. Despite the firm ruling foundation, if we fail to eliminate misconduct from the Party, the tragedy of "Farewell My Concubine" will come true. So we must have a sense of crisis.

- Speech during the Investigation and Instruction of the Program of Mass Line Education and Practice in Hebei Province, (July 11–12, 2013).

Commentary

At the end of the Qin Dynasty, Xiang Yu and his uncle, Xiang Liang, raised an invincible army to fight the Qin government and eventually routed-out the Qin army in the Battle of Julu. After the fall of Qin, Xiang Yu took advantage of his power and divided the territory of the state and conferred 18 seigneurs. In the eyes of the world, Xiang was a brave and strong man who was versed in military affairs and of matchless boldness. With the Battle of Julu, he awed all his compatriots and was claimed to be the "Overlord of Western Chu."

The Feast at Hong Gate was supposed to be the perfect opportunity for Xiang Yu to kill Liu Bang. However, at the feast, the conceited and opinionated Xiang broke his agreement with Fan Zeng after having been deceived by Liu, who swallowed his humiliation to submit to Xiang's will and convinced by Fan Kuai, who spoke sternly out of a sense of justice. Fan Zeng "winked at Xiang repeatedly" to hint that it was time to kill Liu; however, Xiang not only turned a blind eye but also accepted Liu's present gladly and allowed him to escape. He even turned a deaf ear when Fan Zeng angrily rebuked him: "This man is undeserving of jointly planning for a great action." Finally, at the young age of 31, Xiang cut his own throat, ashamed of the defeat he suffered in the contest with Liu for dominion over the state.

According to the *Records of the Historian-Biographic Sketches of Xiang Yu*, Xiang chanted in a heroic but mournful tone as his army was defeated, "I can root mountains up, with matchless might! But my good fortune wanes that my steed can no longer fight. My steed cannot fight, and what should I do? My lady fair, tell me what can I do!" The tragic sight caused tears to trickle down the cheeks of all those who were present.

Sima Qian commented on Xiang Yu, "He simply showed off his exploits and made a parade of his ability without learning from his predecessors," further stating that he was "even unaware of his fault, nor did he blame himself." Coming to the hopeless situation, he even exculpated himself from blame by saying, "It is the heaven that will kill me, not my military strategy." With such a mentality, it was inevitable that he would be defeated.

To warn the whole army against complacency or stagnation in making progress, Chairman Mao wrote in *The People's Liberation Army Captures Nanjing* that "We should exploit our victories in hot pursuit of the tottering foe, and we cannot ape Xiang Yu, the overlord of Chu, who let the foe go just to achieve fame." At the Seven-thousand People Congress held in 1962, he quoted Xiang Yu's tale of "Farewell My Concubine," which was used as a metaphor for losing power, to urge the leading officials to be generous, and remain open-minded to advice from inferiors, saying that if we always refuse the views of others, just like Xiang Yu, it will be difficult for us to avoid the dead end faced by Xiang.

Xi Jinping viewed the issue of work style from the perspective of the ruling foundation and the survival of the Party, and he emphasized that the people's support is crucial to our success. By using the tragedy of "Farewell My Concubine" as a metaphor, he also cautioned Party officials and members that a poor work style will cause us to lose the support of the masses and push our Party and country to end in tragedy. He also said, "If we let a poor work style be, without correcting it in a resolute way, it will develop into an invisible wall that separates our Party from the masses and deprives us of our roots, blood vessels and strength." These sonorous words not only contain a profound summary of historical experiences and lessons but it also expresses the earnest expectation that all comrades will improve their work style and maintain close ties with the people.

Waist Bent When Promoted the Third Time

Of course, daring to take on responsibilities for the cause of the Party and the people is not about personal fame. We cannot confound it with conceit and overbearing. In the Spring and Autumn period, Zheng Kaofu, a senior official of the state of Song, who served several dukes of the States of Song and was highly self-disciplined, engraved a motto on a ding an ancient cooking vessel in his family ancestral temple that read, "Head down when I was promoted the first time, back hunched when promoted the second time, and waist bent when promoted the third time. No one insults me if I keep close to the wall when walking along the street. What I need is only this vessel in which to cook porridge to feed my family." I was deeply touched by this story when I read it. Our officials are all officials of the

Party, and our power is granted by the Party and the people. Thus, we should make ever-bolder efforts and show ever-greater determination in work and conduct ourselves in a modest and prudent manner that is free from arrogance and rashness.

   – Speech at the National Conference on Organizational Work (June 28, 2013).

Commentary

The key to administering a country is incorruption, and incorruption is all about self-discipline. As early as 2,000 years ago, Confucius stated "If one is guided by profit in his action, he will be much murmured against." This means that the person who cares only for his own interests will incur much resentment. Confucius also said "The gentleman seeks neither gratification of his appetite nor a comfortable home. He is quick in action but cautious in speech. He goes to men possessed of the Way to set himself right. Such a man can indeed be said to be eager to learn." Coming to self-discipline, Zheng Kaofu, a seventh-generation ancestor of Confucius, interpreted this proposition long ago.

As a senior official of Song in the Spring and Autumn period, Zheng Kaofu successively assisted Duke Dai, Wu, and Xuan of Song, in ruling the state. Although he was heavily relied upon by the three monarchs and was offered the post of senior minister, second only to the monarch, he remained humble and acted in a respectful and low-key manner. To guard against self-reflection and to direct his descendants, he engraved a motto on a ding in his family ancestral temple, and his story has often been repeated: "Head down when I was promoted the first time, back hunched when promoted the second time, and waist bent when promoted the third time." Among the three postures mentioned in the motto, "back hunched" appears more reverent than "head down", while "waist bent" seems the most reverent. The postures provide a vivid display of how Zheng became more and more respectful as he was promoted. The progressive use of the three positions indeed leads the reader to a sense of humility and respect. After that, there is a sudden turn: "No one insults me if I keep close to the wall when walking along the street." This was because he was protected by the power of personal character and morality.

We can also find the glorious deeds of Zheng in ancient books and records such as the *Records of the Historian—The Aristocratic Family of Confucius* and *Zuo's Commentaries*. In the *Records of the Historian—The Aristocratic Family of Confucius*, Sima Qian wrote, "Zheng Kaofu successively assisted Duke Dai, Wu and Xuan of Song, in ruling the state, during which time he became more respectful every time he was promoted." This is a manifestation of his morality of maintaining strictness in his self-cultivation and an upright manner in the performance of his official duty. Another much-told story is that he taught his descendants and other family members to abide by moral principles and to remain humble and respectful. In *Parental Instructions about Advocating Thrift to Sima Kang*, Sima Guang wrote, "In the olden days, Zheng Kaofu fed his family with porridge. Meng Xizi accordingly inferred that there would certainly be an illustrious and influential personage descended from his family." Meng Xizi was a senior official of the state of Lu in the Spring and Autumn period. He foresaw that a certain celebrity would emerge from Zheng's family. Now, a new historical Peking opera, *Zheng Kaofu*, jointly produced by the Peking Opera Theatre of Beijing and the National Centre for the Performing Arts, has dramatized the stories of Zheng. Zheng's principles of being an incorrupt official, modestly exercising authority, and maintaining his family tradition of loyalty will further influence more people.

Zheng's humility, uprightness, and modesty can restrain others from transgressing the bounds of decency and stop authorities from overstepping the bounds of discipline like a defense line of mentality against the pull of power. At the National Organization Work Conference, Xi Jinping told the story of "Waist Bent When Promoted the Third Time" to remind the leading officials and members of the Party to be strict in their self-development and in the exercise of power and self-discipline and to counsel them to remain humble, as Zheng Kaofu was.

Putting power into perspective and regulating the use of power can be regarded as the first threshold for testing our leading officials. Xi Jinping has put forward many important expositions with regard to the power of leading officials. In a speech at the Central Party School, he condensed the Marxist view of power in the following statement: "The power is from the people and for the people." At the National Conference on Organizational Work, he also emphasized that "Avoiding responsibilities is the greatest disgrace for an official," and he required Party officials to make ever-bolder efforts, to show ever-greater determination in their work, and to conduct themselves in a modest and prudent manner free from arrogance and rash-ness. Furthermore, at the meeting with a class of County Party Secretaries at the Central Party School, he proposed the requirements of the "Four 'With-in-Minds'"—with the Party in mind, with the people in mind, with responsibility in mind, and with self-discipline in mind. These important expositions give the leading officials precise directions for how to correct their views of power.

THE UNTIMELY END OF THE QIN DYNASTY

The First Emperor of Qin was the first feudal emperor to unify China. The founding of the Qin Dynasty was demanded by historical developments. However, after ascending to the throne, the emperor reveled in grandiose things and extorted excessive taxes and levies from the people, making the people furious with resentment. This finally drove Qin to its doom dur-ing the reign of the Second Emperor of Qin. Du Mu wrote in *On the Ah Fang Palace* that "The Qin Dynasty, having no opportunity of lamenting itself, was left to be lamented by later generations; and the later genera-tions who lament Qin but refuse to learn a lesson from it make even later generations lament them." After the establishment of the Tang Dynasty, Emperor Taizong of Tang accomplished the "Prosperity of Zhenguan" by summoning all his efforts to make the country prosperous, taking advice with an open mind and appointing those with talents of both ability and political integrity. However, the later rulers of Tang were carried away with time and indulged in carnal pleasures. For example, Emperor Xuanzong "… slept till the sun rose high, for the blessed night was short. From then on His Majesty no longer held morning court." As a result, an atmosphere of bribery and corruption surrounded the officialdom at all levels, even-tually causing the "Rebellion of An and Shi", during which "rebels beat their war drums, making the earth quake, and the 'song of Rainbow Skirt and Coat of Feathers' broke." The "Rebellion of An and Shi" dragged the dynasty from prosperity into decline. Soon after, Wang Xianzhi and Huang Chao led an uprising and captured Chang'an, and the Tang Dynasty came to ruin.

- Speech at the Second Plenary Session of the 18th CPC Central Com-mission for Discipline Inspection (January 22, 2013).

Commentary

"Although it can be referred to as God's will, does the law of rise-and-fall not have anthropogenic factors?" Ouyang Xiu wrote in the *New History of the Five Dynasties—Preface to the Biography of a Performer*. Upon the analysis of the later Tang Dynasty's course of decadence, from sudden prosperity to sudden death, he reached the conclusions that "diligence improves a nation while indulgence destroys it" and "small mistakes accumulate to form disasters, and indulgence traps the intelligence." Both Qin's ruin during the reign of the Second Emperor and the Rebellion of An and Shi breaking out during Tang provide the historical lesson that indulgence will destroy a nation.

Qin was the first great dynasty in history that unified China. This was an outstanding accomplishment of the First Emperor of Qin, Ying Zheng, who even created the praiseworthy achievement that "carriages have all wheels of the same size; all writing is with the same characters; the unified measurement and monetary units are adopted; and for conduct there are the same rules." Nevertheless, just like what was written in the *Records of the Historian*, "the people suffered from torments for a long time because of the oppression by the Qin government." Ying Zheng began the construction of his mausoleum soon after his enthronement, which was not completed until 208 BC, lasting 39 years and requiring the labor of 720,000 people. It has been determined that the number of people participating in this project was almost eight times that of the Pyramid of Khufu in Egypt. "The reason why the Qin Dynasty came to an end early in the sixteenth year of the reign of the Second Emperor of Qin was that the members of the imperial family were extravagant in preserving their health and had numerous people and objects to be buried with them when they died," according to the *Book of Han*. Jia Yi wrote in *On the Faults of Qin* that "A single rustic nevertheless challenged this empire, and the government was toppled and the emperor was killed by the rebels, becoming a laughingstock in the eyes of all. Why? Because the ruler lacked humanity and righteousness, which reversed the situation with regard to attack and defense." In addition, Du Mu once lamented, "It was Qin and not the world that exterminated the clan of Qin." Simply put, what destroyed Qin was the monarch's extravagance and dissipation as well as his lack of humanity and righteousness.

With respect to the Tang Dynasty's history from prosperity to decay, the principal cause was also that the ruling class indulged in a life of pleasure and comfort, and it became corrupt and degenerate. "Viewed from afar, the hills seemed like brocades in piles. The doors of the palace on hilltops opened one after another. A steed raising red dust won the fair mistress' smiles. But few people knew how many steeds bringing her litchis died on the run." This passage is from *The Summer Palace* by Du Mu, a narration of the story that a steed galloped to bring litchis to the Imperial Concubine Yang. This poem presented an intuitive image illustrating that the ruler of Tang wasted a lot of manpower and money to gratify his appetite. According to the *Old Book of Tang*, "In the imperial palace of Emperor Xuanzong of Tang, about seven hundred workers were employed to do brocading and embroider for the Imperial Concubine Yang, and hundreds of people were employed to carve and forge jewelry for her." From this, we can obtain a hint of the imperial family's extravagance and wastefulness in their daily lives. Indulging himself in worldly enjoyments, Emperor Xuanzong allowed the treacherous officials headed by Yang Guozhong to disturb the affairs of state, thus causing the dynasty, which was then at its peak, to decay when An Lushan raised an army to start the Rebellion of An and Shi.

An iron law proven by history is that integrity allows the regime to prosper, while corruption causes it to decay. Xi Jinping referred to the untimely end of Qin in the reign of its second emperor as well as the fall of the flourishing Tang to emphasize that corruption is a cancer of society and to remind the whole Party to take history as a mirror, to learn the historical lessons, and to fight unswervingly against corruption. As he stated, "Through a thorough review of history in China and elsewhere, our Party has realized that improving Party conduct, upholding integrity and combating corruption are vital for the survival of the Party and the state. Chinese history is littered with examples of serious corruption that led to government failure. Even in today's world, the examples of losing political power because the ruling party became corrupt and degenerate as well as completely out of touch with the people are too numerous to enumerate!"

Having a deep sense of concern about corruption, Xi has said many times that "as the ruling party, the biggest threat we are faced with is corruption," and "if we let the corruption problem intensify, we will inevitably meet the doom of our Party and country." He also emphasized many times that the masses detest various types of corruption and privilege most, and these acts are most destructive to the close ties between our Party and the masses. As early as when he headed the administration of Ningde, Fujian Province, he said, "There is an issue of offence. If you violate the laws and party discipline to occupy a piece of land and build a house on it purely out of self-interest, undermining our Party's authority and image, then it is not the official who investigates and punishes you on behalf of the Party and the people's interests that offends you, but rather, it is that you offend the Party, the people, the party discipline and the laws of the state."

THE TUNE PRESAGING THE FALLEN STATE

In the Northern and Southern Dynasties, Chen Shubao, the Emperor of the state of Chen of the Southern Dynasties, reigned but did not govern and lived off the fat of the land. Later, when the troops of the Sui Dynasty marched south to attack the state of Chen, Chen's army could not withstand a single blow, so that Chen Shubao was captured by the Sui army and finally died of illness. His poem *The Jude Tree-like Backyard Flower* is referred to as "the tune presaging the fallen state" by later generations. In the *Five Poems Written in Jinling—The Capital*, Liu Yuxi, the poet of the Tang Dynasty, wrote, "The monarchs of the six dynasties did their utmost to foster the extravagant climate in Jinling, especially the last king of Chen, who indulged himself in an extremely extravagant and luxurious life in the buildings Jieqi and Linchun. Now the rows of houses have vanished, and the city has become wild and covered with weeds. All of this was caused by the song of the 'Backyard Flower'." After the Anti-Japanese War, the Kuomintang took over many regions. However, they simply took the opportunity to wrest the "five sons", causing the social unrest to die down. Totally losing popular support, they were soon driven away by the revolution led by our Party.

– Speech at the Second Plenary Session of the 18th CPC Central Commission for Discipline Inspection (January 22, 2013).

Commentary

Among the emperors of all the dynasties, Chen Shubao, the last king of the state of Chen of the Southern Dynasties, Li Yu, the last monarch of the Southern Tang Dynasty, and Zhao Ji, Emperor Huizong of the Northern Song Dynasty, were definitively ranked at the top in literary grace and talent.

Chen Shubao had a special fondness for poetry. A banquets, he recited poems and composed verse with the ministers. This played an important role in developing the metrical norms of poetry and laying a foundation for the high point of poetry of the Sui and Tang dynasties. *The Jude Tree-like Backyard Flower* and other poems by him demonstrated his great literary attainments. Li Yu was not only proficient in calligraphy, painting, and music but also had certain attainments in various poetic styles, especially in Ci (a type of lyric poetry in ancient China). "Carved balustrades and marble steps must still be there, but rosy faces cannot be as fair. If you ask me how much my sorrow has increased, just see the overbrimming river flowing east!" This is the poem *The Beautiful Lady Yu*, which has been read through the ages, winning the honorary title of "King of Ci" for Li. Zhao Ji, a rare interdisciplinary artist in ancient times, created the calligraphy font "slender gold" and created a style in bird-and-flower painting.

In the *Comments on the Ancient and Modern Ci Poetry*, a book written by Shen Xiong in the Qing Dynasty, he stated, "The misery of a country is the luck of poets. Good lines will be born when poets witness the vicissitudes of the world." No matter what heights Chen Shubao, Li Yu, and Zhao Ji attained in literature and art, they totally failed in managing affairs of state and bringing prosperity to their states. They eventually ruined their states through fatuity and dissoluteness, which allowed them to be eclipsed. Chen Shubao was addicted to a lewd and debaucherous life, causing his army to be defeated and his government overthrown. For this reason, his poem *The Jude Tree-like Backyard Flower* is referred to as "the tune presaging the fallen state" by later generations, just as Liu Yuxi lamented, "Now the rows of houses have vanished, and the city has become wild and covered with weeds." All of this was caused by the song of the "Backyard Flower". When Du Mu heard a singsong girl sing *The Jude Tree-like Backyard Flower* as he berthed the ship by the Qinhuai River at night, he could not help but lament, "Knowing not the grief of the captive king, by riverside the songstress still sings his song presaging the fallen state."

As the saying goes, "Peril approaches as an extravagant atmosphere emerges." In all the past dynasties, the prevailing extravagance was an omen of the decline of the dynasty. In the later Zhou Dynasty during the Five Dynasties, Dou Yujun, a resident in Yanshanfu, had five sons who were all excellent in character and learning. The five boys passed the highest imperial civil service examination in succession, which led to the common blessing, "Five sons pass the civil examination," meaning "wishing your children a promising future." After the success of the Anti-Japanese War, the key officials of the Kuomintang took advantage of regaining the lost territory to extort gold, houses, paper money, cars, and traitors' wives by trick or by force from the people. The "gold, houses, paper money, cars, and traitors' wives" were then satirically referred to by the people as "the new five sons". As a result, the social unrest died down, and the Kuomintang lost its popular support and finally fled to Taiwan in defeat.

Xi Jinping often cautions Party members and officials against poor work styles and expresses aspirations using ancient poetry, endowing members and officials with a concrete and profound understanding of the work-style issue. He warns of the harm brought by extravagance and dissipation by citing Chen Shubao's "tune presaging the fallen state"; he highlights the importance of upholding the spirit of hard work and perseverance using the verse "From the history of the sagacious states and families, we know that thrift leads to success, and luxury, failure" and he has quoted the verse "The portals of the rich reek of flesh and wine while frozen bodies lie by the roadside" to warn Party members and officials against hedonism and extravagance. In Xi's view, maintaining close ties with the people and preventing the party from becoming corrupt during long-term rule "are major political tasks that we must perform well."

"The tune presaging the fallen state" also implies that the improvement of work style must start with the administrator of the state. Only if the "vital few", the leading officials, straighten up, can "the inferior follow the example set by the superior." Shortly after the 18th National Congress of the CPC, Xi visited and inspected Guangdong Province without heavy security guards or a welcome banner. While inquiring of the poor about their sufferings in Fuping, Hebei Province, he took only light meals with his accompanying personnel. When he braved the rain to conduct an on-the-spot inspection in Yangluo Container Harbor in Wuhan, Hubei Province, he visited the site with his trouser legs rolled up and holding his own umbrella. These deeds of taking the lead and practicing what the Party Central Committee preaches show the officials and masses the steadfast determination of the Party Central Committee to govern and manage the Party and its political commitment by setting itself as an example.

Pei Ju Turned from Obsequious in Sui to Outspoken in Tang

There is a story in the *Abstracts of Ancient Prose*: Pei Ju, the famous official of the early Tang Dynasty, was a loyal and candid minister who dared remonstrate with the emperors. He even had the courage to argue face-to-face with Emperor Taizong of Tang. However, when he was an official of the Sui Dynasty, surprisingly, he had only curried favor with Emperor

Yang of Sui, finding every way to satisfy him. Sima Guang commented on this by saying, "Pei Ju shifted his attitude from obsequious in Sui to outspoken in Tang not because of a change in temperament but due to the likes and dislikes of the monarch. If the monarch disliked listening to criticisms of his faults, then Pei became obsequious, and if he wished, then Pei became outspoken." We can learn from this story that people are willing and pleased to tell the truth only to those who have hope and are able to listen to the truth. Our leading officials must encourage others to tell the truth and embrace the truth in line with the following principle: "Do not blame the critic for an incorrect comment, but take heed from it."

– Adherence to the Ideological Line of Seeking Truth from Facts— Speech at the Opening Ceremony of the Second Batch of Trainees of the Central Party School in 2012 Spring Semester (May 16, 2012).

Commentary

The ancients said, "True words are not fine-sounding; fine-sounding words are not true." Sharp criticisms are unpleasant to hear. The more valuable the words are, the more likely that it will be difficult to accept. It takes breadth of mind to accept criticisms, and it takes courage to offer criticisms. Both history and reality tell us that the question of whether to tell the truth depends entirely on those who listen to it.

Pei Ju, a famous official of the Tang Dynasty, was originally an official of the Sui Dynasty. He was good at figuring out how the mind of Emperor Yang of Sui worked and catering to the emperor's pleasure. Emperor Yang once praised him, "Pei Ju knows me very well. The proposals he submitted were all what I expected. Although I did not specify what was required, he was able to anticipate my needs. He definitely strives to serve the state with heart. If it were not so how else could he do that?" Emperor Yang had a fondness for the grandiose, thus he suggested that a grand Lantern Festival be held in the eastern capital Luoyang. Emperor Yang yearned for a golden age when "all surrounding nationalities are obedient to Sui and many states come and pay respects to it," and he then backed a foreign war. When Sui was defeated, he led his following to surrender to Tang. However, facing Emperor Taizong of Tang, who was willing to heed counsel in court, Pei became a changed man who dared to frankly criticize the emperor's faults and unhesitatingly offer counsel. Emperor Taizong spoke highly of him:

"As an official, Pei Ju dares to make his utmost efforts to argue with me on the basis of reality instead of blindly obeying me. If everyone could do this, we wouldn't need to worry about the poor governance of the state, would we?"

In *A General Reflection for Political Administration*, Sima Guang wrote, "The ancients said, 'If the monarch is sagacious, then the officials are outspoken.' Pei Ju shifted his attitude from obsequious in the Sui court to outspoken in the Tang court not because of a change in temperament but in deference to the likes and dislikes of the monarch. If the monarch disliked listening to criticisms on his faults, then Pei became obsequious, and if wished, he became outspoken. Thus, the monarch is like a sundial, and the official is like the shadow that moves with the sundial." This means that it was not the change in temperament that caused Pei Ju to turn from obsequious in Sui to outspoken in Tang. If the monarch dislikes hearing criticisms of his faults, then an upright official will become a crafty sycophant. In contrast, given a monarch who is willing to listen to the truth, a crafty sycophant will become upright. The monarch is like the body, and the official is like the shadow that always follows the body.

Xi Jinping used the example of Pei Ju to emphasize that the leader is the one who holds the "baton" and conducts his orchestra of inferiors to tell the truth. Only if leaders have the courage to listen to the truth and encourage their inferiors to tell the truth, if they are magnanimous and receptive to criticism and show a cordial attitude "to correct mistakes if you have made any and guard against them if you have none," can speaking the truth and offering sound advice become a common practice for them.

In the speech, Xi stated that to be realistic and pragmatic, leading officials should not only seek truth but also address concrete matters. They should especially speak the truth, make pragmatic suggestions and recommendations, handle concrete affairs, and seek substantial results. "To speak the truth" means to focus on the nature of things, to speak frankly, and follow the truth. This is an important embodiment of a leading official's characteristics of truth seeking, embodying justice, devotion to public interests, and uprightness. Moreover, he highlighted that the premise of telling the truth is to listen to the truth. In addition to the story of Pei Ju, Xi quoted a dictum of the English philosopher Bacon to prove that listening to true words is a type of wisdom, "It is a blessing or good fortune for one to have a chance to hear the truth from someone else so that he may avoid making detours altogether or at least make few detours, to make only a few mistakes or at least prevent serious mistakes."

INFERIORS FOLLOW THE EXAMPLE OF SUPERIORS

The preferences and taboos of leadership are the driving force for the formation of social customs, while the preferences and taboos of the masses are the basis for the formation of folklore. Those in subordinate positions will follow the example set by their superiors. The style and appeal of leading officials not only concern their own character and image but they also affect the Party's prestige and image imprinted on the masses' minds. They play an exemplary role in the formation of the social atmosphere and the cultivation of the masses' life interest. There are many anecdotes about this, two of which still have a strong significance for today. One is a story in *The Collections of Anecdotes in Song Dynasty*. Qian Chu offered a precious belt with rhinoceros horn ornaments as a tribute to Emperor Taizu of Song. Emperor Taizu said, "I have three such belts." Qian asked to be shown the belts, and the emperor laughed and answered, "The Bian River, the Huimin River and the Wuzhang River." Then, Qian felt greatly ashamed and sincerely apologetic. Another story was recorded in *The Casual Literary Notes by Nancun—Foot Binding*. Yao Niang, a concubine of the last monarch of the Southern Tang Dynasty, was slim, beautiful, and good at dancing. The emperor instructed her to bind her feet with silk and then dance trippingly in a pair of white socks on the lotus terrace, presenting a spectacle like dancing in the clouds. Later, the common people followed her example in pursuit of bound feet and felt ashamed of non-bound ones. From positive and negative perspectives, these two stories illustrate that the attitude leaders show toward the details of life are not trifles.

 – *Delight of Life Is Not a Trifle* (February 12, 2007), from *Fresh Ideas of Zhejiang*, Edition 2007, published by Zhejiang People's Publishing House.

Commentary

The setting of an example by superiors for their subordinates has been used as an important measure to correct customs and govern the country since ancient times. The ancients said, "As he puts everything aside, the folk will not have him as their guide." *The Analects* told us, "Government is being correct. If you lead the people with correctness, who will dare to be incorrect?" In the book *Mencius*, it was stated that, "If people of high rank like something, people below will surely like it all the better. The virtue of people above is like the wind, while that of those below is like the grass. The grass is sure to bend toward where the wind blows." There is also a folk saying, "If the upper beam is not straight, the lower ones will go aslant." The stories of the Emperor Taizu of Song and the last monarch of the Southern Tang Dynasty provide strong proof of this from a positive and a negative perspective, respectively.

Qian Chu was a grandson of Qian Liu and the last king of the state of Wuyue during the period of Five Dynasties and Ten Kingdoms. When Emperor Taizu was pacifying the regions south of the Yangtze River, Qian dispatched troops to assist Song in eradicating the Southern Tang Dynasty instead of accepting the request for reinforcements by Li Yu, the last monarch of Southern Tang. After that, he surrendered to Song. According to the historical records, after surrendering to Song, Qian Chu offered precious and scarce objects as a tribute to Emperor Taizu; however, Taizu said, "These are nothing but belongings in my warehouse, which never need to be presented as a tribute!" *The Collections of Anecdotes in Song Dynasty* recorded the story that Qian Chu presented a precious belt as a tribute to Taizu but received a reprimand from him. This story depicted Taizu's uprightness—observing the principle of "country first." In spite of driving the state to its doom, the people of Wuyue felt deeply grateful to Qian Chu because he followed Qian Liu's last words and surrendered to Song to avoid war in consideration of the security of the people. Even today, some monuments to his memory still stand by West Lake, such as King Qian's Temple and the Pagoda to Bless Qian Chu.

There are widely divided opinions on the origin of the undesirable customs of foot binding. According to *The Casual Literary Notes by Nancun— Foot Binding*, it was thought that foot binding dated from the period of Five Dynasties. To enjoy more graceful dancing, on the basis of the aesthetic standard of the Tang Dynasty, during which time shoes with upturned ends were immensely popular, Li Yu had an out-of-the-ordinary idea. He instructed a dancer to wrap her shoes with long strips of cloth and wear a pair of white socks. Soon afterward, everyone followed this example to pursue slim feet. This is strong evidence of the amazing potency of examples set by superior authorities.

When heading the administration of Zhejiang Province, Xi Jinping elucidated the exemplary role of the ruler with these two stories, a positive one and a negative one. Xi Jinping has repeatedly made clear that leading officials at all levels should take the lead in the improvement of work style. At the First Plenary Session of the 18th CPC Central Commission for Discipline Inspection, he quoted the saying "To straighten your shadow, you must stand straight; to require your subordinates to be clean and incorrupt, you should take the lead first" to emphasize that the work style of leading officials, especially high-ranking ones, has an important influence on Party conduct, government conduct, and even social conduct. At the Second Plenary Session, he again noted, "Those who are good at governing society with a ban must be the ones abiding by the ban."

A person must meet a requirement before he proposes it to others, and he must not do what he bans others from doing. Xi Jinping has carried out this idea through actual efforts since his youth. The main reason for the good situation whereby public opinion echoes the aspirations of the Party, which has taken shape since the 18th National Congress of the Communist Party of China, is that the central leadership practices what it preaches and takes the lead. From taking the initiative by observing the "Eight Rules" of the CPC to warning of the "four forms of decadence", launching the campaign for criticism and self-criticism and setting an example of fulfilling the "Three Guidelines for Ethical Behavior and Three Basic Rules of Conduct," the Political Bureau of the Central Committee of the CPC has insisted on setting a good example. This has helped them establish credibility and produced a strong exemplary effect in the whole Party and throughout the country.

Three Not-Cheats

We are all familiar with the story of "Ximen Bao Administered Ye" recorded in the *Records of the Historian*. The story unfolds as follows: "When Zichan was administering the state of Zheng, the people could not cheat him; when Zijian was administering Shanfu, the people had no heart to cheat him; and when Ximen Bao was administering Ye, the people dared not cheat him." During the Spring and Autumn period, Zichan administered the state of Zheng. He was aware of the slightest deceit; thus, the people were unable to cheat him. Zijian was a student of Confucius. When he governed Shanfu, he attached importance to civilizing and enlightening. As a result, although he played Zheng (a Chinese zither) for pleasure everyday instead of performing hands-on leadership, the people, who were civilized and enlightened, thus could not bear to cheat him. Ximen Bao, a methodical man of great wisdom, was an official in the state of Wei during the Warring

States period. Standing with the people, he successfully abolished the evil practice of "marrying girls to the River God," led the people to construct water conservancy facilities and punished crimes with stringent laws; thus, the people dared not cheat him. The truths of these stories help us deepen our understanding of the relationship between officials and the masses and improve our working methods. We should study them in depth.

- Speech at the Grassroots Officials Symposium in Ruian, Zhejiang Province (December 26, 2004), from the *Take the Lead, Take Pragmatic Actions—Thoughts on and Practices in Promoting the New Development of Zhejiang Province*, Edition 2006, published by The Central Party School Publishing House.

Commentary

The assertion that people did not cheat the ruler is another way of saying that they obeyed him. In ancient China, the officials aimed to obtain people's obedience to them given the nature of the times and their limited understanding. It was written in the *Records of the Historian* that "When Zichan was administering the state of Zheng, the people could not cheat him; when Zijian was administering Shanfu, the people had no heart to cheat him; and when Ximen Bao was administering Ye, the people dared not cheat him." There are three administrative policies contained in this sentence. One is hands-on leadership, another is the seeking of assistance from people of wisdom and virtue, and the last is the severe punishment of crimes. Although these governance styles and philosophies varied greatly, they all achieved the people's obedience.

Zichan was a famous politician of the state of Zheng during the Spring and Autumn period. He allowed the people to discuss government affairs and was willing to draw useful suggestions from them. However, he also enforced reform, which he believed was to the benefit of the country, regardless of public opinion. He "cast the statute law on the bronze tripod" to make it public, and vigorously promoted economic reform and concerning himself with all matters, regardless of whether they were important or trivial. Through hands-on leadership, he made Zheng a state where "the people kept the door open all night and no one pocketed anything found on the road," and the people could not cheat him.

Zijian, who was born in the state of Lu in the Spring and Autumn period, was listed among the "72 students of Confucius." When he administrated Shanfu, he played Zheng every day for fun and seldom went out to visit the people, living a leisurely and comfortable life. However, the county was well governed. This was because he employed the administrative policy of maintaining honest, sincere, kind, respectful, and loyal administrators, attaching importance to employing people of virtue and of talent, and he ran the government with a sense of compassion. Because of this, the people felt in their hearts that they could not cheat him, although he played Zheng for pleasure everyday instead of engaging in hands-on leadership.

Ximen Bao was an official in the state of Wei during the Warring States period. When he served as the Governor of Yexian County, he found, upon investigation, that a grassroots official had colluded with a sorcerer and a sorceress to defraud the people of their property in the guise of "marrying girls to the River God." Once, when they were holding a wedding ceremony for the "River God", Ximen declared that there was a need to send a report to the River God and then ordered someone to throw the grassroots official, sorcerer, and sorceress into the river, thus wiping out this deceptive practice. After that, he led the people to construct water conservancy facilities and excavate 12 canals to channel water from the Zhang River for irrigation. Promulgating laws and decrees, he banned witchcraft and punished crimes with stringent laws, so that the people dared not cheat him.

In the view of the later generations, Zichan, Zijian, and Ximen Bao were, respectively, models of hands-on leadership, commission, and strict supervision.

Attitude and emotion support us in performing mass work, and ways and methods are the key to success. If one uses the wrong method, one will obtain a negative result despite a positive attitude. Xi Jinping used the "three not-cheats" to demonstrate the importance of selecting right ways and methods in mass work. "Cannot cheat" shows that an official should be willing to get his hands dirty and be mindful of the slightest detail as well as advocate openness, fairness, and justice to the greatest extent possible. The people's having "no heart to cheat" proves that the talents of wisdom and virtue should be given important positions, the people should be extensively civilized and enlightened, and officials should stimulate the people with actual affect, impress them with their sincerity, and inspire them with lofty values. "Dare not to cheat" shows that law-based governance and stern treatment for offenders are effective remedies for the ills of society.

Only if we punish crimes with stringent laws and enforce those laws with great exertion can evil deeds be stamped out and peace reign over the land.

Xi Jinping was an expert at mass work from his early appointments. During the period in which he served as the Secretary of the CPC Ningde Prefectural Committee, he visited all of the villages of Ningde, even those in the most remote mountain areas, which required traveling a few hours by car and on foot. Not merely inquiring after the villagers' living conditions, he also felt the thickness of their quilts by touch and learned about their dietary conditions. This was the state of "cannot cheat". When he lived and worked in the rural area of northern Shaanxi Province, he performed all types of hard labor and bore all sorts of hardships—farming, hauling a coal cart, building dykes, and carrying manure. He always spared no effort to work for the well-being of the villagers, including reinforcing the riverbank to prevent erosion, organizing a cooperative of blacksmiths to make farming tools, and building a methane tank for gathering cooking gas. In the eyes of the villagers, he was "a tough boy" and "a good secretary for the poor and lower-middle peasants." This is the state of "have no heart to cheat." While working in Zhengding, he seriously rectified the financial problems in the rural area and cracked down heavily on economic crimes. At one point, he and other senior officials in Fuzhou met with more than 700 petitioners in 2 days and solved many of their problems on the spot or set a time limit to find solutions. When he was heading the administration of Zhejiang Province, he attached importance to pollution prevention and controls to ensure environmental safety. This is the so-called "dare not to cheat."

POPULAR SUPPORT

In his book, *The Great Chinese Revolution, 1800–1985* Harvard University Professor John King Fairbank posed a question: "as of 1928 China's future seemed to be with the Kuomintang; ...How did the situation come to be reversed twenty years later?" His answer was as follows: "the Kuomintang leadership was older and had become worn out" and it "... alienated...the Chinese people." Meanwhile, in Fairbank's view, the leaders of the CPC "were...fervently devoted to their cause, and they pioneered..., on the cutting edge of a great national upheaval." He recognized the problem of the common aspiration of the people, which is rare for a bourgeois scholar. His words certainly point to the root cause of victory in the Chinese revolution—the Party's close relationship with the people.

- *The Basic Proficiency of Officials—Maintaining Close Ties with the People* (January 1989), from the *Up and Out of Poverty*, Edition 2016, published by Foreign Languages Press and Fujian People's Publishing House.

Commentary

John King Fairbank, a tenured Professor at Harvard University, was one of the most prestigious China watchers in America. He was referred to as "No. 1 Old China Hand". In his autobiography, he revealed that he had been working on understanding China for 50 years. Coming to China in the 1930s, Fairbank taught at Tsinghua University, and he was acquainted with Liang Sicheng and his wife Lin Huiyin. His Chinese name was given by Liang. *The Great Chinese Revolution, 1800–1985* was his magnum opus, which unfolded the 185 years of political and social changes that occurred in China from 1800 to 1985.

Why did the Kuomintang cause the collapse in the Chinese mainland, and why did the CPC garner victory? This question is still under debate among historians at home and abroad, and it concerns the development of modern China, which is worth deep exploration. As early as 1946, Theodore Harold White and Annalee Jacoby, correspondents of *Time* magazine in China, published the book *Thunder Out of China*, which presented the corruption of the Kuomintang government to the American public in an objective and comprehensive manner. Fairbank wrote a book review for the book, saying, "The *Thunder Out of China* lifts the lid". He made a bold prediction of the Kuomintang-CPC civil war and further stated that the mass line allowed the CPC to go deep into the countryside and mobilized the masses, thus the final victory went to the CPC.

Unlike the American political leaders who were accustomed to attributing the China issue to ideology, Fairbank, who was familiar with Chinese history, noted, based on deep and clear observation, that the one and only key to the survival of a regime is the people's support. These observations and judgments were recorded in *The Great Chinese Revolution, 1800–1985*. Coincidentally, the American scholar Lloyd Eastman also noted in his book *Seeds of Destruction—Nationalist China in War and Revolution, 1937–1949* that the defeat of the Kuomintang was not due to the lack of "American aid", but because of its own malpractices and internal divisions such as corruption and incompetence as well as the loss of discipline. All of these aspects eventually caused it to lose public support and political power.

The book *Up and Out of Poverty* includes some speeches made and articles written by Xi Jinping when he was working in Ningde during 1988 and 1990. Although there are only 120,000 words in this book, we can see Xi's reflections on many important issues, such as the construction of a clean government, the mass line, and common prosperity, as well as his deep understanding of the people's strength. Xi writes, "On our way forward, there will be many problems and difficulties. Exactly where should we start to solve the problems, and on what should we rely to overcome the difficulties? We can discuss different ideas and methods from various perspectives. The fundamental issue, however, is to mobilize and rely on the people." Even to this day, this important judgment generated by Xi Jinping is still of great significance.

The people's support versus opposition is an issue always lingering in Xi's mind. "Never forget that we are the government of 'the people'." "We should always keep closely attached to the people, share joys and sorrows with them, and strive hard together with them." "We should regard the people as though they are our." He has expressed his deep regard for the people and a deep understanding of the relationships between the party and the people on many occasions. He has cited Fairbank's research results as circumstantial evidence to prove that the victory of the revolution in China depends on popular support to admonish the Party members and officials not to forget the Party's original intention of serving the people and always maintaining close ties with the people.

The Yan'an Conversation

The patriot and democracy advocate Huang Yanpei said the following to Mao Zedong: Few people, families, groups, localities, or even nations, have the capacity to break free of this cycle. At first, they carefully focus on every issue, and everyone exerts their best effort. Conditions may be quite difficult at the time, and they must struggle for their very survival. As things gradually change for the better, they gradually lose their focus. Complacency then arises, spreads from a few to the many, and becomes the norm. Even with a great effort, the situation cannot be reversed. Huang hoped that the "members of the Communist Party" would be able to find a new way forward to escape the historical cycle in which rulers in the past had moved from hard work and innovation to becoming isolated from the people. Mao Zedong immediately answered: We have found a new path and we can break this cycle. This new path is democracy and the mass line. When the people are allowed to monitor the government, it dare not become lax. When everyone bears responsibility, the death of the ruler will not cause the government to collapse. Mao Zedong summarized the theory and practice of the Party and made the great and solemn call to "serve the people wholeheartedly," which was written into the Party Constitution as the sole purpose of our Party. We can see that maintaining close ties with the people is determined by the very nature and mission of our Party, and it is also an excellent tradition and style forged and upheld throughout its long revolutionary struggle.

> – *The Basic Proficiency of Officials—Maintaining Close Ties with the People* (January 1989), from the *Up and Out of Poverty.*

Commentary

On the eve of the victory of the Anti-Japanese War, Mao Zedong had a conversation with Huang Yanpei, which was referred to as the "Yan'an conversation". The conversation later became a much-told anecdote on communication between the CPC and democratic parties.

Huang Yanpei was a famous educator and social activist. Making a resolution in his early years to save the nation by way of education, he engaged in an unremitting exploration into China's cause of professional education throughout his life. After the outbreak of the Anti-Japanese War, Huang actively participated in the war, joining the National Political Council as a member of the social elite and endeavoring to uphold democratic solidarity and support the struggle against Japan. In July 1945, to consolidate democratic unity and facilitate the Kuomintang-CPC negotiation, Huang and six other members of the National Political Council visited Yan'an. During the 5-day visit, the simplicity and prudence of the leaders of the CPC as well as the democratic and peaceful climate of the Yan'an revolutionary base area moved him deeply. His response was as follows: "Of course what I saw and heard during these five day in Yan'an was quite close to my ideal."

When Mao Zedong asked Huang how he felt about the visit, he said, frankly, "I've lived for more than 60 years. Let's not talk about what I've heard. Whatever I saw with my own eyes fits the saying 'The rise of something may be fast, but its downfall is equally swift.' Few people, families, groups, localities, or even nations, have the capacity to break free of this cycle… Throughout history, there have been various examples: a ruler ignored state affairs and eunuchs used the opportunity to seize power; a good system of governance ceased to function after the person who initiated it died; some people lusted for fame and fortune through humiliating themselves. No one has escaped the historical cycle." Mao answered decidedly, "We have found a new path, and we can break this cycle. This new path is democracy and the mass line. When the people are allowed to monitor the government, it dare not become lax. When everyone bears responsibility, the death of the ruler will not cause the government to collapse." In Huang's view, "this was reasonable" because "only if the people are empowered to participate in the administration of where they live can each task be assigned to the right person and can each person have a proper post where he or she can play a role. Perhaps it will work to break out of this cycle with democracy."

The "Yan'an conversation" was of great significance in the history of our Party and country. This not only provided a good representation of the deepest sincerity shown by the CPC to democratic parties but it also indicates the exploration that by the CPC into the people's democracy and its aspiration for the people's well-being.

Shortly after the 18th National Congress of the CPC, Xi Jinping visited the central committees of the eight democratic parties as well as the All China Federation of Industry and Commerce and had informal discussions with them. During the discussions, he emphasized that the dialog on the historical cycle of rise-and-fall made by Mao Zedong and Huang Yanpei in a cave dwelling in Yan'an is a very good inspiration and warning to us in the CPC to this day. He recalled the "historical cycle of rise-and-fall," brushed the "two musts" up and cited the tale of "Farewell My Concubine" to warn Party officials of the danger of being derailed by poor work styles simply for the purpose of reaffirming that "we must forever preserve the fighting spirit demonstrated by Chinese Communists when the CPC was first founded and forever preserve our devotion to our people." Keeping the people in mind and striving for the people's well-being is the precious wealth that our Party accumulated during this 90-year course of trials and hardship. Just as Xi declared at the Celebration Ceremony of the 95th Anniversary of the Founding of the CPC, no matter how far forward we go, we can never forget the past, and we can never forget why we embarked on this journey in the first place.

DISPELLING THE SUFFERINGS OF THE PEOPLE

At present, we are placing great emphasis on social stability. What is our most important safeguard? It is the people, the tens of millions who whole-heartedly support the Four Cardinal Principles and reform and opening up. "Governance lies in reassuring the people; reassuring the people lies in observing their suffering." This ancient saying about governance is still worth drawing from today. As long as we understand and address the suffering of the people, "dispelling the suffering of the people is like treating your own severe illness." As long as we truly represent the fundamental interests of the people and "take as our own the mind of the people," the people will gather around us, and we need not worry about social instability. As the poet Gu Yanwu of the Ming Dynasty wrote, "In the mountain Goujian lived/His countrymen their lives would give." He meant that Goujian, the king of Yue, lived in the Kuaiji Mountains and patiently suffered hardships to build up strength against the invading neighbor state of Wu, winning the trust of the people, who then became willing to sacrifice themselves for him. The fundamental interests of our Party's officials conform with those of the people. As long as we stay close to the people and truly share their pains and concerns, we will certainly reaffirm our close ties with the people and win their hearts and minds.

> – *The Basic Proficiency of Officials—Maintaining Close Ties with the People* (January 1989), from *Shake off Poverty.*

Commentary

"The people are the root of a country. When the root is firm, the country is peaceful." Such people-oriented thought has deeply influenced Chinese society for thousands of years. "Governance lies in reassuring the people; reassuring the people lies in observing their suffering." "Dispelling the suffering of the people is like treating your own severe illness." These two ancient adages form a microcosm of people-oriented thought.

In the tenth year of the reign of Emperor Wanli in the Ming Dynasty, to alleviate social contradictions, Zhang Juzheng submitted a proposal to the emperor for ceasing to levy taxes on farmlands throughout the country and exempting the people from payment of overdue taxes. He also asserted, "Governance lies in reassuring the people; reassuring the people lies in observing their suffering." This meant that the key to achieving national stability is to make the people live and work in peace and contentment. To realize this, the ruler must show understanding of and sympathy for their sufferings and hardships. This initiative of "reassuring the people" precisely embodies people-oriented thought.

Su Zhe was a son of Su Xun and the younger brother of Su Shi. Deeply affected by his father and brother in his learning, he mainly embraced Confucianism and admired the "Secondary Saint" Mencius the most. Having dissenting views on the political reformation promoted by Wang Anshi, Su Zhe submitted a memorial to Emperor Shenzong of the Song Dynasty to convey his views on the new law. The *Memorial to His Majesty Emperor Shenzong* contained many of his important viewpoints, including the advice "dispelling the suffering of the people is like treating your own severe illness." He remonstrated with the emperor that a monarch should treat the people's sufferings as his own "severe illness" and dispel their misery with sympathy.

"In the mountain Goujian lived/His countrymen their lives would give" is a verse stemming from the poem, *The Mountain in Autumn*, by Gu Yanwu, a thinker in the late Ming and early Qing Dynasties. In 1645, the troops of the Qing Dynasty marched south and annihilated the regime of Emperor Hongguang of the Southern Ming Dynasty. During the war, several relatives of Gu were murdered in the Jiading Massacre. Thus, he penned this poem in grief and indignation to voice his deep sorrow over the fall of Southern Ming and his resolve for the restoration of his state. Goujian, the king of the state of Yue, in hopes of taking revenge for the insult, dwelled in the Kuaiji Mountain and patiently suffered hardships to build up strength against the invading neighbor state and finally won the trust of the people; therefore, the people were willing to follow him and even to sacrifice their lives for him. The poet quoted the tale of Goujian restoring his state to embolden the monarch and subjects of Southern Ming: as long as they kept the faith of fighting against the enemy and restoring the state, the people would rekindle the fighting will for renascence.

To highlight the importance of mass work, Xi Jinping presented to Party officials the methodology of observing the people's suffering and hardships and dispelling their suffering. As Party officials, they must stand in the shoes of the people to realize how they feel, to experience their suffering, and to detect the difficulties they encounter, and, in doing so, reaching the bottom of their hearts. They should continue to put the issue of people's livelihood at the top of their work, learning more about the expectations of the people, and meeting more of their pressing needs.

"To take as our own the mind of the people" is a view aired by Xi on multiple occasions. He once stated that poverty alleviation was on the top of his concerns and it took up most of his time and effort. To know the feelings of the people, to listen to their will and their desires, and to understand their living conditions, he reached the ice-and-snow-covered frontier, utterly oblivious to the bitter cold at minus dozens of degrees centigrade, and he went deep into the old revolutionary base areas where the land was infertile and the people were still ground down by deep poverty. Moreover, he once wrote that, "As a public servant, the Loess Plateau in Northern Shaanxi is where I became rooted. It nurtured my abiding faith: handling concrete affairs for the people!" "No matter where I go, I will always be the son of the Loess land."

BE INCORRUPTIBLE AND DILIGENT WITHOUT COMPLAINT OF POVERTY OR HARDSHIP

Throughout Chinese history, there have been many examples of honest and hardworking officials. The ancient statesman and strategist Zhuge Liang, who humbly strove to "do his best until death," required himself "not to allow himself or his family to have extra possessions in or out of the household." The Song Dynasty scholar-official Sima Guang "desired to sacrifice himself for his country and attend personally to public matters, working day and night." He was "indifferent to materials things, with no special interest in them" and "wore coarse clothing and ate poor food until the end of his life." If feudal officials were capable of this, who says that our proletarian officials are not? The older generation of proletarian revolutionaries, as represented by Chairman Mao Zedong, was models of honesty and diligence. Our officials at all levels must learn from the older generation of proletarian revolutionaries and strive to "be incorruptible and diligent without complaint of poverty or hardship." In this way, we can always be rooted in the people.

– *The Basic Proficiency of Officials—Maintaining Close Ties with the People* (January 1989), from the *Up and Out of Poverty*.

Commentary

There is a couplet hung on the columns of the door of the east accountant's office in the yamen of Neixiang County, Henan Province. The first line goes "Be incorruptible and diligent without complaint of poverty or hardship," and the second line is "Be respectful and conscientious of what you have heard and learned." The first line means that a truly incorruptible official would not complain about poverty, and a truly diligent official would not complain about hardship. The second line advises us that we should attach importance to the voice of the people and make an effort to practice what we learn. The first line now is utilized by President Xi Jinping in improving Party conduct and upholding integrity because this governing proverb, which preaches both incorruption and diligence, is still of strong realistic significance today.

Zhuge Liang, the Prime Minister of the state of Shu during the Three Kingdoms period, set strict demands on himself and lived frugally throughout his life. He assisted Liu Bei and Liu Shan diligently and conscientiously for 26 years, from his youth, when he had just come from his thatched cottage at the age of 27, until his death at 53 in Wuzhang Plains. By striving humbly to "do his best until death," he set an example to later generations. According to historical records, Zhuge Liang wrote *My Memorial to the King Liu Shan* before his death, in which he said, "My family has eight hundred mulberry trees and 15 acres of farmland in Chengdu. The gains from them are sufficient to afford the daily expenses of my sons and brothers as well as other family members. I myself, as an official, rely entirely on my salary to pay for my living expenses. I am not engaged in any part-time job or business for increasing income. Therefore, when I die, Your Majesty will never fall short of your expectations by finding any spare silk or extra money of mine."

The scholar-official Sima Guang of the Song Dynasty, who once saved a childhood playmate who had fallen into an enormous vat full of water by picking up a rock and smashing a hole in the vat, was famous for resourcefulness and determination. Assiduous and diligent, he "felt the need for more time to do his work and would thus steal some hours from the night," and he devoted nearly all his life to historical record compilation and political participation. The first annals in Chinese history—*A General Reflection for Political Administration*—were compiled under his direction. He remained honest and upright throughout his 40 years of officialdom, from his early years when he served as a local official until he was promoted to high-ranking positions. "He dares neither to often eat meat nor wear clothes made of pure silk." This is a true portrayal of his everyday life. Toward the end of his life, Sima Guang wrote a famous article to teach his son that it is easy to drift to a sumptuous and comfortable lifestyle, but it becomes very difficult then to change back to a simple and unadorned way of living. Many wise sayings can be derived from this article, such as "It is easy when one's living conditions ascend from economical to luxurious; conversely, it is difficult" and "Frugality is the magic weapon of establishing a reputation, while extravagance is the bane of failure," and they still bear significance today.

The older generation of proletarian revolutionaries, as represented by Chairman Mao Zedong, can be seen as models of honesty and diligence. There is an anecdote of Mao Zedong about frugality. In 1936, Edgar Snow arrived at the Shaanxi–Gansu–Ningxia border area as the first Western journalist to conduct an interview there. On this soil, he encountered a phenomenon: Mao Zedong had only two suits of uniforms and one patched overcoat, without any personal property; the officers and soldiers of the Red Army were treated equally and paid a salary of a negligible amount; however, none of them resorted to corruption and favoritism to make a fortune. Thus, Snow reached a conclusion: the CPC and the people's army under its leadership "were unbeatable owing to their steadfastness and perseverance as well as their willingness to bear hardship without complaint."

With the anecdotes of Zhuge Liang and Sima Guang, Xi Jinping exemplified the political attainments that our Party officials must have. Honesty is the foundation for governance, and diligence is the key to good governance. Only the official who has both political integrity and diligence can achieve good governance.

Xi Jinping once composed a poem to a Ci tune to express his admiration for Jiao Yulu's spirit of serving the people, and he wrote an article to extol Gu Wenchang as "an immortal monument in the people's heart". At the summary conference of the Program of Mass Line Education and Practice, he put profound meaning into simple words, "Our Party officials are all the people's public servants, thus we should concentrate on our duties. We should maintain both incorruptibility and diligence, and we should deliver practical services to the people with clean hands." It is thus clear that the excellent qualities of honesty and diligence are the political attainments that weigh most heavily in Xi's heart. The construction of a clean and diligent government is not only a revolution of integrity and efficiency but also one that stretches deep into the roots of some unhealthy notions. Only if one allows the conceptions of honesty, integrity, and diligence to take root in his or her heart can one be a good official and win the support and trust of the people.

CHAPTER 2

Stories of Morals: "Governing the Country After Cultivating One's Moral Character and Managing the Family's Affairs Well"

A HALF QUILT

In essence, the Long March told the story of a deep emotional bond between the Red Army and the people. When passing through Shazhou Village in Rucheng County, Hunan Province, three female Red Army soldiers sought shelter in the home of an elderly villager named Xu Jiexiu. Upon their departure, they cut their only quilt in two, leaving half with Xu Jiexiu. The elderly Xu said, "Who are the Communist Party members? They are those who have only one quilt but give half to the people."

– Speech at the Convention to Commemorate the 80th Anniversary of the Victory of the Red Army's Long March (October 21, 2016).

Commentary

Never give up on the people, and go hand in hand with the people forever. The "quilt cut in half" narratively evidences the close relationship between the Red Army soldiers and the people and symbolizes interdependence between the CPC and the masses.

The story took place in November 1934, when the Central Red Army broke the second blockade of the Kuomintang army and the legions arrived

© People's Publishing House 2020
People's Daily, Department of Commentary,
Narrating China's Governance,
https://doi.org/10.1007/978-981-32-9178-2_2

in Wenming Village, Rucheng County, Hunan province in succession and were quartered on Wenming, Xiushui, Hantian, and Shazhou for a week of rest and recuperation. It was during this period that three exhausted women soldiers of the Red Army sought shelter in a dilapidated cottage at the edge of Shazhou Village. This cottage was the home of Xu Jiexiu and her husband. Being utterly destitute, the couple had only a bedstead made of bamboo, with a meager covering of rice straw and a tattered grass mat serving as mattress. They did not even have a complete quilt. When sleeping, they could only cover themselves in a ragged pile of rotten cotton batting. Such being the case, the woman soldiers, who had abandoned all their baggage during the rapid march with the exception of a single quilt, squeezed up on this bed and shared the quilt with the hostess at night as they slept, while the male host of the cottage had to sleep on the haystack at the door to guard them.

The soldiers not only helped Xu Jiexiu and her husband tend the kitchen fire and cook meals but they also taught them revolutionary philosophies at their leisure. After sharing a bed with Xu, eating at the same table with the couple and performing manual labor together with them for several days, the soldiers had to say goodbye to them and continue to march on. In the early morning of the parting day, they decided to leave their only quilt to the couple, while the couple graciously declined it. The elderly couple continued to decline out of modesty all the way until they saw the soldiers off at the village entrance. Then, one of the soldiers took a pair of scissors from her backpack and cut the quilt in half, and said to Xu, "After we win the victory of the revolution, we will definitely present a complete new quilt to you." Accepting the half quilt, Xu felt a lump in her throat, and her eyes brimmed with tears.

The fellows of the Red Army spread all over the road of the Long March, their stories famously including "the old peasant living in the soviet area who sent all eight of his sons to join the Red Army," "the boatmen who risked their lives to ferry the Red Army soldiers over the Dadu River," and "the Tibetans living in the Qiaoqi Tibetan Town who set three memorial gateways composed of pines and cypresses as well as fresh flowers to greet the Red Army." They were the unsung heroes of the Long March.

At the Convention to Commemorate the 80th Anniversary of the Victory of the Red Army's Long March, Xi Jinping narrated the story of the half quilt that took place during the Long March, asserting that "the Long March succeeded because the CPC and the Red Army stood together with the people, maintained a close bond with the people, and shared weal and woe with the people," and warning the whole Party that to carry forward the spirit of the Long March and to succeed in our present long march, we must put the people at the very center of our hearts and remain committed to serving the people and relying on them in all of our endeavors.

EMPEROR KANGXI DISFAVORED THE LINGZHI MUSHROOM

The rulers of the past dynasties paid close attention to doing pragmatic work and implementing governance with pragmatism. Once, the Governor of Guangxi Province, Chen Yuanlong, reported to Emperor Kangxi that "a cloud-like Lingzhi mushroom over 33 cm high was plucked in a mountain in Guilin," and he quoted the words in the book *Shen Nong's Classic*, "The benevolent monarchs encourage the growth of the Lingzhi mushroom." Kangxi gave the following in reply: "There have been numerous indications of auspiciousness and disaster recorded in the annals of history. However, none of them had a use for the national welfare and the people's livelihood. No auspicious sign is greater than good crops from place to place as well as families living in affluence." He also once wrote, "The auspicious signs recorded in the historical annals, such as the propitious star, colored cloud, kirin and phoenix, and Lingzhi mushroom as well as tales of burning jewelry and jade in front of the hall and the sealed book coming down from heaven to the Chengtian Gate were all unreal and absurd writings, which I consider undesirable. I solely focus on the pragmatic administration of the people's livelihood in all sincerity." The ancient rulers also knew that if officials at all levels were not pragmatic, the people would not live well and live on, and consequently their feudal regimes would collapse.

– Speech at a Meeting for Criticism and Self-criticism of the Political Bureau of the 18th CPC Central Committee on the "Three Guidelines for Ethical Behavior and Three Basic Rules of Conduct" (December 28 to 29, 2015).

Commentary

In ancient China, there was a theory of "telepathy between man and nature," claiming that the auspicious signs in nature symbolize the clean and bright government. The feudal emperors therefore looked forward to the presence of so-called "auspicious signs". This offered an opportunity for sycophants to crawl out and flatter the monarchs with fake auspicious signs.

In 1713, the 52nd year of the reign of Kangxi, Huang Guocai, the Administrative Commissioner of Guangxi Province, reported to the Governor of Guangxi Chen Yuanlong that a cloud-like Lingzhi mushroom over 33.3 cm high had been plucked on a mountain of Guilin that February. He asked a favor of Chen to present this specimen to the emperor. Chen immediately sent a person to deliver it to the imperial palace, with a memorial attached. He indicated the "theory of auspicious sign" by quoting the classics and flattered Kangxi that the mushroom was an outcome of his benevolent governance. Knowing that Emperor Kangxi disliked so-called auspicious signs, but still going out of his way to deliver a harangue on it, Chen Yuanlong said a few words of flattery on Kangxi's birthday. Unexpectedly, Kangxi expressed his displeasure with the statement, and he declared that such a matter was so meaningless that there was no need for him to read the report on it.

Similarly, in the 56th year of Kangxi's reign, the Viceroy of Zhili Zhao Hongxie reported that a Lingzhi mushroom grew in his neighbor's yard. He stated, "A Lingzhi mushroom has arrived to presage auspiciousness under both reigns of Emperor Yao of the state of Tang as well as Emperor Shun of the state of Yu. Yet Your Majesty is much more virtuous and much more benevolent towards the people than Yao and Shun, so that people all over the world are bathing in the bounties bestowed by Your Majesty. Therefore, it is reasonable that the Lingzhi mushroom would grow at this time." Disagreeing with Zhao, Kangxi wrote a comment in red: "What does auspiciousness refer to? A bumper harvest and an abundance of food for the people. These are the most favorable auspices." He also pointed out to Zhao that, "This is a truth that is very easy to understand; thus, there is no need to debate about it."

Kangxi considered "good crops from place to place as well as families living in affluence" and "a bumper harvest and an abundance of food for the people" as the most favorable auspicious signs instead of embracing the vain theory that "the auspicious sign is endowed by heaven." His statements were intended to promote the practice of pragmatic governance in all sincerity.

Xi Jinping told the story of "Emperor Kangxi disfavored the Lingzhi mushroom" with the intention of stressing the practice of carrying out pragmatic governance in all sincerity and warning the leading officials of the

CPC that even the ancient rulers knew that if the officials at all levels were not pragmatic, the people would not live well and live on, and consequently their feudal regimes would collapse. He once recalled the precious insight he had when he was living and working in a production team in Yan'an, "I got to know what 'reality' meant, what 'seek truth from facts' meant, and what 'the masses' meant. This has benefitted me all my life." Therefore, the precept to "always act on the basis of seeking truth from facts" became the basic principle to which he adheres while pondering problems, making decisions, and handling affairs. He often encourages others to "do less unpragmatic work" and "be more pragmatic in planning, starting a business and behaving ourselves." The story of "Emperor Kangxi disfavored the Lingzhi mushroom" properly teaches the leading officials of the Party to be pragmatic and perform solid work.

SELF-CULTIVATION IS THE PRIORITY-AMONG-PRIORITIES FOR STATESMEN

The Chinese have been emphasizing self-cultivation since ancient times. We believe that "From the Son of Heaven down to the mass of the people, all must consider the cultivation of the person the root of everything else"; "Cultivate oneself and thus bring peace and security to the people"; "To enter politics, a person should first cultivate his moral character and enrich himself with virtues"; and "One should behave himself on the basis of a pure thought and from the starting point of self-cultivation." For example, in the Warring States period, Zou Ji, an official of the state of Qi, persuaded the King Wei of Qi to encourage remonstrance against himself by citing the instance when he compared himself in handsomeness with Mr. Xu who resided in the north of the city; Zhuge Liang came to the conclusion in *The First Memorial to the King Before Setting off for War* that "The emperors supported the virtuous and able officials and kept away from the vile and mean ones; thus, the Western Han Dynasty was prosperous. The emperors supported the vile and mean officials and kept away from the virtuous and able ones; thus, the Eastern Han Dynasty collapsed"; Fan Zhongyan contributed great lines through his essay *The Yueyang Tower*—"Be not thrown into ecstasies over success, nor feel depressed over failures" and "To be the first in the country to worry about the affairs of the state and the last in the country to enjoy oneself"; Wen Tianxiang wrote the heroic verse on the subject of life, "Since no one lives forever; I will leave only a loyalist's name in history." "One cannot be led into dissipation by wealth and rank, nor swerved from his aim by poverty and obscurity, nor subdued by power and force." Such characteristics of a great man were advocated by our ancestors.

> – Speech at a Meeting for Criticism and Self-criticism of the Political Bureau of the 18th CPC Central Committee on the "Three Guidelines for Ethical Behavior and Three Basic Rules of Conduct", (December 28–29, 2015).

Commentary

The Confucian culture in ancient China emphasized "the supreme morality internalized as cultivation and externalized as the governance of virtue." "Internalized as cultivation" refers to one's inner morality. It means that one can become a qualified ruler only by cultivating his morality and forging his character. Zou Ji, Zhuge Liang, Fan Zhongyan, and Wen Tianxiang were all historical figures famous for supreme morality and moral integrity.

Zou Ji, an official of the state of Qi in the Warring States period, was tall and very handsome. When he asked his wife, concubine, and guest, respectively, "Who do you think is more handsome, Mr. Xu (who is popular in town for his handsomeness) or I," all three told him that he is more handsome. But one day when Zou Ji eventually met Mr. Xu, he realized that Mr. Xu is actually much more handsome than himself. So he asked himself why his wife, concubine, and friend wouldn't tell him the truth. Then, he concluded the reason for this distorted information: "my wife favored me," "my concubine was afraid of me and therefore wanted to please me," and "my guest asked me for help." In view of this, he realized that to govern the country, the ruler should encourage the free airing of views. Thus, he persuaded King Wei of Qi to encourage remonstrance against himself with an open mind and listen to advice from all parties. This initiative subsequently promoted Qi to hold hegemony over all other contender states. Today, we can find the article *Zou Ji Persuaded the King Wei of Qi to Encourage Remonstrance Against Himself* in Chinese middle-school textbooks. Zhuge Liang's tales are praised far and wide, especially "Three Visits to the Thatched Cottage" and "Longzhong Dialogue", which are highly popular. Zhuge Liang, who was tilling land in Nanyang, received an assignment from Liu Bei at the time of a setback and was dispatched as an envoy at the very moment of a crisis. He did all he could for his state throughout his life, even giving the last drop of his blood. Fan Zhongyan was a writer in the Northern Song Dynasty. Born in a poverty-stricken family, he passed the highest imperial civil service examination through great study. Guided by the principle of "taking the destiny of one's country as one's own," he remained true to the mission, although many times he was relegated due to his outspoken remarks on the monarch. He always went by the following motto: "To be the first in the country to worry about the affairs of the state and the last in the country to enjoy oneself" both when he was heading the local government and defending the frontiers. Wen Tianxiang, a famous official in the late Southern Song Dynasty, was born in turbulent times, when wars raged throughout China. When the army of the Yuan Dynasty was marching south and invading his state, he persisted in fighting the invading army; however, he was ultimately defeated and taken prisoner. Yet he stuck to his values, although he was imprisoned in "a low, dirty, dark and wet cell about 2.6 m wide and 10.6 m deep, with a low and small single-leaf door and a short and narrow white wood window." It was in this impoverished environment that he produced the masterpieces *Passing Lingdingyang* and *Song of Righteousness*, and he became a beacon of values in Chinese history.

Zou Ji, Zhuge Liang, Fan Zhongyan, and Wen Tianxiang have been memorialized by generations throughout the ages due to their noble character, forming a continuous and consistent map of values and setting benchmarks of character-forging.

At a meeting for criticism and self-criticism of the Political Bureau of the 18th CPC Central Committee, Xi Jinping made much of the self-cultivation by the leading officials of the Party. With the tales of Zou Ji, Zhuge Liang, Fan Zhongyan, and Wen Tianxiang, he exemplified that to settle down and get on with their pursuits, Party members and officials, especially senior leaders, must cultivate their moral character and mind.

"Be strict with oneself and lenient towards others"; "Seeing good deeds, I risk everything to achieve such goodness; seeing evil deeds, I immediately recoil as if I had sipped boiling water"; "All of the world's failures are due to action without authorization; all of the world's successes are the result of collaboration"; "The people who are with you because of your power will leave you when you are no longer in power; the people who are with you because of your money will scatter when your money runs out"... Many of the allusions that have been cited by Xi have been about self-cultivation. The saying, "I examine myself, day by day" teaches us the philosophies of self-reflection and self-criticism. "Hold the rules in awe" emphasizes the principle of abiding by laws and adhering to the bottom line "Be cautious about executing power, be cautious when you stay alone, be cautious about the erroneous ideas at the outset, and be cautious about making friends" highlights that we should be cautious about small matters and destroy evils before they pose a threat. With regard to the various aspects of settling down and getting on with one's pursuit, Xi Jinping presented the leading officials of the Party with the epistemology and methodology of morality avocation and self-cultivation.

NEVER HANKER AFTER TRANSIENT SUCCESS

Taking on responsibility calls for conscientiousness. One's plans must be carried out from beginning to end, taking care to refrain from merely going through the motions or treating them as a temporary measure, like a passing gust of wind. On most occasions, a County Party Secretary serves for only a few years; however, that person should not act as if he or she were a temporary worker. Some officials are anxious to achieve quick success and obtain instant benefits within a short term of office to show their capability with ornate achievements and pave the way to promotion. This is wrong. If one's plans change every few years, a county will achieve little of substance. Instead, one should be open-minded about achievements—a good plan, as long as it is feasible, pragmatic, and answers the people's needs, should be passed down from one term of office to the next. Youyu County of Shanxi Province is situated in a windswept location in the Mu Us Desert (Ordos Desert). It is a barren land battered by sandstorms with minimal natural resources. In the early days of new China, its first County Party Secretary led the people to begin an afforestation program to curb encroachment by the sand. Over the past six decades, the successive administrations of Youyu have passed this plan on and on, retaining the same goal, leading the Party officials and people in this county to unremittingly afforest the land. Now, the greening rate of the county has risen to 53%, from 0.3% in 1949, and the "barren land" has been turned into an "oasis". Such perseverance, patience, endurance, and long-term vision are what we should be equipped with when doing any type of work.

– Be a Good County Party Secretary—Speech at the Meeting with a Class of County Party Secretaries at the Central Party School (January 12, 2015).

Commentary

"What is an official's reputation? You can only find the real answer from the chitchat among the people after he has retired from office." No matter how much money we gain, or how high a political reputation we have, we are subject to natural law, and we will eventually perish. What kind of achievement can maintain its glory throughout the course of history? The story of Youyu County, Shanxi Province, gives us an answer.

At the beginning of the founding of new China, the natural conditions in Youyu were very bad, sandstorms and floods wreaked havoc such that the land was sparsely populated and too arid for any plant to grow. Soon after Zhang Ronghuai, the first County Party Secretary of Youyu, assumed office, one sandstorm with overwhelming yellow sand presented a "special gift" to him. In recognition of the rugged natural environment, he embarked on the trek to investigate the environment throughout the county, with a pack on his back, a military map in his hand, and stir-fried noodles. Within only 2 months, he had traveled to more than 300 villages of all sizes and over 1000 brooks across the county and had accordingly coined a resounding slogan: "To subsist in Youyu is to plant trees in Youyu." This slogan determined the county's blueprint for development—afforesting for ecological improvement. Taking the baton from Zhang, Wang Jukun, the second County Party Secretary of Youyu, initiated the 10,000-People Afforestation Campaign. He planted trees with the people. His face became tanned as deeply as that of an average person, and his hands were covered with bleeding blisters as serious as those of average person. They even called him "Secretary Plant-Trees". The next successive secretaries handed this baton on and on and adhered to the blueprint one by one. They all followed the guiding principle, "Plant trees anywhere we can to make somewhere green first." One of them even promoted afforestation throughout his entire 12-year term of office.

Over the course of 60 years, things changed, and so did the leadership of the County Party Committee. However, the blueprint of afforestation remained unchanged. In 2015, the greening rate of the county reached 53%, compared to below 0.3% before the founding of new China, increasing forested area from 533 to 100,000 hectares. With the ecological improvement, economic and livelihood conditions there improved dramatically. With the efforts successively made by the secretaries, this once "barren land" has already become an "oasis".

Xi Jinping recounted the story of desertification control in Youyu to tell the large number of grassroots officials headed by the County Party Secretaries that to achieve accomplishments, they must be open-minded about achievements and have patience and endurance to reap long-term benefits.

Xi Jinping stressed that "a County Party Secretary should be open-minded about achievements," and "a good plan should be passed down from one term of office to the next." These words represent both the philosophy of keeping the ultimate goal in mind all along and the practice of holding on straight to the end. When he governed Ningde, he demanded that the officials should overcome impatience and decrease short-term acts during economic construction. In Fuzhou, he noted, "In economic construction, the lack of long-term planning is prone to cause serious mistakes and even breed permanent regret." In Zhejiang Province, he emphasized that an official should be willing to pave the way for his successor, take over unfinished work from his predecessor, and "do his or her bit to help attain the ultimate goal based on the achievement of the predecessor..."

Telling the story of Youyu, Xi Jinping guided Party members and officials to think about and address the relationships between the individual and the collective as well as between long-term fundamental interests and personal ambitions and interests. He stressed that this concept of political achievement is a form of political ethics, which officials should firmly foster and sustain.

THE GREAT LOVE OF TEACHERS

I have read much of the deeds of many prominent teachers. Many of renown have devoted themselves to students in the spirit of selflessness. Some teachers have given financial assistance to poverty-stricken students with their limited salaries for fear of students dropping out of school. Some have purchased teaching materials at their own expense. Some have carried students on their back to school or held students' hands to help them cross over rapid steams or take dangerous roads. And some have even stuck to their posts despite disabilities. Many of these deeds are deeply moving. They all spring from the great love of the teachers. We should vigorously promote and carry forward the meritorious deeds and noble character of prominent teachers throughout our large-scale education system and even the whole of society.

- To Be a Good Teacher of the Party and the People—Speech at the Symposium with the Representatives of Teachers and Students of Beijing Normal University (September 9, 2014).

Commentary

They impart knowledge in chalk year after year; they transmit love on the platform from generation to generation. Everyone has a cherished mentor in his memory.

As we read the newspaper and browse the Internet, we often feel moved by some story of an exemplary teacher's deeds. In Taizhou, Zhejiang Province, a teacher spent RMB 300,000 yuan over 23 years to aid needy students, while he himself lived frugally and biked to work every day; in Yibin, Sichuan Province, a disabled teacher with a single arm remained at his post in a shabby school house for 30 years; in Shiyan, Hubei Province, a female teacher who has been stationed in a remote mountain for 35 years has carried her students on her back to cross over a river hundreds of thousands of times. The great love of these teachers moves countless people.

Furthermore, some teachers have even served as the moral standards of this era. When the Wenchuan earthquake occurred, Tan Qianqiu, a teacher of Deyang Dongqi Middle School, was giving a class. He quickly organized his students to evacuate downstairs. Learning that several students had not yet left the classroom, he returned to the fourth floor. In the moment when the cement ceiling was about to fall, he shielded four students firmly under his body with open arms. When his remains were found in the ruins, he lay prone on the platform with his arms still open. Zhang Lili, a teacher of the 19th Middle School of Jiamusi, Heilongjiang Province, is hailed as "the most beautiful woman teacher." On the evening of May 8, 2012, out-of-control bus rushed toward students. In the critical moment, Zhang Lili struggled to save her students and entangled herself in the rolling wheels, resulting in severe fractures of both her legs, and was eventually amputated above the knees. These teachers' deeds touched China.

Xi Jinping, who feels eternal gratitude to his own teachers, has made a good example of respecting teachers and attaching importance to education. He sends greetings and wishes to his teachers on the occasion of each Chinese Spring Festival. When he held public office in other places, he would take time to visit his teacher every time he came to Beijing for meetings or Party affairs. On the eve of Children's Day 2014, Xi Jinping visited the students of the Minzu Primary School of Haidian District in Beijing and especially invited Chen Qiuying, his Chinese teacher in middle school, who was later transferred to China Children's Publishing House. He said to Teacher Chen with a smile, "I remember when I was in the first year of middle school, you taught us Chinese and explained the texts very well."

"A teacher's indispensable, and perhaps most important quality, is the love of students," said Zankov, a Soviet educator. Telling teachers' stories on Teacher's Day, Xi Jinping elicited the deepest emotions held in everyone's heart with touching details, which not only conveyed the values of respecting teachers and education but also set an example to all teachers—one should try to emulate those who are wise and good.

In Xi's view, to be a good teacher, one must have ideals and faith, moral sentiment, solid knowledge, and a benevolent heart. With these four virtues, he painted a portrait of the good teacher of the new era. "It is easy to impart expertise to others; however, it is not so easy to teach people how to be a man of virtue with profound knowledge and a noble personality." "A teacher is one who deciphers truths, teaches skills, and clarifies misconceptions." He also cited these ancient sayings to encourage teachers not only to transmit culture and knowledge but also to shape character and values.

STATESMEN'S ASPIRATIONS

Wang Anshi, a statesman of the Northern Song Dynasty, was appointed Governor of Yinxian County, Zhejiang Province (now the Yinzhou District, Ningbo, Zhejiang) at the age of 27. When he served at the post, he not only organized the construction of water conservancy facilities and developed production but also gave the people loans of official grain and defended against corruption. In addition, respecting teachers and attaching importance to education, he stressed the cultivation of talent. During his 4-year term in office, he achieved remarkable results in governance and was widely praised by the people, laying a foundation for the reforms he later introduced. Feng Menglong, a writer of the Ming Dynasty who authored the classic works *Stories to Enlighten the World*, *Stories to Warn the World* and *Stories to Awaken the World*, worked toward the challenging imperial civil service examination until he reached the age of 57, when he was enrolled as a senior licentiate (a professional title in feudal China). He assumed the post of the Governor of Shouning County, Fujian Province at the advanced age of 61, with a term of office of 4 years. He made Shoun-ing a county where the people lived in peace and contentment by enacting the following: alleviating the corvee, reforming the style of governing, set-tling lawsuits based on the principles of justice, breaking with undesirable customs, cleaning up the academic atmosphere, and promoting beneficial policies and abolishing those that were harmful. According to the records of that period, "The prison cells stood empty without any prisoners, and there was no need for a jailer to report on security."

 – Speech at a Meeting for Criticism and Self-criticism of the Standing
   Committee of the Lankao County Party Committee, Henan Province
   (May 9, 2014).

Commentary

The two governors, Wang Anshi and Feng Menglong, achieved equally brilliant feats, although they were born in different dynasties. They jointly demonstrated splendid governance over the years. Wang Anshi dedicated his youth to the people on the border at the beginning of his political career, and Feng Menglong continued to struggle to serve his people into his twilight years.

Wang Anshi was a famous thinker and statesman in the Northern Song Dynasty. He was referred to as the "Chinese reformer of the 11th century" by Lenin. As soon as he took office in Yinxian County, he began to inves-tigate local agricultural production. Learning that the people of Yinxian County were most afraid of drought, "he vigorously organized the people to dredge the waterways and construct water conservancy facilities for water storage to cope with the drought." In the spring of the second year in his term of office, when the grain has not been harvested and the villagers have run out of their food, he lent the grain in the county-owned grain depot to the villagers and agreed with them that after the autumn harvest, they would repay the grain to the county government and pay a small amount of interest. This laid the foundation for the later promulgation of the *Young Crops Law*. He also valued education, establishing the Confucius Temple of Yinxian County as an institute. "From then on, Yinxian County had a county institute," according to historical records. This had a great impact on the eastern Zhejiang school of Chinese culture.

The records state that "During his four-year tenure in Shouning, Governor Feng achieved great political progress. Who would dare say that he only has attainments in literature?" Feng Menglong was a famous writer and scholar of the Ming Dynasty. When he served at the post of the Governor of Shouning County, Fujian Province, he also commenced work based on field investigation. Concerned about the people's lack of food and clothing, he strived to achieve an agricultural production target to "reclaim land by chiseling stones and plant seedlings once a piece of sandy soil [was] reclaimed." He also placed importance on the construction of water conservancy facilities because "in general, the fields will become fertile when they are irrigated by water veins without a jam." Feng also attached importance to establishing customs and habits and disseminating culture, so that advanced culture could be introduced into the relatively backward Fujian Province. He even pursued impartial law enforcement, streamlined administration, and fair and clear punishment. During his 4-year tenure, he gained a good reputation for "promoting streamlined administration and fair and clear punishment, advocating literature first, favoring the people and treating other officials politely."

Wang Anshi was not frivolous in his youth. Feng Menglong did not muddle along in his old age. They jointly present the image of a pragmatic official in the first half and second half of life, respectively.

Xi Jinping once noted that all the grassroots officials of our Party are the reinforcing steel in the foundations of the party's edifice of governance: "They bear heavy responsibilities, yet they stand lower." In the spring of 2014, the second round of the Program of Mass Line Education and Practice got into full swing. The main recipients of this round were the Party members and officials, and the main purpose was to impress the excellent style of work of the Party into the mind of every Party member or official by extending the results of the previous round to the grassroots level. Integrating the grand theme of the second round of the campaign into impressive historical stories, Xi Jinping interpreted the value of remaining pragmatic and the people being served by the grassroots officials.

"Under Jiao Yulu's Paulownia, Their Tears Run in Spate"

Comrade Jiao Yulu lived a simple life, working diligently and frugally, and he practiced the principle "to be the first to bear hardships and the last to enjoy comforts." His clothes, hat, shoes, and stockings were all old and had been washed many times, and all the worn items had been mended and sewn innumerable times. He strictly observed party discipline and never used his power to benefit himself or his relatives. The *Ten Never-Do's for Officials* drafted by him included specific provisions on honesty and self-discipline for officials. Yesterday, standing in front of the display board of the *Ten Never-Do's for Officials* in the Memorial Hall for Comrade Jiao Yulu, I read it again carefully. I think these provisions are on-target and emphasize the rules. Thus, we should not juggle our words, making regulations that are grandiose but vacuous. In addition to the provision "never accept a complimentary opera ticket," the *Ten Never-Do's for Officials* stipulated, "Opera tickets for seats in the front ten rows should not be sold only to officials." This was meant that some favorable tickets should be left for the masses. Once, when he overheard that his son had not paid for a show because he knew the ticket seller, he chastised him never to seek any personal privilege and "freeload", and he ordered him to send the money to the theater. His character of being strict with himself and refusing to be contaminated by evil influence vividly reflected his self-consciousness of strengthening Party discipline.

> – Speech at the Enlarged Meeting of the Standing Committee of the Lankao County Party Committee of Henan Province, (March 18, 2014).

Commentary

In August 1922, Jiao Yulu was born into a poor family in Zibo, Shandong Province. He volunteered to be a militiaman as early as 1945 and joined the CPC in 1946. In 1948, he went southward with a work team, and he later was transferred to Lankao County, Henan Province to be the County Party Secretary of Lankao. In the position of the County Party Secretary of Lankao, he manifested his immovable faith and forged a spiritual monument to the communists.

During 1962 and 1964, Lankao was under "three serious threats"—waterlogging, sandstorm, and saline-alkali land. Together with the officials and the masses of the county, he conducted small-scale experiments. These included digging out the silty soil to repress the sands, digging out the silty soil to repress the alkali, and enclosing the sand dunes. Based on the experimental results, he summarized specific strategies for eliminating the "three serious threats" and explored methods of large-scale paulownia planting. During that period, Jiao Yulu, who was suffering from liver cancer, endured intense pain and yet continued to work. Through painstaking efforts, he led Lankao to achieve remarkable results in eliminating the "three serious threats." He led the masses to plant paulownia to develop windbreaks and for sand fixation. Since then, planting paulownia has become the major industry in Lankao, and the annual output value reached more than RMB 6 billion yuan by 2014. The sand-proof tree became a moneymaker for the people. Although Jiao Yulu spent a short time in office in Lankao, he bequeathed the spirit of Jiao Yulu—treat and love the people as family, struggle hard, remain scientific and pragmatic, brave difficulties, and contribute selflessly. This spirit is of eternal value.

Xi Jinping has repeatedly told the story of Jiao Yulu. He has often recalled when he learned the deeds of Jiao with deep emotion, relating the following: "On February 7, 1966, when I was in the first grade of middle school, the *People's Daily* published a lengthy newsletter from Mu Qing and other comrades—*The Example of County Party Secretaries—Jiao Yulu*. My politics teacher choked with tears many times while reading this newsletter for us. I was especially deeply shocked when I heard that Comrade Jiao Yulu still persisted in his work during later-stage liver cancer, with a stick pressed against the liver area. The other end of the stick made a big hole in the right side of the chair…" Since then, the spirit of Jiao Yulu has been deeply rooted in Xi's heart, inspiring great spiritual power. "Of all the citizens, who does not love a good servant? Under Jiao Yulu's paulownia, their tears run in spate." These are the words of the *Niannujiao—Memories of Jiao Yulu*, written by Xi Jinping to express his respect for and cherish the memory of Jiao Yulu.

The story of Jiao Yulu has been passed down from generation to generation, and his spirit has eternal value. Xi Jinping has repeatedly stressed, "County Party Committees are the 'first line command' of governance for our Party" and that "With their responsibilities growing and becoming more diversified, county governments now play an important role in building a moderately prosperous society in all respects, in driving reform to a deeper level, in implementing the rule of law, and in strengthening Party discipline." At the Enlarged Meeting of the Standing Committee of the Lankao County Party Committee, Xi Jinping led the Party members and officials to review the spirit of Jiao Yulu for the purpose of inspiring the numerous County Party Secretaries to learn from Jiao and strive to be a County Party Secretary like Jiao Yulu, urging them to fulfill the requirements of "with the people in mind, with responsibility in mind, and with self-discipline in mind."

WORDS AND DEEDS

There is a couplet hung in the ancient yamen in Neixiang County, Henan Province: "As an official, do not have prejudice on your job because it is you the officer on whom the civilians rely to address even trivial matters; do not bully the civilians since it is they who raise you up and one of whom you are." It reveals the relationship between officials and the people in words that are easy to read and understand. Even the feudal officials had such political consciousness, us, the communists of today, should have much better understanding of the relation between the people and the power that they grant us. Not long ago, an internal reference from the *People's Daily* introduced the thoughts on politics of Gao Derong, Deputy Director of the Standing Committee of the National People's Congress of Nu Jiang Lisu Autonomous Prefecture, Yunnan Province. I was deeply moved after reading his thoughts. This official of Dulong nationality said, "Leaders are the people who lead the masses to work together, to work out a way"; "If an official or a leader is not pragmatic, he will turn from a conductor into a muckraker"; "We should conduct others with our deeds, not words"; "If you float in officialdom, then you will be more and more impetuous; and if you live amid the masses, then you will be further enriched." I would like to recommend these words to all of you for mutual encouragement.

 – Speech at the Symposium with the Principal Leaders of Heze, Shandong Province and the Counties and Districts Under the Jurisdiction of Heze (November 26, 2013).

Commentary

"As an official, do not have prejudice in your job because it is you the officer on whom the civilians rely to address even trivial matters; do not bully civilians since it is they who raise you up and one of whom you are." This is a couplet hung on the columns of the Self-Examination Hall in the ancient yamen in Neixiang County, Henan Province. It was composed by Gao Yiyong in 1680, the 19th year of the reign of Emperor Kangxi. At that time,

Gao was Governor of Neixiang County. He was born in Jiaxing, Zhejiang Province. In 1679, when he was appointed as Governor, the county of Neixiang was in chaos caused by war such that a great deal of civilians had left their hometown, the land was deserted, and the economy was depressed. Extremely worried about this plight and feeling heavily responsible, he was sleepless at night and composed this couplet by candlelight.

Tolerant and benevolent, Gao took good care of the people. When he traveled to the provincial capital Daliang (present-day Kaifeng), the civilians there pointed to him and said admiringly, "This is Officer Gao, Governor of Neixiang County." When he left the post, the civilians of Neixiang lined the streets to retain him, and someone even ran after him hundreds of miles to see him off. *The Encyclopedia of Decrees and Regulations of Neixiang* compiled during the reign of Emperor Tongzhi provides a comment on him: Gao Yiyong, who reclaimed a large amount of land and cracked down on bandits, made a great contribution to Neixiang.

Gao Derong is a typical leader of today. Always bearing in mind his countrymen of Dulong nationality, he resolutely returned to his hometown twice during his career. The first time he made this decision was when he was young. At that time, he had left the remote mountain area and faced an opportunity to work at his college after graduation. However, he applied to be sent back to his hometown, the remote Dulong River Town, to teach. The second time was after he had reached the age of 50. When he was promoted to Deputy Director of the Standing Committee of the National People's Congress of Nu Jiang Lisu Autonomous Prefecture, Yunnan Province, he applied to the organization once again, "Please set my office in Dulong River Town." Further, he gave an unpretentious and touching reason: "My countrymen of Dulong nationality still live in poverty; thus, I am unable to have peace of mind if I live in ease and comfort away from the mountain."

In addition to caring for the people, Gao Derong also advocated pragmatism. He traveled over a hundred miles in the mountain region per day, from the early morning until night, to visit six villages and dozens of construction sites. This was the normal working mode of this old county mayor. To build a long tunnel under the alpine snow line, he busied himself coordinating the work of various departments and governments at all levels for 3 years until the tunnel was completed.

Working among the masses and serving as a good example for the masses is a fine tradition of our Party. In November 2013, Xi Jinping visited Heze,

Shandong Province, for an inspection. At the symposium with the principal leaders of Heze and of the counties and districts under Heze, he began his talk with the couplet hung in the ancient yamen in Neixiang and linked it to the deeds of Gao Derong, endowing the people-oriented thought of ancient times with contemporary significance and tracing the current spirit of "for the people" back to its historical origin. Telling these stories, President Xi reiterated the pragmatic style and mass consciousness with which leading officials should be equipped, restated the metaphorical relationship between a ship and the water, and recalled the interdependence between the CPC and the masses. His intention was to guide the leading officials to continue to bear hardships and to live and work with the masses through governance that aims at the happiness of the masses. He shared Gao Derong's thoughts with the whole Party: "We should conduct others with our deeds, not words," mirroring present-day misconduct.

The Power of Faith

In the revolutionary wars, martyrs defied all difficulties and dangers and took death calmly because of their unswerving commitment to lofty ideals and faith. Six members of Chairman Mao's family sacrificed their lives for the revolution. The Senior General Xu Haidong's clan sacrificed over 70 members. In Marshal He Long's clan, we can find 2,050 identified martyrs. Why were these revolutionary predecessors willing to devote their lives unselfishly and heroically? Reasons include espousing a noble revolutionary ideal, upholding a lofty political faith, seeking the complete overthrow of the evil old regime in China, and striving to achieve national independence and the people's liberation. I have read *Honest Poverty*, which was written by the martyr Fang Zhimin in the prison, many times. It expresses the older generation of communists' loves and hates. It defines true poverty and wealth and the greatest happiness, and it describes the great faith of the revolutionists and what a valuable life looks like. Every time I read it, I am inspired and enlightened.

- Leading Officials Should Have the Correct Outlooks on the World, on Power and on Career—Speech at the Opening Ceremony of the Central Party School in 2010 Autumn Semester (September 1, 2010).

Commentary

Six family members, over 70 clansmen and clanswomen, and 2,050 martyrs: these astounding figures illustrate the aspiration and faith of communist' values.

Six members of Chairman Mao's family sacrificed their lives for the revolution, including his wife Yang Kaihui, eldest son Mao Anying, eldest younger brother Mao Zemin, second younger brother Mao Zetan, younger female cousin Mao Zejian, and nephew Mao Chuxiong. He sacrificed nearly his entire family for the revolution. When he was informed of Mao Anying's sacrifice on the Korean battlefield, the first thing he said from extreme distress was "This is his fate, as the son of Mao Zedong!" These words expressed the father's solicitude, and they even manifested a communist's immovable faith and spirit of dauntlessness. Marshal He Long often said, "It was the need of the revolutionary cause that all martyrs in our clan died for the country; thus, we do not constantly mention ourselves." This dedicated spirit of sacrifice of family and individual interests for one's country and for the collective benefit precisely advanced the success of the revolution in China.

Fang Zhimin is arguably an outstanding representative of the countless martyrs laying down their lives for our nation. When he was captured on the battlefield, what astonished the Kuomintang soldiers was that, as a criminal the Kuomintang wanted most and a "high official" of the CPC, he did not even have a copper coin in his pocket. After being captured, he refused the coaxing and lure of the high-ranking officials of the Kuomintang, and when the Kuomintang led him through the streets to warn the public, he remained defiant and unyielding. In prison, he produced literary works such as *Beloved China, Honest Poverty, A Record of My Life in Prison* and *A Brief Account of My Revolutionary Struggle* despite the extremely poor conditions. These books have become the spiritual food for later generations, inspiring countless communists. As he wrote in *Honest Poverty*, "Honest although poor, we are living a clean and simple life—this is how we revolutionists can overcome innumerable difficulties!"

At the opening ceremony of the Central Party School in the 2010 autumn semester, Xi Jinping told the stories of the communists of older generations to inspire the present-day Party members and officials to fortify their ideals and beliefs and to consolidate the pedestal of their faith. Faith, the most beautiful word in human society, is the foundation for over 88 million communists to settle down and get on with their pursuit. Xi has repeatedly called on all party members "to stick to the lofty faith to achieve indestructibility" since the 18th National Congress of the CPC.

The column "People's Tribune" of the *People's Daily* once published the article *The Flavor of the Faith*, which narrates the anecdote that when Chen Wangdao was concentrating on translating *The Communist Manifesto*, he mistook ink for brown sugar and ate it unconsciously. This story embodied the sweet flavor of the communists' spirit and faith. To stimulate Party members and officials to maintain their ideals and maintain their faith, Xi Jinping repeatedly told this touching story from the Party's history, repeatedly stressing that " ideals and faith are the spiritual nutrition of communists," and he repeatedly warned that "nothing is more dangerous than to waver in ideals and faith; nothing is more dangerous than the slide of ideals and faith."

"WE MUST SAVE HIM, EVEN IF WE HAVE TO GO BEGGING"

In a remote village, the Party Branch Secretary Zheng Jiuwan fell ill. To cure him, the villagers spontaneously raised tens of thousands of yuan within one day for his operation. They said, "We must save him, even if we have to go begging." Some officials of the village even lamented, "If I fall ill, how many villagers will save me?" The villagers did this to repay the contributions made by Zheng Jiuwan, and the scales in their hearts proved the weight of this grassroots Party official. Through practical actions, he revealed the connotation of the saying, "The civilians value the officials as highly as the officials value the civilians." This is the significance of Zheng Jiuwan as a worthy role model.

- Serve the People, and Win the People's Support (July 24, 2006), from *Fresh Ideas of Zhejiang*.

Commentary

Zheng Jiuwan was Party Branch Secretary of Houjiujiang Village, Shankeng Town, Yongjia County, Wenzhou, Zhejiang Province. In the early hours of October 5, 2005, he suddenly had a cerebrovascular rupture due to long-term overwork and was in danger of dying. To raise money for his operation, the villagers of this remotest village in the town, where the per capita income was only approximately RMB 2,000 yuan, unexpectedly scraped together nearly 70,000 yuan within a single day. One villager, Liu Liangli, had 7,160 yuan, which was prepared for paying for the chicken feed needed by his chicken farm. His wife said, "We can recover, although we will lose all the chickens. But, the Secretary will not come back if his illness is not treated immediately!" Therefore, he donated 7,100 yuan, with only 60 yuan left for his family. After that, he further donated 100 yuan that he borrowed to pay his electricity bill. Chen Jurui, Director of the Women's Congress of the Village, donated over 1,300 yuan from her life savings. This was the money that her daughter had given her at the Chinese Spring Festival and other festivals. Liu Songyun, who was suffering from severe hepatic ascites and whose family was in financial distress, sent 300 yuan to Zheng Jiuwan through others. He had earned the 300 yuan by selling eggs, persimmons, and soybeans and had saved the money to buy medicine… "We must save Jiuwan, even if we have to go begging," said the villagers. Those villagers who were able to walk went to the hospital with water and wheat cakes to wait for him. After the first operation failed, people from all sectors of society made generous contributions of funds. Subsequently, the secretary was out of danger and soon recovered.

"One loving others is always loved by others." Upon joining the CPC, every Party member took an oath of loyalty. Zheng Jiuwan carried out his oath by serving his people throughout his career since he became the Party branch secretary a dozen years ago. There are several touching stories. When he learned that Chen Jurui's husband had undergone a hyperos-teogeny and was in urgent need of money to treat the disease, he imme-diately sent her 2,180 yuan, which he had earned by selling his cattle in preparation for his son's marriage, and he told the patient to have a good rest. After the villager Liu Guangmiao's leg was broken in a tractor accident, not only did Zheng pay several hundred yuan for Liu's medical expenses and give him 50 yuan to buy food but he also helped his family to harvest potatoes and grow winter wheat. Zheng Jiuwan was not very well off to be sure; however, he contributed as much as he could to the villagers.

The touching stories between Zheng Jiuwan and the villagers reveal the interdependent relationship between leading officials of the Party and the masses. Learning about Zheng's deeds, Xi Jinping, as Secretary of the Provincial Party Committee of Zhejiang, gave the following instructions: "The civilians value the officials as highly as the officials value the civilians.

The advanced deeds of Comrade Zheng Jiuwan were actually the embodiments of this saying."

Xi Jinping told Zheng Jiuwan's story in *Fresh Ideas of Zhejiang* to highlight that all members and officials of the CPC should put the people at the very center of their hearts. After the 18th National Congress of the CPC was held, "the people" became key words in all important speeches delivered by General Secretary Xi Jinping: "The people are the source of our strength"; "Highest-level politics are about popular support, and justice is the strongest force"; "The people aspire to a decent life—that is what we are fighting for"; "Rely closely on the people to promote reform and opening up"; and "To realize the Chinese Dream, we must pool China's strength, that is, the strength of great unity among the people of all ethnic groups." At the Celebration Ceremony of the 95th Anniversary of the Founding of the CPC, he gave special emphasis to the CPC's "original aspiration", and "the people" as the very center of the "original aspiration".

Gu Wenchang's Hidden Achievement

The masses and Party officials in Dongshan County, Fujian Province admire Gu Wenchang, their former County Party Secretary. This is because Gu neither pursued "conspicuous achievement" nor attracted public attention when he was in office; instead, he took more than a dozen years to lead local officials and the masses to build a shelter forest along the coast for later generations. This is an immortal monument in the people's hearts. Such a "hidden achievement" is the greatest "conspicuous achievement".

– "Hidden Achievement" and "Conspicuous Achievement" (January 17, 2005), from *Fresh Ideas of Zhejiang*.

Commentary

In Dongshan County, Fujian Province, there is a custom that has been passed down: at an ancestor worship ceremony, pay tribute to Secretary Gu before worshipping one's family ancestors. Each year during the Chinese Spring Festival and other festivals, local families offer sacrifices to pay tribute to Gu Wenchang, the County Party Secretary they most respect.

Today's Dongshan is a beautiful and richly endowed ecological island, offset by flower fields and surrounded by trees. To everyone's surprise, over

60 years ago, it was a desolate sand island where sandstorms wreaked havoc and the land went out of cultivation. There were more than 150 days per year with force-6 strong winds or stronger, and the greening rate was only 0.12%. For one hundred years, sandstorms constantly engulfed people's homes, and smallpox and eye diseases spread around the county. At least one-in-ten residents survived as a coolie or a beggar.

The Australian Pine Tree forest was precisely the key to reviving the island, and a "monument" was built there by Gu Wenchang. Gu Wenchang was born in Linxian County, Henan Province. He traveled southward with troops to Fujian Province in 1950. Then, he worked in Dongshan County for 14 years and acted as the County Party Secretary for 10 years. He was known to say, "Overcome the sandy wind, or be buried by it." With such courage, he led the Dongshan people to struggle against the sandy wind for more than a dozen years by planting Australian Pines around the island as a Green Great Wall. Finally, they triumphed over the traditionally unbeatable sandy wind, making the island a peaceful home for the people.

Later, Gu Wenchang was transferred to the Fujian Provincial Department of Forestry as Deputy Director General. During the Great Cultural Revolution, he was sent to work as a regular worker. Wherever he worked and fought, the people all had the greatest respect as well as endless affection for him. When he was in office, he always stood at the forefront of the struggle against the sandy wind, the forefront of afforestation and the forefront of reservoir construction. In the early days after the founding of new China, he put forward the proposal of renaming "the enemy's and puppets' dependents" as "the war-affected dependents." This benevolent policy won him the support of 100,000 people. He often said to his family and those around him, "As leaders, we must keep straight with clean hands." None of the personnel working for him was promoted or put in an important position by him. None of his five children were awarded assignments to an official position. He did not allow his family to use even a bicycle because it belonged to the public.

"I expect to be with the people and the trees of Dongshan forever" were Gu Wenchang's last words as he approached his end. Now, he is sleeping his eternal sleep in the Chishan Forest Farm where he combated nature. The trees he planted more than 50 years ago tower like a canopy and guard his tomb. They witnessed the passion and loyalty of this good official "with the Party, the people, the responsibility and self-discipline in mind."

Xi Jinping has praised three County Party Secretaries: Jiao Yulu, Gu Wenchang, and Wang Boxiang. In *Fresh Ideas of Zhejiang*, taking Gu Wenchang as an example, he discussed the truth in "hidden achievement" and "conspicuous achievement". There is no immediate payoff when one plants trees; however, it is an effort that will bear fruit after several decades of effort and the "hidden achievement" will grow into a "conspicuous achievement". In Xi Jinping's opinion, "hidden" and "conspicuous" are contradictory and unified contradictions. "Hidden" is the basis of "conspicuous", and "conspicuous" is the result of "hidden". The later generations always engage in work based on the foundation laid by their predecessors. If you do not pave the road and are unwilling to contribute in obscurity, then the "conspicuous achievement" will be out of the question, and the "seemingly conspicuous achievement" in front of you will at best obtain the transient success of an "image project", just like a tree without roots or water without a source.

MARX PRODUCED *Capital: A Critique of Political Economy* POVERTY

A quick look at human history reveals that the people who accomplished great things were those who had great character. Karl Marx finished writing *Capital: A Critique of Political Economy* when he was at his most destitute. In February 1852, he wrote a letter to Engels saying, "A week ago I reached the pleasant point where I am unable to go out for want of the costs I have in pawn and can no longer eat meat for want of credit." However, even then, Marx did not yield. He refused to stop working. Defying hardships while staying true to the doctrine shows the moral courage of a revolutionary proletariat.

– A Chat About Entering Public Service (March 1990), from *Up and Out of Poverty*.

Commentary

Karl Marx, as the spiritual adviser of the communists, told us what the phase "moral courage" means through lifelong struggle. When he started writing *Capital: A Critique of Political Economy* in London, he was experiencing one of the toughest period of his life. His family was plagued with starvation and survival threat because of a lack of a fixed source of income, coupled with the persecution and blockade of the bourgeois government. Under the double threat of starvation and disease, Marx poured out his bitterness in a letter to Engels, saying, "My wife is ill and little Jenny, too. Lenchen caught a disease called 'neurogenic fever'. I was unable to send for a doctor before. And now, still, because I have no money to buy medicine. Over the past eight-to-ten days, we have only had bread and potatoes to eat. Yet it is still uncertain whether we can get them today." Three of his six children died in such poverty, and he had no money with which to buy them small coffins.

Marx lived in poverty throughout his exile in London. When he was too poor to pay the rent, his landlady called the police to seal up his family's bed, clothes, and even the cradle and toys of his children. The children were scared to hide in the corner and secretly shed tears. Marx had no alternative but to look for lodging in the rain. However, nobody was willing to take them in. At the same time, the owners of the drugstore, bakery, and milk shop all came to press them for payment of their debts. Faced with the creditors, Jenny, his wife, took their bed with the intent to sell it off to pay their debts. Unfortunately, just after she had lifted the bed into the cart, the police came again, saying that they had violated the law by transporting things at dusk and that they were trying to evade their debts. For Marx, the only function of money and life was to sustain his revolutionary cause. He once wrote in a letter that, "If I could obtain enough money, slightly more than nothing, to raise my family and finish my book, then I would not mind being sent to the stripping yard, in other words, being executed."

Marx was born into a rich family. He got a doctor's degree at the age of 23 and at 25 married a girl of the nobility, the daughter of the Chief Editor of *Rheinische Zeitung*. He should have been "Duke Marx," "Minister Marx," "President Marx," or "Professor Marx"; however, he gave up all such titles and chose the profession that was, according to him, "best for human welfare." For his work and the revolutionary cause, he lived a vagrant life in utter destitution for 40 years, during which time he witnessed the early death of his children. In March 1883, he died at his desk. With his actions, he embodied the moral courage of a revolutionary proletariat.

Xi Jinping has cited Marx's story of producing *Capital: A Critique of Political Economy* to reiterate a truth: moral courage is a quality that everyone who aims to accomplish great things must have. No matter what difficulties and obstacles one faces, he can overcome them and attain success as long as he holds to his faith and sustains moral courage. At present, Party members and officials are faced with all types of temptation and undermining thoughts amid reform challenges and transformation pressures. Therefore, Party members and officials should brush up on Xi's earnest words, for example, "A quick look at human history reveals that the people who have accomplished great things must have great character" and "Moral courage is a quality every leader must have." These words will specifically encourage a firm belief in their ideals and faith and inspire moral courage so they can refuse to be contaminated by the temptation, stand firm when confronting undermining concepts, and have the courage to struggle against risks and challenges. By doing so, the great vessel of "China" will cleave through the waves and head to open waters.

Water Droplets Drilling Through Rock

Upon settling in the countryside, I saw firsthand the power of dripping water drilling through rock. That image, which captured the spirit of persistence, has stayed with me all these years. It has become a well-worn source for contemplating life and movement.

Rock and water are two opposing elements that are used to symbolize dogged stubbornness and gentle fluidity. Yet despite being "gentle", water will drill through "solid" rock over time.

As a metaphor for people, this is the embodiment of a certain moral character: it is the willingness to rise to fight each time one falls and the courage to sacrifice oneself. A single drop of water is small and insubstantial. It will die a cruel "death" in any battle with a rock. Yet in that brief moment of "sacrifice", although it cannot see its own value and achievement, it is one of countless drops of water that have already fallen and thus triumph by finally drilling through the rock. From the perspective of history or the development of an economically disadvantaged area, we should not seek personal success and fame. Instead, we should strive to make steady progress, one small step at a time, and be willing to lay the groundwork for overall success. When everyone doing their work models themselves on a droplet that is ready to sacrifice itself for the greater good, we need not worry that our work is not important enough to make a lasting change.

...

When I describe my awe upon seeing the power of droplets drilling through rock, I am praising those who have the willingness to rise each time they fall and the moral character to sacrifice themselves for overall success. I wish to express my admiration for those who develop a social plan and have the tenacity to see it through to the end.

    – Water Droplets Drilling Through Rock (March 1990), from *Up and Out of Poverty*.

Commentary

Though the power of water droplets is negligible, they are single-minded and persistent. Hence, they can drill through rock. In the Taiji Cave in Guangde County, Anhui Province, there is a rabbit-shaped rock with a pit formed by the drilling of water droplets. In the Bodhisattva Lamasery of the Wutai Mountain in Shanxi Province, a dripping eave has had droplets drip on to the stone steps, which formed porous pits.

    The Chinese idiom "滴水穿石" (which means water droplets drill through rock) is often used as a metaphor to explain that one can attain great achievements by persevering unremittingly, despite one's negligible power. This idiom was originally used by Zhang Guaiya, a famous official in the reigns of Emperor Taizong and Emperor Zhenzong of Song. When he served as Governor of Chongyang County, the social atmosphere there was very poor, theft was rampant, and the money in the treasury of the county government was frequently stolen. Therefore, he became determined to crack down heavily on this social malady. One day, seeing a low-level official who administered the treasury coming out of the treasury in a panic, Zhang speculated that the treasury official might embezzle the money in the treasury, thus asking his valets to search the official. Finally, a copper coin was discovered in his turban. The official excused himself, saying "It is just a single copper coin. No big deal." Then, Zhang wrote in red with a Chinese brush, "One coin is stolen per day, one thousand coins would have been stolen after one thousand days. A rope can cut wood, and water droplets can drill through rock." This meant that if one steals a single copper coin every day, then one thousand coins would have been stolen after one thousand days; if one ceaselessly attempts to cut a piece of wood with nothing but a rope, the wood will ultimately be cut; and if water droplets drip onto a rock one by one without stopping, the rock will eventually be drilled through. Since then, the vice of theft in Chongyang County was kept in check, and the social atmosphere was significantly improved.

From September 1988 to May 1990, Xi Jinping served as Secretary of CPC Ningde Prefectural Committee. At that time, Ningde was recognized by the State Council as one of the 18 contiguous poverty-stricken areas in China. Xi Jinping traveled through all the nine counties under Ningde within the first 3 months after he assumed office, and after that, he further visited throughout the vast majority of towns and villages there to fully pull eastern Fujian out of poverty. When he left the post from Ningde, 94% of the poverty-stricken households in the region had their problems of needing food and clothing solved. The *People's Daily* even made a special report on this, themed as "Ningde Lifted Itself up and out of Poverty". Impelled by Xi Jinping, Ningde continued to strive in the spirit of "water droplets drill through rock" and "the weak bird starts flying early" (a frequently used Chinese idiom which means a person or group that has to compensate for their weaknesses by working hard). For instance, Chixi Village in the county carried out poverty relief on site during the first 10 years after it set off poverty alleviation; in the second 10 years, it further alleviated poverty by relocating the villagers to the central village; and during the third 10 years, it developed the "tourism + industry" and eventually embarked on the road toward a moderately prosperous society. In 2015, Xi Jinping summarized the poverty alleviation experience of this story of "China's top village in poverty alleviation" in a sentence: "Water droplets drill through rock by persevering unremittingly."

In those years, the reform and opening up policy opened China up to the world, and Ningde was in the initial stage of poverty alleviation, during which time it was impoverished and enfeebled. Xi Jinping told the story of "water droplets drill through rock" to inspire leaders and officials at all levels with confidence, boost their morale, and stimulate them to hold firm their resolve toward poverty alleviation and to continue to persevere. Today, standing at a new historical starting point, China is heading for a higher realm of development. Yet Xi is still anxious about the people in the depressed areas, often saying, "The people who evaluate our achievements in building a moderately prosperous society are the peasants," and "To build a moderately prosperous society in all respects, we should not leave any minority ethnic group behind." By saying these words, he inspired leaders and officials at all levels to achieve overall success in poverty alleviation by developing a great plan and then having the tenacity to see it through to the end.

They Irrigated the Land of China with Their Blood

The first generation of communists in Zhengding advanced the freedom and liberation of their hometown and home country wave upon wave. They were the outstanding children of the Zhengding people, and the land of their hometown was irrigated with their blood. Comrade Yin Yufeng and Hao Qingyu were their prominent representatives.

Yin Yufeng was born in Zhoutong Village, Zhengding County. Joining the CPC in 1924, he was the first County Party Secretary of Zhengding and held the post until his death in 1928. Hao Qingyu was influenced by the progressive ideological trend at as young as age of 14 and soon became a member of the Party. He returned to his hometown in 1924, and from then on, he worked with Comrade Yin Yufeng and other comrades to make great efforts to establish the organization of the CPC. In the summer of 1925, the British and Japanese imperialists brought about the May 30 Incident in Shanghai. Then, Yin Yufeng, Hao Qingyu, and other comrades organized the Zhengding Backup Team for the Shanghai Incident. They mobilized the people of Zhengding to economize on food and clothing to assist the families of the victims in Shanghai, and they led a mass rally and a students' strike, starting an anti-imperialist movement in Zhengding.

In June 1927, they led the famous Zhengding Peasant Uprising on behalf of the Zhengding County Committee of the CPC because the clique that had settled in Zhengding concocted pretexts to collect 3 years' land tax in advance from the people and levy "Taochijuan" (which means compelling the people to make donations to suppress the communizing National Revolutionary Army) on the people. All of these actions aroused discontent among the whole county. On Lunar May 17, the day of the Town's God Temple Fair in Zhengding, more than 10,000 people came to the fair from dozens of miles around. At around 10 a.m., someone raised a big white flag in the theater square with the words, "Zhengding Peasants' Petition Against Taochijuan" in red. Then, the people swarmed in the square from all directions, with holding broadswords, spears, and shovels, and they rushed to the county government in a formidable array. Comrade Hao Qingyu, who had practiced martial arts in his youth, was always at the forefront of the parade. He led the masses and rushed the lobby of the government office and then smashed the screen in the lobby with a double-joined cudgel, scaring all the officers. In the end, under pressure from the masses, the county governor set forth the pledge to "abrogate Taochijuan" and "postpone the collection of the land tax" and announced the pledge to the whole county. This uprising hit the arrogance of the Fengtian clique, and it cultivated and trained the Party officials of Zhengding, laying the foundations for the revolutionary victory to come.

In 1928, Comrade Yin Yufeng, who broke down from constant overwork, died of illness at the young age of 24. Comrade Hao Qingyu grew up rapidly in the struggle of the masses and became an outstanding organizer and leader of the northern peasant movement of our Party. He was arrested in Tianjin in 1931 due to the betrayal of a traitor, and he died in 1935 at the age of 32. All the people like Yin Yufeng and Hao Qingyu, who have made contributions to and sacrificed their lives for the Chinese nation and their hometown, made a glorious mark in the patriotic history of Zhengding County. Many of them did not even leave their names, but they continue to be revered by the new generations and will always inspire later generations to devote their efforts and even lives to achieving the prosperity of the motherland and of their hometowns.

– *Know It Deeply, Love It Deeply* (Preface), from the *Know It Deeply, Love It Deeply*, Edition 2015, published by Hebei People's Publishing House.

Commentary

Lu Xun once said, since ancient times, we have people among us who have toiled hard at work, who have pushed through obstacles to get things done, who have pursued truths at all costs, and who have pleaded to the authorities on behalf of the needs of ordinary people. They constitute the backbone of China. Perhaps their lives have gone, but their spirit will be always in the hearts of the people. Yin Yufeng and Hao Qingyu were such heroic figures.

Hao Qingyu was born in Zhengding County, Hebei Province. He went to Beijing to become a shoemaker in 1918 and joined the CPC in 1924. Together with Comrade Yin Yufeng and others, he did a lot of work for the establishment of the Party organization in Zhengding. To appoint liaisons and disguise the roles of Party members, he founded the "Yuhua Shoes Shop", which played an important role in the development of the Party organization in Zhengding. After that, the Zhengding Party organization was expanded and restructured several times, and it developed from a special branch into the central county committee and then the local committee, becoming the leading force in the people's revolutionary struggle in that area. Having the aim of mobilizing the masses, Hao went deep into the farmland and tirelessly traveled to poor peasants' cottages to propagate the truth of revolution. A communist among the rural instructors described him, "He walked in the fields by day, slept in a haystack at night, satisfied his hunger with prepared solid food and quenched his thirst with cold water."

In the spring of 1928, Hao Qingyu was transferred to Tianjin and appointed as the member and Minister of the Peasant Movement Department of Shunzhi Provincial Committee of the CPC. In the summer of 1930, he assumed the posts of the member of the Standing Committee of Shunzhi Provincial Committee, inspector of Shunzhi Provincial Committee, and Secretary of Baoding Ad-Hoc Committee of the CPC. Recalled to the Shunzhi Provincial Party Committee in March 1931, he was arrested and sent to prison in Tianjin in 1931 due to the betrayal of a traitor. In prison, Hao still displayed unyielding integrity although he was seriously ill. The enemy took advantage of his illness to entice him into putting his fingerprint on an "Anti-Communist Notice", saying, "Let us apply some ink to your finger. Just press a fingerprint here, we will send you out and to the German hospital to treat your illness, otherwise you will be sent to the overbridge (an execution ground)!" Hao Qingyu replied without hesitation, "You Kuomintang surrender to Japan and oppress our people, you should reflect on that. I will resist against Japanese aggression to the end and never repent. You can send me anywhere as you wish!" In September 1935, Hao Qingyu died in prison.

With regard to these heroes of Zhengding whom Xi Jinping introduced, their deeds may be little known and their names may be unknown to the public; however, they strove against the oppressors of history; they irrigated our great land with their blood as they pursued their faith. They constitute the backbone of China, and their integrity and spirit will lead us, a nation with a long history, to revive. Xi Jinping learned about their deeds while he was heading the administration of Zhengding, and he encouraged their spirit in the officials of Zhengding. To this day, these deeds can still bring spiritual energy to Party members and officials. Xi Jinping attaches great importance to heroes, and he cherishes them. He has emphasized on many occasions that we should revere heroes, defend them, learn from them, and care for them. At the Ceremony of Awarding the Commemoration Models of the 70th Anniversary of the Victory of the Chinese People's War of Resistance Against Japanese Aggression, he recited a host of heroic teams, including the "Langya Shan Five Heroic Men", the "Liulangzhuang Company" of the New Fourth Army, the "Eight Female Soldiers" of the Northeast Counter-Japanese United Army, and the "Eight Hundred Heroes" of the Kuomintang Army, to pay tribute to the heroes in the name of the state. As Xi said, all national heroes, including those who resisted against Japanese aggression, are the backbone of the Chinese nation, and their deeds and spirit are powerful forces that inspire us to move forward.

CHAPTER 3

Stories of Inspiration: "Learning Is Beneficial to the Talent, Just as Grinding Can Make the Knife Sharp"

"Work Like Farm Cattle"

Literary and artistic production is about arduous creation that does not allow even the slightest falsehood. None of the fine works that enjoy widespread popularity and enduring fame was created in an impatient or impetuous state of mind. They were all forged by the creators straining their heart and mind without seeking fortune. As the old saying goes, "To come up with an appropriate character, I lost several beards (because I like stroking my beard as I compose verses)" and "It cost me three years to compose these two lines. So every time I read them, the tears stream down my face." On the tombstone of Lu Yao, it says, "Work like farm cattle, and dedicate like the soil." Tolstoy also said, "If someone tells me I can write a novel in which I have no problem airing a view that I think is correct on all social issues, then such a novel will take me less than two hours. But if someone tells me that this novel will be read by children twenty years later, and it will even make them cry or laugh, or they will love life because of it, then I will devote my whole life and all my strength to this novel."

– Speech at the Opening Ceremony of the 10th Congress of the China Federation of Literary and Art Circles and the Ninth Congress of the Chinese Writers Association (November 30, 2016).

© People's Publishing House 2020
People's Daily, Department of Commentary,
Narrating China's Governance,
https://doi.org/10.1007/978-981-32-9178-2_3

Commentary

Throughout the ages, the great literary and artistic works have been based on accumulated strength, and their literary and artistic quality manifests their creators' inner enrichment. A work that is circulated for generations or is an eternal masterpiece must be created through perseverance, without hurry and haste, and it must cost all the creator's strength and energy. It can be said that staying calm and steady in work without distraction is an essential quality of all the literary and artistic masters who have been credited with universally praised works.

Jia Dao was a famous poet of the Tang Dynasty who had a painstaking style. In the middle-Tang Dynasty, the painstaking-style poets, typified by Meng Jiao and Jia Dao, held an extremely rigorous and serious attitude toward the creation of poetry and focused on weighing characters and deliberating about expressions. While composing the line "Birds nestle in the trees by the pond, a monk knocks at the door awash in the moon", Jia Dao deliberated whether to use the expression "knock" or "push" for a long time. He even made friends with Han Yu for the purpose of weighing the words, which led to the much-told story of "Jia Dao knocked and pushed." After finishing the poem *Farewell to Monk Wuke*, Jia Dao added a verselet as the annotation of the line "With his lonely silhouette being reflected in the pool, he rested on trees many times." The poet said, "It took me three years to compose these two lines. So every time I read them, the tears stream down my face. If the lines fail to gain the appreciation of my closest friends, I have no alternative but return to my mountainous hometown and live in seclusion." This annotation interprets his spirit of painstaking composition. Speaking of the painstaking style, there have been many more lines on this subject. For example, "To come up with an appropriate character, I lost several beards (because I like stroking my beard as I compose verses)" by Lu Yanrang; "What made you so thin since we did part? Did the verse-composing wring your heart?" by Li Bai in *Joking with Du Fu*; and "I like refining my verses, to the extent that the people read them and marvel at them" by Du Fu.

"Work like farm cattle, and be dedicated like the soil." This was the motto of Lu Yao, which also mirrored his personality and spirit. Lu Yao lived in an era when literary concepts such as the modernist school and stream of consciousness were all the rage, and literary novel forms and techniques emerged overwhelmingly; however, he insisted on the writing technique of traditional realism. He began *The Ordinary World* in 1975 and finished it in May 1988 upon going through hardships. Awarded The Third Mao Dun Literature Prize, this novel provides a panoramic view of the social life in China's urban and rural areas and the great changes in the Chinese people's thoughts and emotions in the era of reform. Leo Tolstoy was a critical realist writer and thinker in Russia in the nineteenth century. He successively overhauled his novel *Anna Karenina* 12 times and produced up to 20 versions of the beginning part of *Resurrection*, another of his novels.

The development of culture is interrelated with the future of the country, and the inheritance of culture is connected with the development of the country. Xi Jinping believed that to achieve the great renewal of the Chinese nation is a great cause that surpasses the ancients and amazes contemporaries, which calls for a great spirit of perseverance and great works to boost popular morale. He places great expectations on literary and artistic work, and he has repeatedly identified the problems that exist in these fields. For example, we have many fine works but few top masterpieces, some works are alienated from people and life, and some are insignificant, designed merely to entertain readers or to provide audiences with history. Xi Jinping cited the ancient, contemporary, and foreign writers' celebrated dictums and stories about a dedicated attitude, creation without hurry and haste and hard work just to urge the writers and artists to bear the responsibility of presenting fine works that enjoy a widespread high reputation and enduring fame, and not to pursue quick success with shoddy works. At the Symposium on Literature and Art held in 2014, he also related that in Gustave Flaubert's novel *Madame Bovary*, there was a page that took him 5 days to produce, and when Cao Xueqin was producing *A Dream of Red Mansions*, he reviewed it ten times and made additions and deletions five times. With these stories, he sent word to the writers and artists that fine literary and artistic works can hardly be produced without the spirit of diligently striving for excellence.

"Serve the Country with Utmost Loyalty"

Speaking of reading literature, I perused literary works mostly in my teens, and I shifted my focus to political books afterward. When I was very young, about 5 or 6 years old, at which time my mother worked in the Central Party School, once she took me to buy books from the Xinhua Bookstore on the way from the Party School to Xiyuan. That day I was unwilling to walk because of laziness, so she carried me on her back. We wanted to buy picture-story books about Yue Fei, and there were two versions of books about him. One was a book series, *The Legend of Yue Fei*, with one book contained in it entitled "Yue Fei's Tattoos", and the other version was about the story, "serve the country with utmost loyalty." Mother bought both versions for me. Returning home, she told me the story that Yue Fei's mother tattooed the characters "精忠报国" on his back, which meant serve the country with utmost loyalty. I said, "Having characters tattooed on his back! That must have been painful!" My mother replied, "Painful, of course. But the idea was forever etched in his mind." From then on, I have kept the words "serve the country with supreme loyalty" firmly in mind as my lifelong goal.

– General Secretary Xi Jinping's Affinity for Literature (*People's Daily*, October 14, 2016, Page 24).

Commentary

The passionate love for our nation is a cultural heritage running through Chinese history of several thousand years, which is deeply rooted in the heart of every excellent Chinese citizen. The story "Yue Fei's mother tattooed characters on his back" illustrates the advocacy of family tradition and education in China as well as the Chinese people's passionate love for our motherland.

Yue Fei, whose courtesy name was Pengju, was born in 1103 in Tangyin County, Xiangzhou (present-day Tangyin County, Henan Province). He was a famous general in the resistance against Jin's invasion in the Southern Song Dynasty, among the "Four Great Generals of Zhongxing Period", and he was also a famous militarist and strategist in Chinese history. He joined the army during the last Northern Song Dynasty. From 1128 to 1141, he led his invincible troops to fight several hundred battles of all scales with Jin armies, and he eventually "reached the position of general." In 1140, Yue Fei commanded his troops to fight northward to strike back at Wanyan Wuzhu from the Jin Dynasty, who broke the treaty of alliance with Song by attacking Song. Yue Fei reconquered Zhengzhou, Luoyang, and other places successively and marched troops into the town of Zhuxian after defeating Jin armies in Yancheng and Yingchang. Defeated in the town of Zhuxian, Wuzhu lamented, "To shake Yue's army is much more difficult than to shake a mountain." However, although they had the advantage over the enemy, Emperor Gaozong of Song and Qin Hui, then Chancellor of Song, sued for peace, and even sent 12 "gold-character plates" to force Yue Fei's army to retreat. Forced by the isolated and helpless situation, Yue Fei withdrew the troops. At the time when Song and Jin were conducting peace negotiations, Yue Fei was jailed due to the frame-up by Qin Hui, Zhang Jun, and their wing. In January 1142, Yue Fei was executed on a groundless charge of rebellion, and his eldest son Yue Yun and Zhang Xianyi, a military officer under his command, were killed together with him. During the reign of Emperor Xiao of Song, Yue Fei was vindicated and was reinterred in Xixialing near West Lake.

When Yue Fei marched northward to fight against the Jin armies, he wrote the poetic masterpiece *The River All Red*: "Wrath sets on end my hair, I lean on railings where I see the drizzling rain has ceased. Raising my eyes towards the skies, I have long sighs, my wrath not yet appeased. To dust is gone the fame achieved at thirty years; like the cloud-veiled moon the thousand-mile land disappears. Should youthful heads in vain turn grey, we would regret for aye. Lost our capitals, what a burning shame! How can we generals quench our vengeful flame! Driving our chariots of war, we'd go to break through our relentless foe. Valiantly we'd cut off each head; laughing, we'd drink the blood they shed. When we've reconquered our lost land, in triumph would return our army grand." (Translated by Xu Yuanchong) This Ci was imbued with a spirit that seemed to conquer mountains and rivers, which fully manifested Yue Fei's patriotic emotion and lofty aspirations to serve his country and recover his homeland.

Yue Fei's virtues of loyalty, patriotism, and integrity were inherited from the instruction by his parents and teachers. The historical story of "Yue Fei's Tattoos" was first read in the hand-copied book of the Qing Dynasty, *Views on Legends*, as well as *General Yue Fei* by Qian Cai. According to the *History of Song—Biography of Yue Fei*, when Yue Fei suffered an undeserved grievance, he ripped his jacket to reveal the four tattooed characters of "serve the country with the utmost loyalty" on his back. This proved that he was clearly innocent of the charges. This story has had a profound influence on later generations and has been passed down to the present.

Xi Jinping once compared the formation of values to "buttoning up our coat", saying that "Young people should 'button right' in the early days of their life." Yue Fei's story "serve the country with utmost loyalty" was the "very first button" in Xi Jinping's teens. At the Symposium on Literature and Art, Xi Jinping recalled the influence of *The Legend of Yue Fei* on him while discussing his affinity for literature. The affection for the motherland reflected by the story always inspires him to cherish the people and never stop fighting. Communists' passionate love for our motherland is clearly illustrated by how we cherish the people and deliberate on how our country can prosper and continue to renew its aspirations'.

BORROWING A BOOK FROM 30 MILES AWAY

During my state visit to Russia last March, I mentioned at the symposium with Russian sinologists that I had read the works of many Russian writers such as, *What Is to Be Done?* by Chernyshevskiy. I was young that I read this book, and it gave me a great shock. When I paid a state visit to France this March, I discussed the influence of French literature and art on me. Many of our Party's older generation leaders had studied in France. Influenced by them, in my youth I had a strong interest in French literature and art. In Germany, I discussed my experience of reading *Faust*. When I was living and working in the countryside of Shaanxi Province as an educated youth, I heard that another educated youth had the book *Faust*. So I walked 30 miles to borrow the book from him. Later, he also walked 30 miles to get the book back. Why did I talk about these reminiscences with the foreigners? I did so because literature and art are world languages. They are all about society and life. It is thus easiest to achieve mutual understanding and spiritual communication in this way.

– Speech at the Symposium on Literature and Art (October 15, 2014).

Commentary

No era will be without its heroes, and everyone has a place for his role model in his heart. Rakhmetov, the leading character in the novel *What Is to Be Done?*, was exactly such a hero who was etched on the Russian' soul, and he also served as a role model who influenced a generation of Chinese.

Nikolay Chernyshevsky was a Russian revolutionist, philosopher, writer, and critic. Vladimir Lenin praised him as "the young helmsman in the storm of the future", and Vladimir Plekhanov compared him to "Russia's Prometheus". He was arrested by the Czarist government in 1862 for propagating progressive thoughts and criticizing the reality of Czarist Russia. In 1864, he was sentenced to 7 years of hard labor and exiled to Siberia for life. In captivity and exile, he produced many excellent works imbued with a passion for revolution, including *What Is to Be Done?* and *Prologue. What Is to Be Done?* revolves around three themes: freedom of labor, women's liberation, and secret revolutionary activities. It suggests that the people can only rid themselves of adversity through struggle. The leading character, Rakhmetov, had been a woodcutter, sawyer, stonemason, and boat tracker. To strengthen his revolutionary will and devote himself totally to his ideal, he chose to live a life of extreme frugality.

Xi Jinping recalled that his generation was deeply influenced by the Russian classics. *What Is to Be Done?* was one of them, which caused a great shock in his mind. According to Xi Jinping, "The leading character Rakhmetov lived an ascetic life. To temper his will, he even slept on a blanket full of nails, causing himself to bleed all over. At that time, we believed we needed to train to attain willpower like this, so we all slept on a heatable brick bed without a mattress. When it rained, we were exposed to the rain; when it snowed, we rubbed the snow on our bodies and took a cold bath by a well. This was all due to the influence of this book."

Faust is also a work of profound influence. It has been said that "One cannot write a history of world literature without discussing Johann Wolfgang von Goethe; similarly, it is difficult to understand Goethe without reading *Faust*." *Faust* is a poetic drama written by Goethe on the basis of a German folktale. The devil entices Faust to sign a pact with him: the devil will do everything that Faust wants during his lifetime, and in exchange Faust must devote his soul to the devil after death. With this pact as the background, Goethe interpreted many significant issues concerning worldly ideals and the future of humanity, and he declared the victory of the enterprising spirit of human beings. Xi Jinping has mentioned on multiple occasions his anecdote of reading *Faust* by borrowing the book from 30 miles away, which vividly demonstrates the power of literature.

Describing his affinity for literature and recalling the influence of reading at the different stages of his life, Xi Jinping conveyed an air of erudition and an amiable charisma. These qualities were cultivated by extensive reading. His story demonstrates the value of a good literary work: a good literary work should take root in people's lives and be able to enlighten us as to all aspects of human experience, including career and life, prosperity and adversity, dreams and expectations, love and hate, and existence and death.

Literature and art are the language of the world. Literature is a bridge of communication. As Xi Jinping shares his experiences of reading, he also communicates the value of shared knowledge and the possibility of cultural exchange. We should be inclusive of other civilizations, and we should take time to study them. Literary works are the best way by which the countries and nations of the world can engage in mutual understanding and exchange. As Xi said, "When we talk about literature and art, we are talking about society and life. It is the easiest means for us to understand and communicate with each other."

WHY DID CHINA'S SCIENCE AND TECHNOLOGY LAG BEHIND

I have been wondering about why our science and technology gradually lagged behind in the late Ming (1368–1644) and early Qing (1644–1911) dynasties. Studies show that Qing Emperor Kangxi was very interested in Western science and technology. He invited Western missionaries to give him lectures on astronomy, mathematics, geography, zoology, anatomy, music, and even philosophy. More than 100 books on astronomy were introduced to him. When did he study these subjects, and for how long? He continuously studied them for 2 years and 5 months sometime between 1670 and 1682. He began his study quite early and learned quite a lot. The problem was that, at that time, although some people were interested in Western learning and had learned quite a lot of it, they did not apply what they had learned to social and economic development. Rather, they simply discussed the knowledge. In 1708, the Qing government asked some foreign missionaries to draw a map of China. It took them 10 years to complete The Map of Imperial China—the first of its kind at that time. However, this important work was confined to the imperial storehouse as a top-secret document, away from the public eye. Therefore, it had no impact on social or economic development. However, the Western missionaries who had drawn the map took the data back to the West and had it published. Hence, for quite a long time, the West knew China's geography better than the Chinese people did. What can we learn from this story? It means that science and technology must be combined with social development. No matter how much one has learned, it cannot possibly have any impact on society if the knowledge is merely set aside as a novelty, refined interest, clever trick, or doubtful craft.

- Transition to Innovation-driven Growth (June 9, 2014), from the Xi Jinping: The Governance of China, Edition 2014, published by Foreign Language Press.

Commentary

Qu Yuan, a Chinese patriotic poet from southern Chu during the Warring States Period, had a work entitled Tian Wen. The literal meaning of the title is "questions to heaven," and this work consists of over 170 questions on astronomy, geography, nature, and life, which was praised as "an eternal extraordinary masterpiece." In regard to "questions to heaven", there are some about Chinese history. One of them is the "Needham Question": why did modern civilization in science, technology, and industry not originate from China, the most advanced country in science, technology, and economy at that time?

It is undeniable that an important factor allowing for China's suffering from foreign aggressions as a poor and weak country in modern times was that China has repeatedly missed the scientific and technological revolutions, and it has not applied its advanced knowledge to economic and social development. Although "The Golden Age of Three Emperors—Kangxi, Yongzheng and Qianlong" has been praised by people through the ages, by taking a comprehensive look at the history of the world, it becomes clear that the so-called "golden age" was, to a large extent, merely an "illusion." When China was under the Kangxi administration, Europe ushered in an era of the highest achievement in the history of science, during which time Francis Bacon, Newton, Descartes, and other great philosophers and scientists emerged. Emperor Kangxi was also very studious. He got along with foreign missionaries including students and teachers, often spending 3–4 hours a day with them to become acquainted with many types of precision instruments and delving into various subjects with them. He liked mathematics, and especially liked exploring the use of all types of mathematical measuring tools, such as semicircle instruments, dividers, and geometric polyhedron models. According to the French missionary Joachim Bouvet, for 2 years, Kangxi spent all his spare time on mathematics. Although he was praised by the missionary as "the greatest emperor" and "the wisest emperor", he only considered the development of science to be his hobby instead of thinking about the methodology and worldview lurking within science and spreading scientific knowledge from the West across China.

As the ruler refused to "shake hands" with Western industrial civilization and share advanced technologies and knowledge across China, our nation walked into the bitterly painful era as a semicolonial and semifeudal country.

During Xi Jinping's state visit to Europe in March 2014, the Chancellor of Germany, Angela Merkel, presented him with the first accurate map of China drawn by Germany in 1735. Few people know that Emperor Kangxi had organized missionaries to complete an unprecedentedly advanced map of China—The Map of Imperial China—as early as more than a decade before the German map. After The Map of Imperial China was completed, Jean Baptiste Regis, a member of the Society of Jesus who had participated in the drawing of the map, sent it to his home country of France. Subsequently, The New Map of China was produced based on The Map of Imperial China and was published publicly in Europe. In 1840, when the British sent military ships to China based on The New Map of China and bombarded the gate of the Qing Empire, The Map of Imperial China was still shelved in the Forbidden City, without playing a practical role in promoting economic and social development.

Not only does Xi Jinping read history books and have knowledge of Chinese history but he also enjoys thinking about and studying questions of governance—not simply for the sake of discussing science and technology but to apply them to social and economic development. This is the essence of innovation that he obtained from the story of the relationship between Kangxi and science, and it has also served as his solution to China's "Achilles' Heel." If we simply discuss science, we cannot promote our nation's development. It is said that "Science and technology must be combined with social development." Only if we free ourselves from the "ivory tower" and avoid isolation in innovation can scientific and technological innovation produce greater motivation for and create more miracles of development, just like "a fulcrum that is said to be able to level the earth."

In Xi Jinping's speech at the 17th General Assembly of the Members of the Chinese Academy of Sciences and the 12th General Assembly of the Members of the Chinese Academy of Engineering, he noted that our scientific and technological achievements could not be smoothly converted into productivity because there are institutional bottlenecks in the scientific and technological innovation chain and loose connections among the various links in the innovation and conversion process. Xi Jinping said that if we decide that scientific and technological innovation is a new engine to drive our development, then reform is the ignition system that is essential to start the engine, thus we should take more effective measures to improve the ignition system and let the new engine run at full speed.

WHERE DID THE TIME GO?

Speaking of hobbies, I like reading, watching movies, traveling, and strolling. As can be seen in this post, I have almost no private time. In China, there is a song titled "Where Did the Time Go?," which became popular during the Chinese Spring Festival this year. For me, the question is where my private time goes. Of course, I spend almost all of it on my work. The only thing I have managed to keep as a hobby is reading, which has become my way of life. It invigorates my mind, gives me inspiration, and cultivates my moral force. I have read many works by Russian writers such as Ivan Krylov, Alexander Pushkin, Nikolai Gogol, Mikhail Lermontov, Ivan Turgenev, Fyodor Dostoevsky, Nikolay Nekrasov, Nikolay Chernyshevsky, Leo Tolstoy, Anton Chekhov, and Mikhail Sholokhov. Many wonderful chapters and stories in those books have remained in my memory.

In terms of sports, I like swimming and mountaineering. I learned to swim as early as 4 or 5 years old. I also like football, volleyball, basketball, tennis, and martial arts. Among the ice and snow sports, I love watching ice hockey games, speed skating, figure skating, and freestyle skiing. Ice hockey is my favorite. It not only calls for personal strength and skill but also teamwork and collaboration, which makes it a great sport.

- Xi Jinping Gave an Exclusive Interview with Russian Television (February 7, 2014) (People's Daily, February 9, 2014, Page 1).

Commentary

"Where did the time go? I had not yet enjoyed youth before I got old. Raising and cultivating my children for a lifetime, my mind is full of their cries and laughter…" The Spring Festival Gala of CCTV 2014 made the song Where Did the Time Go popular. The song extolls parental love. In February 2014, Xi mentioned the song in an exclusive interview with Russian TV, triggering a nationwide discussion on "Where Did the Time Go".

So where does Xi Jinping's time go? Just as he said, he spends all of it on his work. According to incomplete statistics on the basis of the public reports issued in 2015, in that year alone, Xi Jinping attended at least 61 important meetings, including 14 meetings of the Political Bureau of the CPC Central Committee, 11 meetings of the central leading group for deepening overall reform, ten working meetings, three meetings of the standing committee of the Political Bureau, and 23 other important meetings and conferences. During that year, he took part in the nine regular study sessions held by the Political Bureau and made eight trips for state visits.

Xi Jinping spent most of his spare time reading. Sergei Brilyov, Russian television host who conducted an exclusive interview with Xi in Sochi, said he "particularly liked" Xi's eyes because "he saw the light of thought from them." The "light of thought" can be partly attributed to reading. Xi regards reading as a lifestyle: "Whenever I was free, I would pick up and read a book, and every time I found it to be beneficial"; "A book is like a treasure. Once you explore the secrets hidden within it, you will benefit from it throughout your lifetime."

Xi Jinping visited Russia and three African countries for the first time a week after assuming the presidency. In consideration of his overly tight schedule, the Chinese Embassy in Russia intended to shorten the length of some of his activities to provide some rest time for Xi, "but President Xi persisted in keeping the original schedule." "Although I feel weary, I enjoy it," said Xi. This is Xi Jinping, a president who races against the clock as he works diligently for the country and the people and strives after the Chinese Dream of rejuvenating of the nation.

Xi Jinping's story about time is an inspiration to all Party members and officials. We should make full use of our spare time to study for the enrichment of our minds while sparing no effort to perform our duties. Our nation always stresses that one should pursue self-cultivation by reading books, and one should cultivate morality as one enters politics. As our traditional culture advocates, study and morality cultivation are not only the foundations for one to gain a foothold in society but also the key to handling government affairs. Xi Jinping once profoundly asserted that "Leading officials' power of personality is more and more critical for leadership, and a predominant way to generate the power of personality is to study by reading books."

HEROES EMERGE FROM A NATION'S YOUTH

A quick look at world history suggests that many thinkers, scientists, and writers produced their important creations in their youth, the full-flowering of their life, during which time they were quickest witted in their lifetime. When *The Communist Manifesto* was published, Karl Marx was 30 and Friedrich Engels was 28. Isaac Newton and Gottfried Wilhelm Leibniz discovered calculus at the ages of 22 and 28, respectively. Charles Darwin embarked on his voyage around the world at the age of 22 and famously produced *The Origin of Species* thereafter. Thomas Edison invented the phonograph when he was 30 and the electric light when he was 32. Marie Curie discovered that radium, thorium, and polonium were radioactive when she was 31 and later won the Nobel Prize for their discovery. Albert Einstein proposed the special theory of relativity when he was 26 and general relativity at 37. Li Zhengdao and Yang Zhenning proposed the parity nonconservation of weak interaction when they were 30 and 34, respectively. Jia Yi, the political commentator of the Western Han Dynasty, was only 32 when he died. Wang Bo, the author of the masterpiece *A Tribute to King Teng's Tower*, also died young at age 27.

– Speech at the Collective Talks with Members of the New Leadership of the Central Committee of the CCLY (June 20, 2013).

Commentary

"If we have chosen a position in life in which we can above all work for mankind, no burdens can hold us back because they are sacrifices for the benefit of all; then we shall experience no petty, limited, selfish joy, but our happiness will belong to millions, our deeds will live on quietly but perpetually at work, and over our ashes will be shed the hot tears of noble people."

This is an excerpt from *Reflections of a Young Man on The Choice of a Profession*, an essay by Karl Marx when he was 17 years old. At the time, Marx was graduating from high school and had come to a fork in his path. He had to make up his mind whether to go to college or get a job. Some of his classmates wished to be poets, scientists, or philosophers, some intended to be clergies or priests, and some hoped to live a luxurious life as capitalists. Unlike those who were motivated by self-interest and pursued individual happiness, Marx considered a career choice on the basis of his understanding of society and his philosophy toward life. Hence, came this masterpiece.

Isaac Newton, Charles Darwin, Albert Einstein, and Marie Curie all made great discoveries and inventions at a young age. The youthful days are the best time for one to engage oneself in creation because, during this period, one is quick-witted and full of energy, able to accumulate knowledge and experience in a fast and efficient way, and one dares to follow one's heart and make a difference with courage and determination. At the same time, the youthful days are also a peak time for the generation of new discoveries, creations, and knowledge. This is almost a universal law.

There have been many young and promising talents in Chinese history. For example, Jia Yi became well known for his literary skills in his youth. His precociousness caught the attention of Emperor Wen of Han. The emperor made him a "professor" when he was only 21 years old, and he thus became the youngest professor in the imperial court at the time. When Jia later served as Grand Tutor to Liu Yi, Prince of Liang, he wrote the *Countermeasure Against Public Security Issues*, which contains the memorials he submitted to the emperor on government affairs including the invasion of Xiongnu on the border of Han, unsound regulations, and the separatist regimes established by the dukes and princes. The *Countermeasure Against Public Security Issues* was praised by Mao Zedong as the greatest political essay of the Western Han. Another example is from Wang Bo, a scholar of the Tang Dynasty who had been smart and studious since his childhood. According to the *Old Book of Tang*, he began writing beautiful literary pieces at the age of six and was reputed as a child prodigy. Although he drowned at the young age of 27, he left many great lines for posterity, for example, "If you have a friend from afar who knows your heart, distance cannot keep you two apart"; and "A solitary wild duck flies alongside the multi-colored sunset clouds, and the autumn river shares a scenic hue with the vast sky." He was grouped with Luo Binwang, Lu Zhaolin, and Yang Jiong as the "Four Paragons of the Early Tang."

Xi Jinping pays great attention to the development of young people. At the collective talks with members of the new leadership of the central committee of the Chinese Communist Youth League (CCYL), he entrusted them to take the lead in studying hard, working hard, enhancing self-discipline, and maintaining close ties with the youth. As a fine example is probably the most convincing argument, he has told stories about luminaries such as Marx, Newton, and Wang Bo who achieved great accomplishments in their youth to encourage the new leadership of the CCYL central committee and even the Chinese youth to resolutely strive for success in extraordinary causes.

Xi Jinping likes to go among the young people, and he often exhorts them to maintain their spirit of struggle and dedication. He successively wrote to the Youth League Branch of the Grade 2009 undergraduate classes of the School of Archaeology and Museology, Peking University, Benyu Volunteer Team from Huazhong Agricultural University, and the representatives of the Baoding University graduates engaged in teaching assistance in West China to inspire them to combine their personal ideals into national and ethnic causes and strive to use their talents for our nation. At a symposium with the teachers and students of Peking University, he also offered the metaphor of "button up our coat" to exhort them to attach importance to value formation, saying "The life buttons are required to get off to a good start." Our younger generation has a promising future, and it will accomplish much. In Xi's view, "It is a law of history that 'the waves of the Yangtze River from behind drive on those ahead', and it is the responsibility of young people to surpass their elders."

The Revolutionary Youth

In the history of our Party, many outstanding leaders have established the revolutionary ideal in their youth: to fight for the people. Comrade Mao Zedong determined to devote himself to the prosperity of the Chinese nation early in his youth. He founded Xinmin Institute with He Shuheng and Cai Hesen at the age of 25 and attended the First Conference of the CPC at 28. When he was 34, he headed the Autumn Harvest Uprising and led the insurrectionary army to establish the first rural revolution base of China on the Jingang Mountains. Comrade Zhou Enlai headed the Tianjin Patriotic Student Movement when he was just 21 and participated in the founding of the Chinese Communist Youth League in Europe when he studied in France on a work-study basis at the age of 24. He also led the Nanchang Revolt and the building of the army of the CPC at 29, and he was elected to the standing committee of the Political Bureau of the Sixth CPC Central Committee the next year. Comrade Deng Xiaoping went to study in France under a work-study program at 16 and joined the Chinese Communist Youth League in Europe 2 years later. He took the post of the Secretary General of the CPC Central Committee when he was 23 and headed the Baise Uprising and built the Seventh Army of the Chinese Workers' and Peasants' Red Army when he was 25.

- Speech at the Collective Talks with Members of the New Leadership of the Central Committee of the CCLY (June 20, 2013).

Commentary

Youth is fleeting and cannot be remade; thus, how can we make the most of our lot and have a wonderful life? This is "a question of youth" that has been asked by young people throughout the ages. In hope of rescuing our nation from peril, Mao Zedong, Zhou Enlai, and Deng Xiaoping all resolutely devoted themselves to the revolutionary cause, imprinting the mark of youth on the history of our Party. This mark represents their ardent faith in the Party as well as the courage to rescue our nation.

"I, your son, am determined to go out of my hometown, and I will not return until I succeed in a certain field of study. If I die in a place far from home, it will not be necessary to bury me in my hometown because every place I set foot is a good place to lay my bones." At the age of 17, Mao Zedong left his hometown for Xiangxiang County, Hunan Province to study there. Before his departure, he wrote this poem on a slip of paper and stuck it in his father's account book to communicate his ambition and determination. From then on, the sufferings of the people and the hardships of the nation became the chief concern of young Mao Zedong. In his 20 s, he successively founded Xinmin Institute and the Students' Union of Hunan, started the publication of the *Xiangjiang Review* and participated in the founding of the early organization of the Changsha Communist Party. He attended the First Conference of the CPC at 28. The young Mao Zedong was just like what he wrote in *Changsha—To the Tune of Qin Yuan Chun*, "When, students in the flower of our age/Our spirit bright was at its height/Full of the scholar's notable rage/We criticized with all our might/Pointing to stream and hilWriting in blame or praise/We treated like dirt all mighty lords of old days."

In Europe in the 1920s, when the CPC had just been founded, there was a political force made up of young Chinese called the "Chinese Communist Youth League in Europe." In 1915, Cai Yuanpei and Wu Yuzhang headed the founding of the Diligent Work-Frugal Study Movement and called on Chinese students to study in France on a work-study basis. Some of those students later became Marxists in France including Zhou Enlai, Zhao Shiyan, Cai Hesen, Li Weihan, Wang Ruofei, Li Lisan, Xiang Jingyu, Chen Yi, Chen Yannian, Chen Qiaonian, Nie Rongzhen, Deng Xiaoping, and Li Fuchun. They established the Paris Communist Party in 1921 and founded the Chinese Communist Youth League in Europe the following year. At that time, 24-year-old Zhou Enlai was in charge of propaganda in the executive committee of the party and 18-year-old Deng Xiaoping joined the organization as a newcomer. *Our Years in France* is a television series that presented their experiences in France, which was very popular among Chinese audiences for a while.

After returning to China, Zhou Enlai served as the Director of the Political Department of the Whampoa Military Academy and headed the establishment of the CPC-controlled Ye Ting's Independent Regiment, a revolutionary armed force established for the Northern Expedition. When he was 29, he led the Nanchang Revolt, the Party's first military action against the Kuomintang reactionaries, greatly contributed to the building of the people's army. Deng Xiaoping, who returned to China after studying in the Soviet Union, became involved in the revolutionary movement in China. He assumed the post of Secretary-General of the CPC central committee at the age of 23, led the Baise Uprising and built the seventh battalion of the Chinese Workers' and Peasants' Red Army at 25.

Telling the stories of the revolutionary youth of Mao Zedong and other revolutionary predecessors, Xi Jinping has inspired contemporary youth to adhere to their ideals and to struggle unremittingly for our nation's prosperity and our people's happiness. Recollecting the older generation of communists' soul-stirring struggle in their youth and encapsulating China's past century, which was full of ups and downs before the young people, he aimed at enlightening them to their mission and responsibilities, indestructible faith, and the determination of and confidence in struggle. China's strength is embodied in the strength of the youth, and China's dream is to be realized through the struggle of the youth. As Xi noted, the youth are fresh troops on the front lines to build a moderately prosperous society in all respects. They are a generation with many calls for their kind effort, from obtaining a decisive victory in building a moderately prosperous society in all respects to finding a solution to the issues and contradictions emerging from the process of reform and development. As long as the thousands upon thousands of young people release their youthful dreams and keep their morale high, China will certainly radiate new glory.

KEEPING UP WITH THE TIMES

In modern times, previously held knowledge is becoming outmoded at an ever-increasing pace by a whole range of new knowledge, new things, and new states of affairs arising all over. Academics have noted that before the eighteenth century, the body of human knowledge doubled within a period of approximately 90 years. Since the 1990s, there has been an exponential acceleration in this process—the body of human knowledge is now estimated to double every 3–5 years. Thus, over the past 50 years, human beings have produced knowledge of an amount exceeding the aggregate generated over the previous 3000 years. It is also believed that in the age of agro-farming, a few years of study sufficed for one's lifetime; in the age of industrial economy, one had to study for at least a decade to obtain all the knowledge necessary for one's life; and in this age of the knowledge economy, one can only keep up with the times through lifelong study. If we fail to improve our knowledge in a wide variety of areas, if we do not take the initiative to learn about science and culture, if we are unwilling to conscientiously update our knowledge and improve our knowledge structure, develop the broadest possible perspective and broaden our horizons, our professional competence will become stagnant. As a consequence, we will not be able to grasp the initiative and prevail. Ultimately, the future will pass us by.

> – Speech at the Celebration Assembly of the 80th Anniversary of the Central Party School and the Opening Ceremony of Its 2013 Spring Semester (March 1, 2013).

Commentary

"In the vibrant woods, the young leaves hurry the defoliation of the current ones; in a rushing river, the waves ahead make way for those behind." The supersession of the old by the new is a general law of the universe. In the process of knowledge production, the supersession speeds up dramatically. Research by UNESCO shows that before the eighteenth century, human knowledge was updated every 80–90 years; from the nineteenth to the early twentieth century, the validity term of knowledge was shortened to 30 years; from the 1960s to the 1970s, the validity term for common subjects was 5–10 years, and by the end of the twentieth century, knowledge was being updated every 5 years in most subjects. As we enter into the twenty-first century, our knowledge is updated every 2–3 years.

A scholar once put forward the term, "the half-life of facts," derived from the principle of radioactive decay with regard to the development and change of knowledge. If one who has a lot of knowledge or is specialized in a certain field no longer studies, he will experience truth decay due to the half-life of facts. This means that the basic knowledge he grasps is still useful; however, half of his knowledge has already become outdated and replaced by new knowledge. Today, knowledge is undergoing "fission" at a tremendous pace. It is estimated that knowledge maintained a half-life of 50 years before 1950; however, in the twenty-first century, this duration has been shortened to approximately 3.2 years. For a senior IT engineer, half of his knowledge will become obsolete in 1.8 years. By the same token, if one never studies or stops studying for a long time, it is difficult for him or her to keep pace with society. It is often the predicament that many people "have no alternative when the tried and trusted methods fail, or they dare not to adopt stricter measures when soft ones prove inadequate." This is precisely because they do not equip themselves with the latest knowledge and skills that could help them escape the trap of "the half-life of facts."

It is our Party's tradition to attach importance to study. As early as the Yan'an Period, Mao Zedong had identified the issue of a "competence crisis". He drew an analogy between studying and "running a shop"—when your goods are sold out, you have to replenish your stock to keep the shop running. According to this analogy, "to replenish" is to learn.

"To a large extent, we Chinese Communists have relied on learning for our achievements, and we will surely continue to do so in the future." At the Celebration Assembly of the 80th Anniversary of the Central Party School, Xi Jinping stressed the importance of study in this way. It was said in *The Garden of Stories* that, "If you want to enhance your ability, you must study; if you want to make the blade sharp, you must sharpen it." This is a saying cited by Xi Jinping in *Fresh Ideas of Zhejiang* to exhort the leading officials to study more and to place study and reading high on their list of priorities. In the foreword to the training material for the fourth group of national officials, Xi Jinping highlighted that "We should study hard to improve our knowledge in a wide variety of areas and strive to enhance our abilities in practice. We should update our knowledge at a faster pace, optimize our knowledge structure, develop the broadest possible perspective and broaden our horizons. We must study to avoid the bewilderment that results from inadequate knowledge, the blindness that results from insensibility, and the chaos that results from ignorance. We must also study to overcome professional deficiencies, the dread of incompetence and outdated capabilities."

Xi also once proposed a "storage battery theory": now it is no longer the era that one needs charge oneself only once throughout one's lifetime; if one wants to be energized continuously, one must charge oneself unremittingly like an efficient storage battery. Unlike dull sermons, such a vivid summation is not only easy to understand and practice but it also inspires the audience, who interprets study as a lifestyle and necessity for progress, not a mandatory task.

LEARNING BY THINKING

Our ancestors left many stories on diligent study to us. To study, they tied their hair on a house beam or jabbed their thigh with an awl to keep themselves awake, or they made use of the neighbor's light by boring a hole in the wall or read by the light of bagged fireflies or the reflected light of snow. These stories have been passed from person to person with approbation, and such a spirit of diligence is worth bearing in mind. We should all calm down and delve deeply into books without distractions and engage in thorough discussion. "If one learns from others but does not think, one will be bewildered. If, on the other hand, one thinks but does not learn from others, one will be imperiled." This saying of Confucius makes a very good point. Learning and thinking are interrelated and mutually reinforcing. We must not separate them from each other. In the process of learning, we should connect the problems that we have encountered in actual work and think them over repeatedly. This is helpful in cultivating and improving our theoretical thinking and strategic thinking abilities. The Central Party School holds trainee forums and political experience exchange activities every semester, which supports further study and discussion of the governing experience. Participants also engage in exchange and sharing of their learning experiences during class breaks or free time for mutual enlightenment.

  – On the Study of the Trainees of the Central Party School—Speech at the Opening Ceremony of the Central Party School in 2012 Autumn Semester (September 1, 2012).

Commentary

In *An Exhortation to Learning*, Hsun Tzu said that "Truly, if you do not climb a high mountain, you will be unaware of the height of the sky. If you do not look down into a deep gorge, you will be unaware of the thickness of the earth." Learning is a powerful approach to changing one's destiny and to seeing the world around us. Studying diligently has been regarded as an excellent quality since ancient times.

According to the *Stratagems of the Warring States*, Su Qin studied diligently and strived for progress from his youth. It is said that "Every time he felt too tired and sleepy, he jabbed his thigh with an awl. As a result, blood flowed to his feet." The *Book of Han* also tells a story of diligent study: "Sun Jing, whose style name was Wenbao, was diligent and studious. He studied from morning until night. To keep himself from dozing off, he tied his hair to the house beam." These two stories are combined into a Chinese idiom that means "to tie one's hair on the house beam or stab one's thigh with an awl to keep oneself awake."

In the Western Han Dynasty, the writer Kuang Heng made use of his neighbor's light to study by boring a hole in the wall. According to *A Miscellany of the Western Capital*, Kuang Heng was born in a poor family and had no money to buy a candle for reading at night, so he bored a hole in the wall to make use of his neighbor's light. Similarly, in the Jin Dynasty, Che Yin read by the light of bagged fireflies, while Sun Kang by the reflected light of snow. Deprived though they were, they studied around the clock, unwilling to waste a single second. There have been many other similar stories. Confucius read *The Book of Changes* over and over so that the leather cords holding the pages broke many times. In the Eastern Jin Dynasty, young Zu Ti rose upon hearing the crow of a rooster every day to practice swordsmanship. In the Northern Song Dynasty, Yang Shi and his friend You Cu once sought the advice of a scholar named Cheng Yi. When they arrived at Cheng's house, it snowed very heavily, and they were informed that Cheng was sleeping. In order not to disturb the instructor, they waited outdoors in the snow until Cheng woke up.

In study, we should also pay attention to method and manner. In this regard, *The Analects* provides advice of considerable referential value. The book states that "If one learns from others but does not think, one will be bewildered. If, on the other hand, one thinks but does not learn from others, one will be imperiled." This means if one learns without thinking, he will acquire nothing because of bewilderment. If one thinks without learning, he will be imperiled because of bewilderment. *The Analects* also proposed that one should "Learn widely and be steadfast in one's purpose, inquire earnestly and reflect on what is at hand, and there will be no need to look for benevolence elsewhere." By doing so, we will ultimately become benevolent.

Introducing the ancients' deeds of studying diligently and their ways of studying, Xi Jinping encouraged the trainees of the Central Party School to study hard and continue to think. As early as when he worked in Zhejiang Province, he proposed the idea to "take an initiative to start a 'revolution of study'." He thinks highly of the role of "thinking" in study: "Thinking is a further step to deepen one's reading. It is an inevitable step to gain access to cognition, and it is the key to capturing the essence of a book." Albert Einstein said, "Studying requires continual thinking and rethinking, which is a learning method that has helped me become a scientist."

TO HAVE A GOOD GRASP OF ORIGINAL WORKS

In the preface to *Capital, Volume III*, Friedrich Engels noted "When a man wants to address scientific questions, he should above all learn to read the works he wishes to use just as the author had written them, and above all without reading anything into them that they do not contain." For the majority of Party members and officials, it is inevitable that they will encounter some difficulties at the initial stage of reading some original works. However, Marxism is the scientific truth that guides the working class to understand the world and to transform the world. As long as we make great efforts to read these works, we will definitely come to have a good grasp of it. "The method of analysis that I have employed, and which had not previously been applied to economic subjects, makes the reading of the first chapters rather arduous," said Karl Marx after the publishing of *Capital, Volume I*. "This is a disadvantage I am powerless to overcome except by forewarning and forearming those readers who zealously seek the truth. There is no royal road to science, and only those who do not dread the fatiguing climb of its steep paths have a chance of gaining its luminous summits." Lenin said that the task of helping college students to fully comprehend the question of the state is "a most complex and difficult one." He once recommended that students should "devote some time to reading at least a few of the most important works of Marx and Engels." He said, "Some of you may at first be dismayed by the difficulty of the exposition, I must again warn you that you should not let this worry you; what is unclear at a first reading will become clear at a second reading, or when you subsequently approach the question from a somewhat different angle." He emphasized, "Anybody who desires to study it seriously and master it independently must attack it several times, return to it again and again and consider it from various angles to attain a clear, sound understanding of it." Comrade Mao Zedong stressed that to take a scientific attitude is to seek truth in facts, stating that "The absence of a scientific attitude, that is, the absence of the Marxist-Leninist approach of uniting theory and practice, means that Party spirit is either absent or deficient." The learning methods above are still applicable for how we should study the classical works of Marxism today.

- Leading Officials Must Value the Study of the Classical Works of Marxism—Speech at the Opening Ceremony of the Second Batch of Classes for Advanced Studies at the Central Party School in 2011 Spring Semester (May 13, 2011).

Commentary

As revolutionary instructors, Marx, Lenin, and Mao Zedong made great efforts in pursuit of truth.

Marx read and wrote all year around. His method of taking a break was simply walking up and down the room, so that there was a trace trod through the carpet from the door to the window in his room, just like a path through the grass. When he was writing *Capital*, to finish two dozen pages on British labor law, he studied all the blue books in the library that contained the reports of the British and Scottish commissions of investigation and factory inspectors.

Lenin continued to read and write, even when he was in prison. To evade notice by the prison guards, he poured milk into his bread, which he used as makeshift ink. When the milk dried, it became invisible. When a guard came into his cell, he ate the little "ink bottle". Once he wrote in a letter that, "I have eaten six 'ink bottles' today." In Volume 40 of the *Collected Works of Vladimir Lenin* compiled by the Marxist-Leninist Institute of the CPSU Central Committee, approximately 400 out of the 500 pages are composed of Lenin's comments on, notes to, and excerpts from the works of Marx, Engels, and others.

Mao Zedong repeatedly read *Capital*. The People's Publishing House even printed a large-character edition of the work especially for him. He also read *The History of the Communist Party of the Soviet Union and Outline of the Sociology* by Li Da more than ten times in addition to reading through *The Communist Manifesto, Capital, Selected Works of Lenin, Critique of the Gotha Program, The State and Revolution*, and other works repeatedly. He also made comments on and put annotations in many chapters and paragraphs. Every time he read a book or an article, he circled, underlined, drew arrows, and other marks at places that he considered important, and he wrote many comments in the margins. When he was dying, three editions of *The Communist Manifesto* were still laying beside him: a thread-bound large-character edition and two other editions that had been published in wartime.

At the opening ceremony of the second group of classes for advanced studies at the Central Party School in spring semester 2011, Xi Jinping taught the trainees how to address difficulties in reading and understanding original works by introducing the experiences of Marx, Lenin, Mao Zedong, and other revolutionary instructors in "reading original works." As he said, "Officials, especially high-ranking ones, should master the basic theories of Marxism as their special skill and diligently study Marxism-Leninism and the thought of Mao Zedong, especially Deng Xiaoping's Theory, the important thought of the Three Represents and the Scientific Outlook on Development."

THE XUNWU INVESTIGATION

When Comrade Mao Zedong was conducting an investigation in Xunwu County, he directly convened the people from all sectors and held a fact-finding meeting, collecting a great deal of first-hand information, including the yields and prices of all categories of products in the county, the numbers and proportions of employees in various industries in the urban area, the scope of businesses and the incomes of the shops, the land areas and incomes of the peasants in different areas, as well as the political attitudes of all groups of people. He made all of these categories crystal clear. Such an in-depth and pragmatic style is worth attaining.

- A Talk on Investigation and Study—Speech at the Opening Ceremony of the Second Batch of Classes for Advanced Studies at the Central Party School in 2011 Autumn Semester (November 16, 2011).

Commentary

The exhibition "The Road to Rejuvenation" at the National Museum of China has on display a precious lithographed book. The book is the *Investigation Work* written by Mao Zedong in Xunwu County in May 1930. The title was later changed to *To Oppose Dogmatism*. In the article, Mao Zedong first put forward the idea that "He who makes no investigation has no right to speak" and "The victory of China's revolutionary struggle depends on the Chinese comrades' understanding of the situation in China." The Xunwu investigation, whether in terms of revolutionary guidance or scientific research, is a brilliant example for our Party to carry out investigations.

The Xunwu investigation was the largest scale social investigation initiated by Mao Zedong in the agrarian revolution period, and it was also his first investigation focusing on an urban area. In May 1930, Mao Zedong led the Red Army to march from Huichang to Xunwu, Jiangxi Province. Located at the Jiangxi' border area that neighbors on Guangdong and Fujian provinces, Xunwu was a main distribution center of commodities. In Mao's view, "I have not yet fully understood the rich peasant issue in China, and I am only a layman in commerce, so I must make great efforts to carry out this investigation." Thus, he set out to investigate the commercial state in the urban area of Xunwu when the troops mobilized the people to join the agrarian revolution in the neighboring counties.

"Which tofu shops make the best tofu and sell best in Xunwu? And which shops brew the best wine here?" These were some of the questions Mao Zedong asked before the investigation, which stumped the local officials. The investigation team headed by him visited 47 stores and 94 shops engaged in handicraft. They took part in labor with the masses and communicated with them. Based on this investigation, the Red Army established the urban policy that would "eliminate the exorbitant taxes and protect trade," correct the left-leaning errors and solve the problem of supply shortage.

The report of this action, the *Xunwu Investigation*, consisted of five parts: the political division of Xunwu, transportation, commerce, original agrarian relationship, and agrarian struggle. The report provided an overview of the situation of Xunwu through statistical data, an introduction of historical evolution, an industrial survey and class analysis. From the report, we can not only read the 131 imported products being sold in the variety stores in the county and obtain a glimpse of the operation of the shops making jewelry and those repairing clocks and watches but also get a sense of how the rural ancestral hall distributed grain and meat at festivals. Such meticulous material, informational, and scientific analysis and comprehensive study were featured in the report.

"Investigation is the foundation for achievement and the way toward success. He who makes no investigation has no right to speak, and, of course, has no right to make decisions." In his distinctive style, Xi Jinping always attaches great importance to investigation and advocates in-depth and pragmatic investigation. By quoting the instance of the Xunwu investigation initiated by Mao Zedong, he exhorted the officials that, to conduct an investigation, one must go to grassroots communities, find out what the people think and want, and correct their perceptions according to the people's social practices.

Many classes of the Central Party School are required to conduct special investigations. At the opening ceremony of the second group of classes for advanced studies at the Central Party School in the 2011 autumn semester, Xi Jinping gave the trainees a special lesson on investigation. In the talk, he put forward many important judgments and made some working demands. For instance, investigation is not only a working method but it is also a big problem concerning the success of the Party's and the people's cause; to measure whether an investigation is well done, we should consider the actual effect of the investigation as well as the application of the investigation's results and judge whether the problems have been solved.

THE 114-CHARACTER EPITAPH

Comrade Mao Zedong composed an epitaph for the Monument to the People's Heroes in only 114 Chinese characters, which, however, describes the whole modern history of China. In 1975, Comrade Deng Xiaoping drafted the report that was to be made by Premier Zhou Enlai at the first plenary session of the Fourth National People's Congress in only 5,000 characters. Later, when discussing this matter, Deng Xiaoping said, "Chairman Mao designated me to head the drafting of the report and limited it to five thousand characters. I finished the task. The 5,000 characters indeed work very well, don't they?"

- Get Rid of the Bad Style of Writing and Promote the Good Style—
  Speech at the Opening Ceremony of the Second Batch of Trainees of
  the Central Party School in 2010 Spring Semester (May 12, 2010).

Commentary

From September 21 to 30, 1949, the first plenary session of the Chinese People's Political Consultative Conference was held in Peiping (now Beijing). To commemorate the heroes of the people who laid down their lives in the people's war of liberation and the people's revolution, the conference decided to establish the Monument to the People's Heroes outside Tian An Men in China's capital of Beijing. Mao Zedong composed the following epitaph for the monument: Eternal glory to the heroes of the people who laid down their lives in the people's war of liberation and the people's revolution in the past 3 years! Eternal glory to the heroes of the people who laid down their lives in the people's war of liberation and the people's revolution in the past 30 years! Eternal glory to the heroes of the people who from 1840 laid down their lives in the many struggles against domestic and foreign enemies and for national independence and the freedom and well-being of the people! Short although the epitaph is, it is concise and powerful and expresses the admiration for and memory of the people's heroes.

From January 13 to 17, 1975, the first plenary session of the Fourth National People's Congress was held in Beijing. This was the only session of the Fourth National People's Congress held during the Cultural Revolution. In consideration of the physical condition of Zhou Enlai, Premier of the State Council at the time, Deng Xiaoping, then the First Vice Premier, received the commission by Mao Zedong to preside over the drafting of the government's work report on behalf of Zhou Enlai. Not only did Deng compress the report to only 5,000 Chinese characters but he also led the drafting team to overcome all the obstacles and to put Zhou's thoughts about the "Four Modernizations" into the report as a focal point. Once the grand goal of "Four Modernizations" was reported, it immediately raised the confidence of the whole Party and the people to break through the shackles of the "Cultural Revolution". Deng Xiaoping thus said, "The five thousand characters indeed work very well, don't they?"

Xi Jinping said, "We should abandon empty talk while advocating short, pragmatic and novel writing styles." This is what Xi Jinping preaches, and it is also what he practices. He employed a simple writing style as early as 1984, when he published his first signed paper, *Young and Middle-aged Officials Should Respect the "Veterans"* in the *People's Daily* as the County Party Secretary of Zhengding, Hebei Province. When he served as Provincial Party Secretary of Zhejiang during 2003 and 2007, he published a total of 232 brief comments in the special column "Fresh Ideas of Zhejiang" for the *Zhejiang Daily*. Composed of only 300 to 500 characters without empty rhetoric or a bureaucratic tone, these works put forward strong viewpoints by quoting the classics, told the truth in an easy-to-understand way, and struck at the heart of the issues. Many of the thoughts and expressions in the articles are still worth considering to this day.

The writing style of an official reflects his or her work style as well as capability and qualification. Hence, Xi Jinping attaches great importance to the issue of writing style. There is a misconception of writing style: the length of an article is proportional to its grade. Xi Jinping cited the 114-character epitaph of the Monument to the People's Heroes and the 5,000-character government work report drafted by Deng Xiaoping on behalf of Zhou Enlai to prove that a short essay can also contain rich content, and an author should aim at integrating profound meaning in as succinct an article as possible.

Xi Jinping once quoted an allusion in *Chuang Tzu*: "What is long is not considered as excess, and what is short is not regarded as wanting. A duck's legs, although short, cannot be lengthened without dismaying the duck, while a crane's legs, although long, cannot be shortened without leaving the crane miserable." This means that although a duck's legs are short, it would bother the duck if they were lengthened; although a crane's legs are long, the crane would suffer if they are shortened. The same is true for writing. He noted that today there are too many articles that look like "the lengthened leg of a duck", and hence advocating for short articles, short speeches, and short files as today's main task in the improvement of one's writing style.

Read the Communist Manifesto 100 Times

To study the works of Karl Marx, Vladimir Lenin, and Mao Zedong, we should read them carefully and thoroughly and make real effort in our study. At the end of 1939, Comrade Mao Zedong said to a comrade who was studying in the Marxist-Leninist College that "You must read the books on Marxism-Leninism often. I have read *The Communist Manifesto* more than one hundred times. Every time I come up against a question, I looked for answer in it. Sometimes I just select one or two paragraphs to read, and sometimes I read the book through. Every time I read it, I receive new inspiration from it. I also referred to it many times while writing *On New Democracy*. Our purpose of reading the Marxist theories is to apply them. And to apply them properly, we must read them repeatedly and carefully." Comrades Deng Xiaoping, Jiang Zemin, and Hu Jintao have all repeatedly stressed the importance of carefully studying original works in different periods.

- Party Officials Should Love Reading, Be Good at Reading, and Read Good Books—Speech at the Opening Ceremony of the Second Batch of Classes for Advanced Studies at the Central Party School in 2009 Spring Semester (May 13, 2009).

Commentary

The Communist Manifesto is the first programmatic document for the international communist movement, marking the birth of Marxism. Although it is not long, it shocked the whole world as a "spiritual atomic bomb" when it was published. In terms of theory, it is permeated with the basic spirit of historical materialism, providing a scientific methodology for understanding human society. In terms of practice, it served as the party program of the first international communist organization, which included the chanted slogan "Workers of the world, unite!", providing a guide to action for the proletarian revolution. Friedrich Engels noted that *The Communist Manifesto* "is the most widely dispersed and international book among all Socialist literature" and that it is the first "comprehensive party program covering both theory and practice" for the Proletarian parties all over the world.

The Communist Manifesto also had an extraordinary impact on China's revolution and the CPC. Mao Zedong once revealed to Edgar Snow that it was under the influence of *The Communist Manifesto* that he became a Marxist who preached Marxism and, to a certain extent, practiced it by the summer of 1920. Once at a meeting, Zhou Enlai, who was in his later years, walked up to Mr. Chen Wangdao, the translator of the first Chinese version of *The Communist Manifesto*, and asked Chen if he could find the first Chinese version because he wanted to have one more look at it. Deng Xiaoping first read *The Communist Manifesto* when he studied and worked in Paris and then joined the Communist Party and the revolution. "My primer was *The Communist Manifesto*," he said with deep emotion in his 1992 Southern Tour.

It is not easy for our Party officials to study the original works of Marxism-Leninism. Xi Jinping told Mao Zedong's story of studying *The Communist Manifesto* with the intention of informing the officials that the pith and marrow of Marxism can be only acquired through diligent study, even for the leaders of our Party. By doing so, he proved the importance of reading original works carefully and increased the officials' confidence in studying the classics. Xi has spoken of *The Communist Manifesto* on multiple occasions, "Marxism is the 'scripture' for us communists. He who only thinks about 'how to make a pilgrimage', instead of 'studying the scripture', would be misled!"

According to the villagers of Liangjiahe Village, Xi Jinping has read *Capital* as early as when he worked in the countryside. When he studied for a doctorate at the School of Humanities, Tsinghua University during 1998 and 2002, he majored in Marxist theory and ideological and political education. While heading the drafting of the political report to the 18th National Congress of the CPC, he asked to put these words into the report: "Belief in Marxism and faith in socialism and communism are the political soul of Communists, enabling them to withstand all tests." As he stressed, the officials must fully understand the importance of "studying the theories of Marxism-Leninism in a general and in-depth manner," and they should read the classic Marxist works carefully and thoroughly.

THE THREE STATES OF STUDY

The famous scholar Wang Guowei once described the three states of study with three poetic lines, respectively. The first is "Last night the western breeze blew withered leaves off trees. I mount the tower high and strain my longing eyes"; the second is "I find my gown too large, but I will not regret; it's worthwhile growing languid for my coquette"; and the third is

"In the crowd once and again I look for her in vain. When all at once I turn my head, I find her there where lantern light is dimly shed." (All the three lines above are translated by Xu Yuanchong.)

We officials must reach these three states in theoretical study. In theoretical study, first, we should aim high, endure loneliness, and settle down to diligently inform ourselves on important works, which can be compared to the line, "mount the tower high and strain my longing eye." Second, we should assiduously and unswervingly and make real and painstaking effort. During this process, we should not regret, although "our gown becomes too large and we grow languid." Third, in study, we should learn to think for ourselves and understand the true essence of theories; in practice, we should apply what we have learned and further grasp the true essence of the readings. We may look for the essence in vain at first; however, we will finally find it when we least expect it. Only in this way can our officials take the lead in studying thoroughly and persistently, and only in this way can they provide fine examples of diligent studying and thinking, fine examples of emancipating the mind and keeping up with times, and fine examples of accomplishing things by applying what one has learned.

– Three States of Theoretical Study (July 13, 2003) From *Fresh Ideas of Zhejiang.*

Commentary

The theory of "the three states of study" is derived from a paragraph in *Jen-Chien Tz'u-Hua* by Wang Guowei, a master in sinology. He said, "Everyone who has achieved great things or is of profound learning has surely reached three states in study. 'Last night the western breeze blew withered leaves off trees. I mount the tower high and strain my longing eye.' This is the first state. 'I find my gown too large, but I will not regret; 'it is worthwhile growing languid for my coquette.' This is the second state. And the third is 'In the crowd once and again I look for her in vain. When all at once I turn my head, I find her there where lantern light is dimly shed'." These lines depicting the three states of study and career are ingenious quotations of the verses of Yan Shu, Liu Yong, and Xin Qiji, which describe romantic scenarios.

The first state derives from the *Butterflies in Love with Flowers—Orchids Shed Tears with Doleful Asters in Gray Mist* by Yan Shu, a poet of the

Northern Song Dynasty: "Orchids shed tears with doleful asters in gray mist; silk curtain chill, a pair of swallows fly away. The moon, knowing not parting grief, sheds slanting light through crimson windows all the night. Last night the western breeze blew withered leaves off the trees. I mount the tower high and strain my longing eye. I'll send a message to my dear, but endless ranges and streams serve us far and near." In the first part of this Ci poem, the poet takes advantage of the scene to express the hero's pain of parting. Stemming from such pain, the second part draws a vivid picture that illustrates his lovesickness—"strain his longing eye from the tower high." Wang Guowei expressed his thoughts through this Ci poem: a person engaged in scholarship who aims to achieve great things should first persist in his or her pursuit and look far ahead from a high plane to determine his or her goal, direction, and path.

The second state stems from the *Butterflies in Love with Flowers—I Lean on the Balcony in a Light, Light Breeze* by Liu Yong, another poet of the Northern Song Dynasty: "I lean on balcony in a light, light breeze; as far as the eye sees, on the horizon's dark parting, grief grows unseen. In fading sunlight smoke rises over grass green. Who understands why mutely on the rails I lean? I'd drown in wine my parting grief; chanting before the cup, strained mirth brings no relief. I find my gown too large, but I will not regret;'it is worthwhile growing languid for my coquette." The theme of this Ci poem is homesickness and lovesickness, emphasizing the hardships of love and the poet's lack of regret. By depicting the scenery, he expresses his feelings of loss and grief far away from home and his yearning for whom he is in love with, enabling readers to sense his sincere affection. Wang Guowei used the two lines in this Ci poem as a metaphor for the pursuit of great achievements and great learning, which expresses that no one can achieve great things or great learning in the course of a single walk; thus, we must pursue our aims unswervingly and without regret.

The third state stems from the poem *Green Jade Table—The Lantern Festival Night* by Xin Qiji, a Ci poet of the Southern Song Dynasty: "One night's east wind adorns a thousand trees with flowers and blows down stars in showers. Fine steeds and carved cabs spread fragrance en route; music vibrates from the flute; the moon sheds its full light while fish and dragon lanterns dance all night. In a gold-threaded dress, with moth or willow ornaments, giggling, she melts into the throng with trails of scents. But in the crowd once and again I look for her in vain. When all at once I turn my head, I find her there where lantern light is dimly shed." The first part of this Ci poem depicts the scene of joy and peace at the lantern show of the Lantern Festival, while the second part illustrates that the hero searches for the lady to whom he lost his heart, portraying a subtle beauty without a trace of vanity. Wang Guowei cited this line to exhort us that in the process of study, we cannot gain insight without unremitting exploration and research.

Citing "the three states of study," this talk on theoretical study by Xi Jinping encouraged learning using beautiful lines to inspire officials to take the lead in studying theoretical knowledge thoroughly and persistently. The theory of "the three states of study" exhorts us that, in theoretical study, first, we should not only aim high, endure loneliness and settle down to diligently study important works but we should also think for ourselves to understand the true essence of theories and apply what we have learned.

Do not Be Pessimistic, or Idle the Time Away

There is a young man named Zheng Chunlin in the Qiji Group of our county. He has a disability in one leg due to infantile paralysis. Yet he is neither pessimistic nor does he idle the time away. Instead, he went to Beijing and studied painting as well as photography at his own expense, and he then established a mobile painting and photo studio in his hometown to provide door-to-door services to paint screen walls and kang boxes (kang is a type of heatable brick bed that is common in Northern China) and taking photos for the local people. One night a teacher from a nongovernmental school went to his house to have a photo taken for urgent use and requested that the photo should be ready the same day. However, a roll of film must be developed only after it has run out because it can only be developed one time. To fulfill the teacher's urgent need, he developed a single photo for this customer, with the rest of the film being nullified. He cannot perform physical labor because of the disability in the leg, so he started a family business at home. He raised more than 20 minks and voluntarily taught other young people the skill of raising minks, leading more than a dozen families to become employed in this business. Over 2 years, he earned nearly 10,000 yuan, which in 1983 was a lot. He even built the first small building in the Qiji Group with the income he earned. If all the young people in our country could be as selfless and dedicated as he is, and exert their talents to develop their hometown, then Zhengding will soon experience an earth-shaking change.

– To Vitalize Zhengding, To Be the Young Generation Hardworking and Promising (August 10, 1983), from *Know It Deeply, Love
It Deeply.*

Commentary

It is said that "A fine example excels twenty instructions from books."
The example is the driving force of progress. Having a disability in one
leg due to infantile paralysis, Zheng Chunling did not abandon himself to
despair but studied painting as well as photography at his own expense and
acquired wealth by raising minks, after which he even led other villagers
to earn money through this family business. With an extraordinary desire
to advance and his executive ability, he set an extraordinary example of
alleviating poverty and helping fellow villagers. Even to this day, his story
serves as a stimulus to encourage people to advance, which makes him an
inspiration for us all.

In August 1983, Xi Jinping, who at the time served as County Party
Secretary of Zhengding, stated that "The youth are the most active and
vigorous force in society as a whole. They are those on whom we will
depend to vitalize Zhengding." He also described some of the weaknesses
and shortcomings of some young people. For example, some of them "do
not have the ability to do what they hope to do" or "blindly perceive that
they are inferior." He went on to say that "Some of them just want to pick
the roses in the distance as they tread on those that grow underfoot. They
forget that to achieve great things, we must start from minor matters and
get involved with what is right in front of us." In his view, if the youth
look down on the grassroots work and ordinary posts, and if they idle their
time away daydreaming about "great achievements" instead of completing
the immediate tasks at hand, then none of their dreams will come true.
Therefore, in his speech, he shared Zheng Chunlin's story of starting a
business and helping his fellow villagers get rich. He encouraged the youth
of Zhengding to concentrate on their own duties and work hard, and he
exhorted them to head toward their bright futures by starting with minor
matters.

In the speech "To Vitalize Zhengding, To Be the Young Generation that
is Hardworking and Promising," he also shared another inspirational story.

Huang Chunsheng, who was of a low degree of education, began to cultivate an improved variety of cotton in 1969. Lacking the relevant knowledge, he started learning from scratch. He studied the units on plants in middle-school textbooks. Then, he taught himself with the relevant teaching materials from Hebei Normal University and Hebei University and read a number of journals about agricultural science and technology. He even made special trips to universities, colleges, and research institutions to consult experts and professors. After several years of hard work and assiduous study, the cotton variety "Jimian 2" cultivated by him won second prize for scientific and technological achievements of Hebei Province and covered a planting area of nearly 66,666 hectares all over our country. In view of his achievements, he was praised as the "self-taught expert" in cotton breeding.

Xi Jinping told Zheng Chunlin's story to teach the youth that only if they perform their duties in a down-to-earth manner and strive for excellent performance in their own posts can the wisdom and talents of all young people be integrated into a tremendous force to advance the development of society as a whole. As long as they concentrate on their own duties and work hard on minor matters, they will certainly have a bright future. We can recognize this truth in Zheng Chunlin's story.

Time and again, Xi Jinping has encouraged the youth to seek out experience in grassroots work. He wrote to the college-graduate village official Zhang Guangxiu and expressed his ardent expectation of all college-graduate village officials, emphasizing that they should "love and take root in grassroots communities; open their minds and enhance their abilities in grassroots posts; and aim to promote rural development, bring benefit to peasants and enjoy a youth without regret." In his letter in reply to a Benyu Volunteer Team from Huazhong Agricultural University, he also encouraged the young generation to insist on advancing together with the motherland and devoting themselves to the cause of the people, and he inspired them to make greater contributions to the realization of the Chinese dream on the basis of their youthful dreams and through their actions.

THE RETURN OF A PRODIGAL CHILD

Here is another story about the return of a prodigal child. Zhou Chu was a famous prodigal son in Chinese history. When he was young, he had surprising strength and a fiery temper, and he liked riding horses and hunting with a bow and arrow. He often harassed and mistreated the local people.

At that time, a fierce tiger on the southern mountain and an alligator in the river often hurt the people; thus, the fierce tiger, the alligator, and Zhou Chu were collectively referred to as "the three pests" by the locals. Later, Zhou Chu rectified his errors by thoroughly following the instructions of the famous scholar Lu Yun. He not only rushed to kill the tiger on the mountain and the alligator in the river but he also became erudite and cultured by studying diligently. In the end, he died a glorious death for his state in battle. This shows that to err is human. One is a good person if he corrects his error quickly. This corroborates the old saying: "A prodigal who returns is more precious than gold."

- Talents Play an Immeasurable Role in Economic Development (April 25, 1983), from *Know It Deeply, Love It Deeply*.

Commentary

Zhou Chu was a brave warrior in the late Three Kingdoms Period and the Western Jin Dynasty. He was "of extraordinary strength" when he was young; however, he had a bad reputation in his hometown because "he paid no attention to small matters and did just as he pleased without restraint." The local people referred to him as well as the fiery tiger in the southern mountain and the alligator in the river collectively as "the three pests," and Zhou was regarded as the "top pest." Realizing that he himself was disreputable, Zhou made a resolution to correct his errors. So, he went to Wu Prefecture to ask for advice from the Lu brothers—Lu Ji and Lu Yun. Unfortunately, Lu Ji was away. However, Lu Yun enlightened him, saying, "The ancients highly valued the practice of correcting mistakes quickly. You are promising, and what is more important for a person is to have an ambition. As long as you are ambitious, you will certainly enjoy a widespread good reputation." As a result, with a guilty conscience, Zhou Chu corrected his mistakes and consequently became a celebrated scholar due to his diligent study. Later, he was sent to the northeast to suppress the rebellion of the Di and Qiang nationalities, and he finally died in battle because his troops were hopelessly outnumbered. He was praised as "a loyal officer of great virtue and loyalty and a martyr of great moral integrity."

The anecdote about Zhou Chu and the return of a prodigal was widely spread. We can read about "Zhou Chu eliminating the three pests" in both the *Book of Jin* and *A New Account of the Tales of the World*. There is also a contemporary Beijing opera titled "Eliminate the Three Pests". Although Zhou Chu's deeds are said to be somewhat fictitious, the story of "Zhou Chu eliminating the three pests" has the specific cultural function of guiding values and advocating self-cultivation. It has been said that "A gentleman's error is like an eclipse of the sun or the moon. When he errs, all people give attention to him, while when he corrects it, all people look up to him." As in this saying in *The Analects*, a human being is bound to make mistakes; as long as he corrects his mistakes, he is worthy of praise and admiration.

There is another story about correcting mistakes in the chapter titled "Amender" of *A New Account of the Tales of the World*. Dai Yuan was engaged in plundering from trade caravans. Lu Ji tried to persuade him away from evil, saying, "You are so talented. But why are you a plunderer?" Following Lu's advice, Dai broke away from the evil path and turned over a new leaf, and he later became a general who subdued the west.

In March 1983, Zhengding County, Heibei Province developed the *Nine Measures for Establishing a New View of Talent Employment for the New Period and Recruiting Talented People*. However, in the process of carrying out the measures, some Party officials did not obtain a full understanding of "recruiting talented people," and some were skeptical about or took a wait-and-see attitude toward the measures. In April of the same year, Xi Jinping highlighted the importance of talent at a county, township, and village official meeting with the theme of "vitalize the economy with open policies." He asked leaders at all levels and all officials to establish a new view of talent employment, to implement the nine measures conscientiously and to vigorously seek and attract talents, to vitalize the economy of the county.

Xi Jinping told Zhou Chu's story to emphasize that "To err is human. One is a good person if he corrects his error quickly." For those who have made mistakes, we should not ignore their virtues while judging those mistakes, and we should notice their advantages and strong points while analyzing their disadvantages and shortcomings. Quoting the old saying "We should highly value a person's morality and forgive him his harmless errors, and we cannot expect anyone to be perfect," he exhorted the officials to emancipate their minds, break through the stereotypes, and eliminate prejudice to appoint people on their merits and acquire talented people through different channels and by different methods.

CHAPTER 4

Stories of Governance: "Solid Work Makes the Country in Great Order, While Boasting Makes It Disordered"

THE DIZZY ONWARD MARCH OF CHINESE MOBILE PHONES

In recent years, some enterprises in our country have engaged in a successful exploration of supply-side structural reform. For example, various cell phone brands, including foreign brands such as Motorola and Nokia, as well as some domestic brands, competed fiercely in our cell phone market, pushing some enterprises to the edge of bankruptcy. Such being the case, some Chinese enterprises have upgraded production and promoted original innovation while aiming at the high-end market and launching high-end smartphones. Satisfying customers' demands for more diversified functions, higher operating speeds, clearer images, and a more fashionable appearance, these smartphones have won an increasing market share at home and abroad. The international cell phone market also endures fierce competition. Once-monopolistic brands such as Motorola, Nokia, and Ericsson no longer hold sway or even exist. After New Year's Day, I visited a Chongqing company, whose thin-film transistor liquid crystal display provides a success story on supply-side reform. Over the past years, the industries of intelligent terminal products such as laptop as well as Chinese-brand automobiles have boomed in Chongqing, which has formed the world's largest electronic information industrial cluster and China's largest automobile industrial cluster. One of every three laptops in the world was made in Chongqing. This proves that we will definitely hew out our way

© People's Publishing House 2020
People's Daily, Department of Commentary,
Narrating China's Governance,
https://doi.org/10.1007/978-981-32-9178-2_4

of the struggle to industrially upgrade as long as we promote supply-side reform while aiming at specific markets.

> – Speech at the Study Session on Implementing the Decision of the Fifth Plenary Session of the 18th CPC Central Committee, Attended by Officials at the Provincial/Ministerial Level (January 18, 2016).

Commentary

The smartphone opened the door to the mobile Internet era. The changes in the mobile phone market show us the improvement of China's innovation capacity and the effectiveness of our supply-side structural reform. A few years ago, Nokia, Motorola, and some other foreign brands dominated the Chinese mobile phone market. However, in recent years, they have presented continuously declining shipments and market shares; conversely, our domestic brands rose suddenly as a new force. In 2015, domestic mobile phones won a user attention rate of 51.3%, surpassing those of foreign brands. This means that the domestic mobile phone manufacturers are catching up with foreign manufacturers in terms of market influence. In the first three quarters of 2016, 371 million smartphones were delivered to dealers in the Chinese market. Huawei, OPPO, VIVO, iPhone, and Mi ranked as the top five brands in shipment volume, with four among them being Chinese brands. What is more, the Chinese brands are taking positive actions to go global. In the first half of 2016, Lenovo and Mi, respectively, ranked second and third among the best-selling brands in the Indian mobile phone market, and Huawei doubled its shipments to Europe.

Another success story about supply-side structural reform involves laptop production in Chongqing, a Chinese city. From the negotiations on introducing laptop manufacturers, Chongqing took just 7 years to become the world's largest manufacturing base of laptops. In 2014, Chongqing produced nearly 200 million units (sets) of smart terminal products, among which the laptops reached 61 million sets, accounting for one-third of global laptop production. BOE Technology Group Co., Ltd., the Chongqing company to which Xi Jinping paid an inspection visit, is one of the world's leading suppliers of semiconductor display technologies, products, and services, with a marketing and service system covering Europe, the US, Asia, and other major regions. The 8.5-generation thin-film transistor produced by BOE is of great strategic significance that has helped China's semiconductor display industry to catch up with the international levels of advancement and push the development of China's electronic information industry as a whole. At the same time, BOE has prioritized innovation, with 5,116 patent applications published in 2014 and 6,156 in 2015. Today it has accumulated over 40,000 workable patents. Innovation is not only the primary requirement of the development concept in this new era but it is also the necessary measure to further supply-side reform.

Sharing the story of changes in the domestic mobile phone market, Xi Jinping introduced Chongqing's breakthroughs in the laptop and self-branded car industry and illustrated the significance of the improvement of China's innovation capacity and the effectiveness of supply-side structural reform. This revealed a law of economic development to officials at all levels: the market always makes positive responses to successful paradigm-shifting innovation on the supply side. Simply put, it is the supply side that fundamentally pushes the development of a country.

How can we adapt to and navigate the economic new normal when faced with the pressures of an economic downturn? How can we achieve the requisite transformation and upgrading of our economic development? Xi Jinping has repeatedly stressed the need to strengthen structural reforms on the supply side: "This is an important innovation and an inevitable requirement for adapting to and leading the new normal of economic development, and an active choice to adapt to the new situation of the competition in comprehensive national strength after the international financial crisis." He has additionally stated that "Every technological and industrial revolution will boost productivity, creating unimaginable supply capacity." This requires officials at all levels to enhance their initiative and enthusiasm for promoting supply-side structural reform, implementing the "five tasks" properly, and making great effort to improve the quality and efficiency of the supply system to promote the transformation and upgrading of China's economy.

"Prepare to Suffer Losses"

In 1945, Comrade Mao Zedong produced a report on the Seventh National Congress of the CPC, in which he discussed the following issues that required consideration in preparation for the difficulties challenging China at the time: first, international hostility; second, domestic hostility; third, several of our major bases had been seized by the Kuomintang;

fourth, nearly ten thousand soldiers could be wiped out by the Kuomintang; fifth, the puppet troops had welcomed Chiang Kai-shek; sixth, a civil war had broken out; seventh, China would be trapped on the road to Greece by our own "Ronald Scobie;" eighth, "The People's Republic of Poland was not recognized," meaning that the status of the Communist Party had not been recognized; ninth, tens of thousands of Party members had either defected or lost contact with Party organizations; tenth, some Party members had become tired and pessimistic; eleventh, catastrophic natural disasters had struck; twelfth, financial difficulties; thirteenth, the enemy had deployed its main force in North China; fourteenth, the Kuomintang had been assassinating Party members in leading positions; fifteenth, disputes in the Party's leadership; sixteenth, we would remain in disfavor with international proletariat organizations; and seventeenth, we would encounter other unpredictable difficulties. Mao went on to say, "Many things cannot be predicted. But we, especially the senior leading cadres, must be prepared to tackle extremely difficult situations and adversity. We must be clear-headed about this." Comrade Deng Xiaoping also repeatedly stressed, "At the same time, we should base our work on the possible emergence of serious problems and prepare for them. In this way, even if the worst should happen, the sky will not fall." We have heard of many such profound views from comrades Mao Zedong, Deng Xiaoping, Jiang Zemin, and Hu Jintao. They represent and convey important political experience and wisdom in governing our Party and country.

> – Speech at the Study Session on Implementing the Decision of the Fifth Plenary Session of the 18th CPC Central Committee, Attended by Officials at the Provincial/Ministerial Level (January 18, 2016).

Commentary

Mao Zedong was a strategic master in bottom-line thinking in the history of the CPC. In his view, we should always be prepared for the most difficult and the worst while striving for the best result. This is a methodology of thinking, of working, and of leadership. The story told by Xi Jinping reflected such bottom-line thinking.

In opening the Seventh National Congress of the CPC, the Party experienced a great change. Through the Yan'an Rectification Movement, the whole Party achieved a great awakening and reached a new level of unity in thought and action. It developed into an experienced and powerful party with 1.21 million members, becoming "the core force to lead the Chinese people to resist Japanese aggression and save our nation." It was also said that "the core force leads the liberation of the Chinese people" and "the core force will defeat the invaders and build up a new China." Under its leadership, the people's army expanded in size to 910,000 soldiers, the people's militia to 2.2 million people, and the population of the liberated area reached 95.5 million. As Mao Zedong said, "The CPC has never been stronger than it is now. The revolutionary base areas have never had populations and troops larger than those they have today. The prestige of the CPC among the people in the areas ruled by Japan or the Kuomintang has hit a record high. And the strength of the people's revolutionary force in the Soviet Union and other countries has also reached an all-time high. It should be said that it is entirely possible to defeat the invaders and build up a new China under these conditions."

Nevertheless, while the people could cheer for such favorable international and domestic situations, in his report to the Seventh National Congress of the CPC, Mao cautioned the Party to be prepared for the suffering of losses. He noted that our Party needed to be prepared for even more difficulties as they faced a bright future, and, unexpectedly, he even agreed with the viewpoint "There is a possibility that China will become a semi-colony of the US." Meanwhile, he also outlined 17 potential difficulties. They were the embodiment of Mao Zedong's way of thinking and art of leadership: "base our policies on the worst possibilities." They were also examples for us to adhere to as we make good use of bottom-line thinking.

At present and in the coming period, we are facing and will face many contradictions, risks, and challenges at home and abroad. Various sources of contradictions and various risk points are interwoven and interact with one another. In this context, Xi Jinping has told stories about Party leaders such as Mao Zedong and Deng Xiaoping and how they took advantage of bottom-line thinking. In doing so, he requires leaders and officials at all levels to make good use of the method of bottom-line thinking and to prepare for the worst while striving for the best result.

During the Program of Mass Line Education and Practice, Xi Jinping warned, "If we fail to eliminate misconduct from the Party, the tragedy of 'Farewell My Concubine' will come true." At the Celebration Ceremony of the 95th Anniversary of the Founding of the CPC, he also urged that "We must be ready at all times to respond to great trials, withstand great risks, overcome great obstacles, and address great challenges." He has stressed repeatedly that "If we fail to take precautions against contradictions, risks and challenges in a timely manner and cope with them properly, the results will be conduction, superposition, evolution and an upgrading of them, upon which the negligible ones will grow into great ones, those occurring locally will form a system of contradictions, risks and challenges, those affecting the world will evolve into those affecting our country, and those in the fields of economy, society, culture and ecology will turn into political contradictions, risks and challenges. These will eventually endanger our Party's ruling position and endanger national security."

We are engaged in a great struggle with many new historical features. Therefore, Party officials at all levels should enhance risk awareness, make good use of bottom-line thinking, and follow Xi Jinping's instructions: "Prepare for any form of contradictions, risks and challenges."

THE CHINESE MIRACLE

In ancient China, agriculture was the foundation on which our nation developed. As a result, for a long time, ancient China led the world in farming. In the Han Dynasty, it had a population topping 60 million and a cultivated area exceeding 53 million hectares. In the Tang Dynasty, Chang'an City covered an area of more than 80 sq km, with a population of over 1 million. Additionally, the palaces in the city were resplendent and magnificent, the pagodas of Buddhist temples soared high, and the eastern and western markets were quite prosperous and bustling. For this reason, a poem by the Tang poet Cen Shen wrote, "There are one million households in Chang'an City." In the Northern Song Dynasty, China developed into the richest country in the world at that time, with its national tax revenue reaching up to 160 million strings of coins [one string contained 1,000 coins]. At that time, none of the cities of London, Paris, Venice, or Florence had a population of 100,000, but China hosted nearly 50 cities with such a population size or larger.

At the start of the Industrial Revolution, we began to fall behind, accompanied by the development of the West. After the Opium War, China's self-sufficient natural economy gradually disintegrated, and at the same time, it missed the opportunity of the Industrial Revolution. Although progress was made in our industry, and some foreign capital entered China—for instance, the concessions in Shanghai, Tianjin's industry, and Wuhan's military industry—China as a whole was an impoverished, backward, and war-torn country, falling way behind. This situation remained for more than 100 years.

Following the founding of new China in 1949, the people began large-scale industrial development under the leadership of the CPC. Mao Zedong proposed that what we should do was "to modernize our industry, agriculture, science, culture and national defense." In the 1950s, remarkable achievements were made in our national construction. Later, however, because of the "Leftist" errors in the Party's guiding thought, we entered the 10-year-long turmoil of the Cultural Revolution. At that time, we had not yet understood the law of socialist construction. All of these aspects hindered large-scale industrial development.

It was the Third Plenary Session of the 11th CPC Central Committee in 1978 that opened the door of reform and opening up that drove us to a new historical era. Over the past 38 years, despite all kinds of difficulties, China created a miracle—it has maintained rapid economic growth for a period longer than any other country since the end of World War II. China's economy ranked 11th in the world at the beginning of the reform and opening up; in 2005, 2006, and 2007, it surpassed France, the UK, and Germany in succession to reach the fifth, fourth, and third places, respectively; in 2009, it moved into the second place by overtaking Japan. In 2010, the scale of its manufacturing industry surpassed the US, ranking first in the world. Within a few decades, we have completed the development course that had took several hundred years in the developed countries. This was a miraculous achievement in world history.

- Speech at the Study Session on Implementing the Decision of the Fifth Plenary Session of the 18th CPC Central Committee, Attended by Officials at the Provincial/Ministerial Level (January 18, 2016).

Commentary

The heyday of the Tang and Han Dynasties is not only imprinted in the collective memory of the Chinese people but it also occupies an important position in the history of human civilization. It represents the peak of universal civilization at that time.

It is said that, in its heyday, the area of the territory of Tang reached 12.51 million square kilometers, which spread all the way to the Korean Peninsula in the east, the Aral Sea in Central Asia in the west, Hue, Vietnam in the south, and Lake Baikal in the north. In regard to the prosperous Tang, it leaves people with an impression of elegance and magnificence as well as inclusiveness and open-mindedness. It was a highly civilized dynasty holding to the principle that courtesy demands reciprocity and sustaining a culture of nobility and confidence. At that time, Chang'an was an international metropolis, attracting businessmen from Central Asia, South Asia, Japan, Arabia, and other countries and regions, most of which were the "Hu merchants" from Central Asia, Persia, and Arabia. These foreign businessmen not only engaged in trade in China but they were also allowed to marry and start a family; they were even given the opportunity to serve as government officials. According to the data, 29 of the prime ministers of Tang were foreigners, while the number of foreigners serving as officials were as many as 3,000. There is a detailed analysis of Tang' prosperity and openness in the *Study in History* by Wang Guowei: "In the South China Sea, there are merchant ships from the Arab Empire. In Chang'an, there are Zoroastrian temples built by Persians. Foreigners flock here like they are returning home because the Tang Dynasty is in the middle of its heyday."

This prosperity continued to the Song Dynasty. We can learn of the Song's spectacular development in industry, commerce, and urban development from the world-famous painting *Riverside Scene at Qingming Festival*. However, in the Ming and Qing dynasties, while the western countries were at the beginning of industrialization, the feudal dynasties of China became increasingly conservative and rigid. They cut off our nation from the outside world, causing us to miss a golden opportunity to modernize. Although some movements were initiated in modern times such as the Westernization Movement and the initiative to save the nation represented by the Chinese people's pursuit of industrialization, they all ended in failure because they took the wrong paths. Since the founding of new China, especially since the reform and opening up, we Chinese people have found the correct road of developing socialism with Chinese characteristics. Along this path, we have promoted industrialization in our country, which has a long history of agriculture that enabled modern civilization to grow from our ancient civilization. We have also accomplished a feat that is unprecedented in human history—leading one billion people to modernization.

History is the best textbook and the most effective medicine for sobering up society. Xi Jinping is a person who pays special attention to gaining experience and drawing lessons from history. Using history as a mirror and having an extensive view of history, in his speeches he often provides analysis on the present and speculates about the future. Tracing the forward movement of the long river of history, he has recalled the brilliant achievements of ancient China, reflected on the humiliation undergone by modern China due to backwardness and analyzed the swift progress achieved by contemporary China by taking opportunity of tight corners. This has provided a panoramic view of Chinese history as it developed from ancient times until today. When he presents figures, details, and stories about the course of China over time, we can clearly feel the strong pulse of history and obtain a sense of China's past, present, and future.

As for history, Xi Jinping has a grand field of vision and has a coordinated graph in his mind. This coordinated graph is composed of 5000 years of brilliant agricultural civilization, more than 100 years of humiliating history, full of ups and downs, and nearly 40 years of heart-stirring reform and opening up. It is a continuum, from which can we more accurately grasp the direction of China's reform and development and obtain a deeper understanding of the significance of the new concept of "innovative, coordinated, green, open and shared development" for China's future. As Zhu Xi, a Chinese philosopher of the Song dynasty, put forward, "The more you know about a thing, the more solid action you can take on it." Xi has put the new concept of China's development in the context of history. By examining the dimensions of both time and space and contrasting the past and the present, he intends to provide a clearer display of the truth and the contemporary significance of the new development concept, and make it possible for the new concept to serve as a spiritual force as well as practical guide for the transformation of the objective world.

The World's Top Eight Pollution Incidents

In the last century, the top eight pollution incidents that occurred in Western countries greatly affected the eco-environment and public life. The Los Angeles Photochemical Smog in the 1940s killed nearly 1,000 people and caused more than 75% of local people to suffer from pinkeye. In December 1952, when the Great London Smog broke out, it caused approximately 4,000 deaths in only a few days during its first outbreak. In the ensuing 2 months, nearly 8,000 people died of respiratory diseases. Later, the city was stricken by 12 severe smog attacks in 1956, 1957, and 1962. In Japan, a factory discharged wastewater containing methylmercury directly into

Minamata Bay, such that nearly 1,000 people who ate contaminated fish and shellfish suffered from severe mercury poisoning and up to 20,000 people were exposed to the threat of mercury poisoning. This was the Minamata Disease of Japan. The book *Silent Spring* by American writer Rachel Carson gives a detailed account of the situation.

  – Speech at the Study Session on Implementing the Decision of the Fifth Plenary Session of the 18th CPC Central Committee, Attended by Officials at the Provincial/Ministerial Level (January 18, 2016).

Commentary

Marx and Engels wrote, "The subjection of 'nature's forces on man, machinery, the application of chemistry in industry and agriculture, steam-navigation, railways, electric telegraphs, the clearing of whole continents for cultivation, the canalization of rivers, whole populations conjured out of the ground—what earlier century had even a presentiment that such productive forces that slumbered in the lap of social labor?" In *The Communist Manifesto*, Marx and Engels explained the impact of industrial civilization on the development of human society in such a powerful way. Science and technology create amazing material wealth for us; however, they are accompanied by great damage to the ecological environment.

The world's environmental pollution incidents, in extreme ways, present the tragic consequences of environmental pollution, thus alerting people to the painful consequences. The world's top eight pollution incidents are the Meuse Valley Fog in Belgium, the Great Smog in London, Yokkaichi Asthma in Japan, Yusho Disease in Japan, Minamata Disease in Japan, the Los Angeles Photochemical Smog, the Donora Smog in the US, and Itai-itai Disease in Japan.

The Meuse Valley Fog in Belgium was the earliest pollution incident among the world's top eight pollution incidents, and it was the first recorded air pollution tragedy in the twentieth century. Along the Meuse River, a 24 km river valley was dotted with heavy industrial plants that engaged in processes such as coking, steelmaking, power generation, glass making, zinc smelting, sulfuric acid production, and fertilizer production. On December 1, 1930, a dense fog came to shroud Belgium, especially the Meuse Valley. On the third day of this freakish weather, thousands of people suffered from respiratory diseases. This incident killed a total of 63 people, 10.5 times the normal death rate in the same period of the previous years. Unfortunately, at that time, the disaster did not garner people's attention. Human beings continued to drive industry forward triumphantly at the expense of the environment. The consequences were the tragedies of environmental pollution.

Silent Spring is a book promoting global environmental protection. For the first time in human history, it voiced the question of the absolute correctness of "human's declaration of war against nature," and it raised awareness of ecological civilization.

Xi Jinping expressed his high attention to environmental protection and green development by relating the world's top eight pollution incidents and introducing *Silent Spring*. The lingering smog "is hurting our ability to breathe"; groundwater pollution has aroused widespread concern; vegetation deterioration is leading to desertification. The many ecological environmental problems accumulated over the years not only impair people's livelihood but they also tend to breed social ills. Xi Jinping stressed, "Our country's contradiction in the ecological environment was not generated overnight, but rather it was an outcome of long-term accumulation. Yet we cannot aggravate it. We communists should have such a breadth of vision and aspiration." This points the way for the rapidly modernizing China: we should open up a new path in which ecology and development complement each other by comprehensively implementing "green development," without following the footsteps of the West in adopting the practice of "treatment after pollution."

LIU QING SETTLED IN HUANGPU VILLAGE FOR LITERARY INSPIRATION

In 1982, when I was preparing to leave for Zhengding County, Hebei Province, for a new appointment, many friends came to bid me farewell, including Wang Yuanjian, a writer and playwright from August First Film Studio. He urged me, "In the rural area, you should learn from Liu Qing, staying close to and going deep among the local farmers." To immerse himself in rural life, Liu Qing resigned from his position of Deputy Party Secretary of Chang'an County, Shaanxi Province, while remaining a member of the standing committee of the country Party committee, and he had moved to Huangpu Village. He lived for 14 years, concentrating on the creation of his novel *The Builders of a New Life*. His immersion in rural life in the Guanzhong area of Shaanxi explains the lifelike characters in his books. Being so well acquainted with farmers, he was able to immediately know whether they would be happy about any new policy concerning agriculture or rural residents.

– Speech at the Symposium on Literature and Art (October 15, 2014).

Commentary

Liu Qing, whose former name was Liu Yunhua, was a famous contemporary writer of China. Born in a poor peasant family, he began writing in the 1930s and published his first novel, *The Story of Cultivating Millet*, in 1947. In 1960, Liu Qing completed his epic novel *The Builders of a New Life* on the basis of his 14-year rural life, which established his position in the history of Chinese literature.

2016 was his centenary year. Different from other writers who revel in digging into books indoors, he took the initiative to settle in Huangpu Village, Chang'an County, Shaanxi Province for 14 years. As a result, he knew people of all types in the countryside as well as their customs and way of thinking. These provided him with inexhaustible source material for creating *The Builders of a New Life*. He was, as it were, a paragon of the spirit of the Yan'an Forum on Literature and Art and an example to the world of literature and art of "going deep into life and going deep among the populace."

Liu Qing knew well the joys and sorrows of the villagers, so he succeeded in creating a number of literary characters such as Liang Shengbao, old man Liang San, Guo Shifu, Yao Shijie, and Guo Zhenshan, and he showed China's magnificent history of socialist transformation of agriculture through these vivid characters. Not describing the characters in a dull, flat way, he skillfully depicted their complex inner worlds. It is said that without his 14 years of rural life, he couldn't have completed *The Builders of a New Life*, which conveys a believable world.

His experience of living among the populace endowed the work with timeless vitality and influence. In the history of Chinese contemporary literature, there are four representative works of 17-year literature: *Keep the Red Flag Flying*, *Red Crag*, *Red Sun* and the generally acknowledged red classic, *The Builders of a New Life*.

"The 'for whom' question is the most fundamental—a question of principle." In 1942, Mao Zedong put forward a basic direction that shocked and enlightened the world of literature and art: literature and art should be used to serve workers, peasants, and soldiers as well as the people. Upon 70 years of kaleidoscopic changes, the notion of "to serve the people" has been imprinted on the values of socialist literature and art. At the Symposium on Literature and Art held in October 2014, Xi Jinping recounted Liu Qing's story of going deep among the populace to reiterate the fundamental values that "literature and art should serve the people" in this day when people's views and values are undergoing profound changes and diverse cultures are emerging. These fundamental values will guide the development of socialist literature and art. Xi Jinping said "You should adhere to people-oriented creation." In his view, the people are not an abstract symbol but real persons, with flesh and blood, with emotions, with love and hate. They have dreams. Sometimes they argue among themselves, and sometimes they struggle to break free from a situation. Therefore, we should not merely pay lip service to the slogan of people-orientation, nor can we further our own feelings about the people. The world is shared by everybody, while China belongs to we Chinese. Only by deepening our roots into our people can Chinese literature and art achieve an inexhaustible power of growth.

The "Governor" Is Coming

I once stated that a County Party Secretary should visit all the villages in the county, a municipal or Prefectural Party Secretary should visit all the districts and townships in the city, and a Provincial Party Secretary should visit all the counties and cities in the province. I did it. When I served as County Party Secretary of Zhengding, I visited all the villages under Zhengding, sometimes even by bike. And when I served as Party Secretary of Fuzhou and Ningde, I traveled to all townships under them. At that time, although there were four towns in Ningde with no access to road transportation, I visited three among them. I did not visit the other because I was transferred to another place and had no chance to pay the visit. There was a town named Xiadang, which for me to get to I had to cut my way through brambles and thistles and travel over mountains and rivers. The Party Secretary of the town led the way for us and cut weeds in our way with a chopper. He said this way was the nearest one, along the river. "'Governor' is coming," the civilians said along the way. They called the Party Secretary "governor," an appellation of the prefectural governor in ancient China. The civilians welcomed us with barrels of cold drinks made of local herbs and mung bean soup, and they said, "Have a drink. You have had a hard time getting here." Xiadang Town is under Shouning County, where Feng Menglong, the author of *Stories to Enlighten the World, Stories to Warn the World* and *Stories to Awaken the World,* had served as Governor in the Ming Dynasty. He traveled through Shouning throughout the first half-year of his tenure. I thought to myself on the way, if a governor of great talent in the feudal times could overcome untold hardships to get there, should we communists be less competent or conscientious than a feudal official? Arriving there, I saw that the office of the Township Party Committee was set in a reformed bullpen, and it was very small. As you know, galley bridges prevail in South China. In those days, we decorated a bridge as a temporary office by putting several bamboo chairs on it and partitioning it with a simple screen. We had meetings, meals, rests, and baths all on the bridge. Now, Xiadang Town has a totally new look. At that time, I saw several churches there. Who built them? The western missionaries of the eighteenth century. No matter what their purpose was, their sense of mission to missionary work was comparable to the sense of mission of our CPC! When I was Party Secretary of Zhejiang Province, I put forward the strategy of "making full use of eight advantages and implementing eight major measures" for the development of Zhejiang after visiting all the counties, cities, and districts in the province. What does that mean? That means we must have a thorough understanding of the situation and grasp first-hand information. Do not merely wait for someone to collect information for you. We are not infants who need to be fed by others. Nowadays, the means to understand a situation are becoming more and more diversified, including telephone, Weibo, and WeChat. They are all very effective. Thus, we have a better approach to mass work.

- Speech at the Enlarged Meeting of the Standing Committee of the Lankao County Party Committee of Henan Province (March 18, 2014).

Commentary

Feng Menglong was an outstanding writer and opera writer in the Ming Dynasty. His *Stories to Enlighten the World, Stories to Warn the World* and *Stories to Awaken the World* are praised as classical representatives of the vernacular short stories of ancient China. However, little is known about how he was also an incorruptible official who was diligent in political affairs and loved the people. In 1634, Feng Menglong, who had already reached 60, assumed the post of Governor of Shouning County, Fujian Province. During his 4-year tenure, he earned a fine reputation for "promoting streamlined administration and fair and clear punishment, advocating literature, favoring the people and treating other officials politely."

At the beginning of his tenure, he conducted a thorough investigation into Shouning to understand the actual situation there. Concerned about agricultural production, he became aware that many fields in Shouning were reclaimed by chiseling stones, and seedlings could be planted once the sandy soil was reclaimed. He knew well that in general, fields will become fertile when they are irrigated by water veins unimpeded; if the water veins are backed up with silt, the fields will turn barren. Upon investigation, he found that although fertilization is necessary for agricultural production, it should be forbidden to produce manure by burning leaves because when people have burned fallen leaves on the mountains in winter, the smog produced would cover certain areas, and the fire could also burn the trees because when they burned the fallen leaves and withered grass on the open ground, they often caused fires. This was first-hand information that he obtained through field investigations.

Xi worked for 2 years in Ningde, the jurisdiction under which Shouning is situated; thus, he traveled to some of the places where Feng Menglong had traveled. The same as Feng, Xi Jinping traveled through all the nine counties under Ningde within the first 3 months after he assumed office, and after that, he further visited throughout the vast majority of towns and villages there, including Xiadang Town under Shouning County. When Xi Jinping visited Xiadang Town for the first time on July 19, 1989, it was a town that lacked roads, running water, light, revenue, or a government office. The people living in the town had to walk more than 10 km over mountains to get to any adjacent town or village, and they had to shoulder items or carry them on their backs to sell them to or buy them from the outer world. To get to the town, Xi Jinping walked on the rugged mountain roads for several hours. On July 26, 1989, he visited Xiadang Town again after a 3 km walk in the rain to inspect the flood situation in Xiapingfeng Village and to express his sincere solicitude for the disaster-affected people. Such investigations embodied the practical working style advocated by him—we must obtain first-hand information through in-person practice.

Feng Menglong "travelled through Shouning throughout the first half-year in his tenure", and Xi Jinping "cut his way through brambles and thistles and travelled over mountains and rivers" to inspect the towns and villages. Xi Jinping narrated these stories precisely to reiterate the importance of investigation and to stimulate officials to go deep into the grass-roots and stay close to the populace.

Xi has stressed that "Investigation is the foundation for doing things and the way toward success. He who makes no investigation has no right to speak, and, of course, has no right to make decisions." He has encouraged officials to experience grassroots work, "It is better to see a thing than to hear it, but it is further better to practice it than to see it." Citing the old sayings, "For food, only the one who tastes it knows whether it is sweet or bitter; for a road, only the one who takes it knows whether it is smooth or bumpy" and "What is learned from books is superficial after all. It is crucial to have it personally tested somehow," he teaches the officials to base judgement on practice and calls on them to resist untrue statements and not to be engaged in hypocrisy.

It Takes Time to Achieve Maturity in a Governance System

From the start of the Bourgeois Revolution in 1640, Britain took several decades to evolve the Glorious Revolution of 1688. It then took an even longer time to mature its system. It took nearly 90 years for the new system of the US to become stabilized, from the American War of Independence, which broke out in 1775 through the close of the Civil War in 1865. During more than 80 years after 1789, at the start of the Bourgeois Revolution in France, to 1870, with the fall of the Second Empire and the founding of the Third Republic, France never stopped vacillating between restoration and anti-restoration. Even Japan, which had begun the Meiji Restoration as early as 1868, did not attain the system it has today until the end of World War II.

- Speech at the Study Session on Implementing the Decision of the Third Plenary Session of the 18th CPC Central Committee and Comprehensively Deepening the Reform, Attended by Officials at the Provincial/Ministerial Level (February 17, 2014).

Commentary

Is the maturity of a governance system a sudden change accomplished at one stroke or an endogenous evolution advanced gradually? When the Western countries celebrate the theory of "the end of history" and promote their governance system and values to the whole world, they forget that the present-day governance system they employ was not inherent but the outcome of decades of or even a century of struggle, turbulence, and change.

None of the developed countries, including the UK, the US, France, and Japan, has eschewed such a process. Taking France as an example, during the French Revolution in 1789, the French people shouted the slogan "Liberty, Equality and Fraternity." However, they did not have this vision realized at one go after the success of the Revolution. In the period of Jacobin dictatorship, 1,376 people were executed in Paris within just 48 days, from June 10, 1794, when the Law of 22 Prairial was enacted, to July 27, on which day the Thermidorian Reaction broke out: "The passion of the crowd died away in a pool of blood... The revolution devoured its own children." Historians have described the Revolution as such. After the Revolution, France continued to vacillate between revolution and restoration, between republic and monarchy, and between democracy and autocracy for 150 years. According to the studies, France underwent eight revolutions during 1800 and 1949 and did not achieve real stability until the end of World War II. The long period France went through to stabilize its governance system proved that it takes time to achieve a system's maturity. Another example is from the US. After the victory of the American War of Independence, the US did not establish as a "union" with inner cohesion but rather it was more like a group of loosely connected states. It maintained this condition until the Lincoln Administration won the Civil War. The Lincoln Administration defended the unity of the US by force, laying the foundation for the country as a complete political entity. This course took nearly 90 years.

From the governance system development of countries such as the UK, the US, France, and Japan, Xi Jinping arrived at a conclusion: a governance system cannot mature overnight because it requires a process of gradual improvement. Hence, this naturally speaks to China's future: like that of the Western countries, the development of China's governance system will go through a gradual improvement and gradual maturity.

Xi has also stressed repeatedly that the type of governance system best suited for a country is unique, which is "developed and gradually improved over a long period of time on the basis of our historical heritage, cultural traditions, and social and economic development." By introducing the historical changes in the governance systems of some developed countries, he reveals the internal logic of the maturity of governance systems and shows us historical thinking and historical vision.

DISCIPLINE MUST NOT BECOME A DUSTY DOCUMENT

For our Party, the question is how to strengthen Party discipline and run it with strict discipline. The key is strict discipline. In October 1964, Comrade Zhou Enlai stated in a speech at the Conference of Performers of the Song and Dance Epic *The East Is Red* that Comrade Mao Zedong defined our Party as "a party that is subject to discipline, armed with the theories of Marxism-Leninism, adopts the method of self-criticism and stays close to the masses." "It is no coincidence that Comrade Mao Zedong places discipline at the forefront. This is the very first precondition for our Party to adhere to the revolution, defeat the enemy and win the victory," said Zhou. Officials fall into wrong paths because they breach discipline. Thus, we must strictly and comprehensively enforce Party discipline. Our compliance with Party discipline should be unconditional. We must turn our words into action and ensure that Party discipline is fully implemented and that any violation is investigated. We must not allow our discipline to become a dusty document resting on the top shelf.

– Speech at the Third Plenary Session of the 18th CPC Central Commission for Discipline Inspection (January 14, 2014).

Commentary

The East Is Red is a song and dance epic directed by Zhou Enlai to celebrate the 15th anniversary of the founding of the People's Republic of China. Produced within just 2 months, this film assembled more than 3,500 performers. It premiered at the Great Hall of the People in Beijing on October 2, 1964, after which it was played 14 times in front of a packed hall. The splendor of the occasion surpassed anything heretofore seen. This song and dance epic dramatizes the history of modern China, from the founding of the CPC to the establishment of new China, during which time the Chinese people, under the leadership of the CPC underwent an extremely hard and bitter revolution and struggle and finally achieved national independence and the people's liberation. *The East Is Red* is a moving musical that compresses the course of hard struggle during which our Party grew from a small and weak party into a huge and powerful one.

Zhou Enlai was not only concerned with the production of the film but he also valued the ideological effect on the performers. To give the performers a better idea of the painstaking process of the CPC leading the Chinese people to establish new China, he presented a report on the history of the CPC in the Great Hall of the People for several hours. The vivid report made them understand that the victory of the revolution was hard-won, which stimulated them to further cherish their current life, led them to reach consensus, and further excited their enthusiasm for the performance.

"Places discipline at the forefront"—these words in Zhou's report can be regarded as the CPC's "password" to one victory after another. Mao Zedong, Zhou Enlai, and many proletarian revolutionaries of the older generation all highly valued discipline. They not only bequeathed a wealth of theories but they also practiced what they preached to defend the authority of discipline. In the autumn of 1927, some soldiers of the CPC dug potatoes out of the civilian fields on their way to the Jinggang Mountains. This event aroused Mao Zedong's reflection. Shortly after, he declared the Three Rules of Discipline to the army, one among which was "Do not take a single needle or piece of thread from the masses." It was the potatoes that drew forth the Three Rules of Discipline and the Six Points for Attention. Zhou Enlai also enforced strict discipline on himself and those around him. During the Yan'an Rectification Movement, the South Bureau set a Day of Party Activities every week. A responsible official of a department was a senior Party member who joined the Party early in the Great Revolution period; however, every time he attended a meeting, he carried a cane chair and sat in it with his legs crossed while listening to reports. Seeing this, Zhou Enlai once asked him to stand up and said to him in earnest, "Are you observing and studying discipline in this way?" "The earlier you joined the Party, the more you need to observe discipline!"

Xi Jinping's telling the stories of the older generation of proletarian revolutionaries and citing the classic sayings of Mao Zedong and Zhou Enlai was fully intended to stress the extreme importance of "discipline". From the war-ridden revolutionary years to the nation-building period in full swing, to the vigorous reform era, strict and impartial discipline was always an important weapon for our Party to win one victory after another.

Xi Jinping has a clear understanding of and made explicit requirements to strengthen Party discipline. In his first meeting with Chinese and foreign journalists as General Secretary, he stated forcefully, "It takes good iron to make good products," and he demanded that "The whole Party must stay on full alert." Since the 18th National Congress of the CPC, the Party has been carrying out complementary campaigns of anti-corruption and work style rectification, which have not only gouged out tumors from the Party and purified the inner-Party's ecological environment but it has also strengthened our Party. These approaches have converged in our strong strategy of strengthening Party discipline, demonstrating our firm determination and great courage in carrying the campaigns through to the end. They have also refreshed the work style of our Party and our government and invigorated our Party and our people. As Xi said, "We must not allow our discipline to become a dusty document resting on the top shelf." This is the key point of our strategy.

LITERARY CHINA

More than 900 years ago, when Su Dongpo was banished to Danzhou, Hainan Province, he produced many poems about the scenery of Hainan, such as "The moon brightens as the clouds are dispersed that any embellishment is superfluous in the night sky because the sky and the sea are pure and limpid enough," "The torrent spring down three thousand feet from high, pairs of cranes fly low" and "The jewel-like flesh breaks through the red litchi skin, while the mandarin oranges overflow with sweet juice." When I visited Hunan Province, I also praised the beautiful scenery there before the local comrades. Comrade Mao Zedong wrote in the *Reply to a Friend* that, "Dongting Lake's snow-topped waves surge skyward; the long isle reverberates with earth-shaking song. And I am lost in dream, untrammeled dreams of the land of hibiscus glowing in the morning sun." Fan Zhongyan, the writer of the Song Dynasty, wrote the lines in *The Yueyang Tower* that "The sky and the lake are tinged with the same hue, making up an infinitely huge canvas of light blue, on which white gulls are hovering in bevies and fish shimmering with silvery scales. And the lake shores adorned with irises and sandbars dotted with orchids are all enshrouded in a sweet and lush green. Sometimes the broad firmament is clear of all mist, a bright moon shines over the vast lake gleaming with a golden glow, and

the moon's reflection in the watery mirror reminds one of sunken jade."
(Translated by Dai Kangxuan and Xie Baikui, 1996) What a lovely view!
During that trip, I also visited Xiangxi and recalled the scenery of Xiangxi
described by Shen Congwen in his *Border Town* and *Xiaoxiao*.

– Speech at the Central Conference on Rural Work (December 23, 2013).

Commentary

When a reader comes across beautiful scenery in a literary work, he is pulled
into a realm of spiritual travel. He can follow Su Dongpo to take a trip of
banishment to the southern border of the country; he can climb high with
Fan Zhongyan to enjoy a distant view; he can get an idea of Chairman Mao
Zedong's passion for poetry; and he can stand in front of the fine view that
Shen Congwen enjoyed to feel what he felt.

Wonderful scenery may stir one to compose poems, and it may even
give the viewer comfort. Su Dongpo was banished to Danzhou, Hainan
Province, in his 60s, before which he had been banished to Huizhou, a
city south of the Five Ridges. In Danzhou, he lived a life rougher than in
Huizhou. When he first arrived there, he sought shelter at a public house
that was worn down by years without repair, so that he could not take
cover from rain. Having no way out, he was forced to build a thatched cottage manually in the forest of Arenga pinnata. He named his cottage "Hut
of Arenga Pinnata". Living in the hut, "although he could only satisfy his
hunger with yams and quench his thirst with water, he took delight in writing." Lonesome though the island where he lived was, Su Dongpo recorded
the wonderful landscapes in lines such as "The torrent springs down three
thousand feet from high, pairs of cranes fly low" and "The jewel-like flesh
breaks through the red litchi shell, while the mandarin oranges overflow
with sweet juice," and he cultivated a magnanimous mind without a care.
He even left the lines "I do not hate the plight I experienced in this desolate
area in the South at all, although it has many times pushed me to the edge
of death because it has enabled me to enjoy an unsurpassably wonderful
trip" when he was saying goodbye to the 3 years of tribulation in Danzhou.

The Yueyang Tower is a masterpiece in the history of Chinese literature
that Fan Zhongyan composed after being banished to Dengzhou, Henan

Province. Being thrown into similar straits, his friend Teng Zijing was banished to Yueyang, Hunan Province. Yet Teng did not become dispirited. He made great efforts to rebuild the Yueyang Tower and invited Fan, who was thousands of miles away from him then, to write a memorial article for the tower. Viewing the *Painting of Autumn Night by Dongting Lake* sent from Teng and spreading the wings of imagination, Fan grabbed his pen with a flourish and finished the famous work *The Yueyang Tower*. The philosophy he set forth in the article, "To be the first in the country to worry about the affairs of the state and the last in the country to enjoy oneself," has been revered by the Chinese people from generation to generation as a spiritual treasure of our nation. In modern times, we find that Mao Zedong also liked taking advantage of a scene to express his emotion. He expressed his yearning for an ideal society through the verses "I am lost in dream, untrammeled dreams of the land of hibiscus" in *Reply to a Friend*. We also have a pure land in our deep soul, which originated from *Border Town, Xiaoxiao* and other works by Shen Congwen.

Xi Jinping quoted these immortal lines about beautiful scenery on the occasion of discussing ecological civilization construction at the Central Conference on Rural Work because we need to delineate the "beautiful China" that lives in our memory. That is what we are yearning for and about which we must care with all our heart. Those immortal words will show us the way to the "beautiful China". Xi Jinping once indicated the direction of our urbanization—"to enable the people to have green hills and blue streams in sight and to bear the image of their homeland in mind." Is this not a vision for building a beautiful China? Retaining the beautiful China in literary works is also to preserve the sweet memory and pursue a bright future for our Chinese nation.

THE LOST 200 YEARS

Looking back on modern history, we are more keenly aware of the extreme importance of seizing opportunities and catching up with the times. The 100 years between the mid-eighteenth century and mid-nineteenth century were the beginning and flourishing period of the industrial revolution. However, during this period, the rulers of the Qing Dynasty sequestered our country from the outside world and maintained sheer parochial arrogance. As a result, they missed the development opportunities brought by the industrial revolution, so that the economic and technological levels of China lagged far behind the pace of development in the world. From the mid-nineteenth to mid-twentieth centuries, this was another 100 years, in which time the Western aggressors drove their military ships to China and bombarded the gates of the Qing Empire, and our country degenerated into a semi-colonial and semi-feudal country. The aggression of foreign powers, the corruption of the Qing government, and the continuous war deprived our country of stability and pushed our people to the edge of starvation. Under these circumstances, we had neither conditions for national construction nor those to keep abreast of the times. From the 1960s to the 1970s, a technological revolution and an industrial revolution sprang up in the world. A number of East Asian countries and regions seized this opportunity and made a great development. However, at the same time, our country lost itself in the Cultural Revolution and missed an opportunity once again. After the Third Plenary Session of the 11th CPC Central Committee, we seized the opportunity, and our country and nation caught up in great strides such that we accomplished today's achievements.

– Speech at the Second Plenary Meeting of the Third Plenary Session of the 18th CPC Central Commission (November 12, 2013).

Commentary

During the 200 years from the mid-eighteenth to the mid-twentieth centuries, the West embarked on a journey of industrialization, and the world experienced great changes while China took a turn from the imperial age toward modern civilization.

When opportunities knocked at the door of China, this age-old nation was out of touch with reality and thus missed them. A few details in the first 100 years mentioned by Xi Jinping reflected the seclusion and extreme arrogance of the rulers of Qing. At that time, the UK was the largest exporter and largest importer to China. The value of the UK's export to China accounted for approximately 90% of the total value of that of the Western countries', while that of the UK's import from China was over 70%. However, the Qing government was blind to this and even referred to the British and Dutch as "ang mo". The diplomatic corps from the UK brought much of value to China: scientific instruments such as the orrey, globe, Herschel telescope, Parke lens, and barometer as well as industrial machinery including the steam engine, cotton-spinning machine, carding machine, and loom. They even brought along a hot-air balloon pilot. The emperor was given the opportunity to take a tour of the sky. Hence, he would be the first person in the eastern hemisphere to fly up into the sky. However, the emperor was not interested in the so-called new-fangled machines of the industrial revolution but in the exquisitely wrought toys such as an "automaton" and or "robot dog", wasting an opportunity to gain access to the industrial revolution.

From the mid-nineteenth century, in response to the calls of people with lofty ideals, initiatives to save the nation by engaging in industry spread through China. The famous industrialist Zhang Jian held the following view: "Saving the nation is a pressing matter of the moment... If we compare the country to a tree, then education is the flower, the navy and army are the fruit, and industry is the roots." In those days, China's national industry did make great progress. The No. 1 mill and No. 2 mill of Zhang Jian's Nantong Dasheng Cotton Mill earned 1,600 million taels of silver from 1914 to 1921. However, continuous wars and turbulence held back China's independence and reunification. The industrial progress was merely a fleeting development. We had no opportunity to catch up with the times.

At the Second Plenary Meeting of the Third Plenary Session of the 18th CPC Central Commission, Xi Jinping presented a clear panorama of the 200-year development of China by tracing this history. From the perspective of the world and based on the characteristics of the times and history, he conducted an in-depth analysis of China's successes and failures in its modernization and revealed "the extreme importance of seizing opportunities and catching up with the times."

In contrast with the lost 200 years, since new China was established, especially in over 30 years of reform and opening up, China has spared no effort to catch up with the world. Today we have lifted reform to a higher level, and the question of "where will China go?" once again attracts worldwide attention. It is in this context that Xi Jinping discussed the modern history of China to testify that "Reform and opening up is the critical strategy that decides the fate of China in contemporary times and is an important weapon for the CPC and the Chinese people to catch up with the times in great strides." Thus, he built the foundation for the consensus on reform.

THE SIGH OF ZHANG ZHIDONG

Historical experience tells us that the success of reform largely depends on whether people of all walks of life in the country reach a consensus. Shang

Yang's reforms in the Warring States Period, Wang Anshi's reforms in the Song Dynasty, and Zhang Juzheng's in the Ming Dynasty all achieved certain effects under the historical conditions of those times. However, the autocratic monarchy, constantly intensified social contradictions, intricate interest relationships, and political strife within the governments overwhelmingly hindered reforms and even brought ruin and shame upon the reformers because the interests of some vested interests were undermined by the reforms. Zhang Zhidong, one of the representatives of the Westernization Movement in the Qing Dynasty, was a man with the mindset of reform. In the late years of the Qing, it became difficult to end the social contradictions, and overall reform became imperative. Under these circumstances, opinions varied, and no unanimous conclusion could be drawn. "The traditionalists give up eating for fear of choking, while the innovators lose their sheep as they wander astray. The traditionalists, who have no ability to subdue the enemy and manage contingency, are tactless, while the innovators, who doubt fame and edification, do not grasp the essence," lamented Zhang Zhidong.

– Speech at the Second Plenary Meeting of the Third Plenary Session of the 18th CPC Central Commission (November 12, 2013).

Commentary

"Reform" is a key word in the long history of China. Some dynasties became rich and strong through reforms, while some declined and fell because reforms were impeded. "The changes of natural phenomena need not be feared, the rules established by ancestors need not be necessarily followed, and people's discussions need not be minded." The ancients had such great courage. "The later generations who lament Qin but refuse to learn a lesson from it make later generations lament them." The ancients thus also lamented.

Shang Yang's reforms in the Warring States Period, Wang Anshi's reforms in the Song Dynasty, and Zhang Juzheng's in the Ming Dynasty were all famous reform initiatives in Chinese history. Shang Yang started reform by building credibility. He gradually abolished the "nine squares" system of land ownership in China's slave society, with one large square divided into nine small ones and the eight outer ones being allocated to serfs who had to cultivate the central one for the serf owner, initiated the system of prefectures and counties, which was a system of local administration and rewarded the people who took part in farming, weaving, and fighting. His reforms supported the prosperity of the state of Qin's economy and strengthened its army, making it the most powerful state in the late Warring States Period and laying the foundations for it to unify China. However, after the death of Duke Xiao of Qin, who supported Shang Yang, the aristocracy of Qin no longer hid their strong opposition to reforms because the reforms impaired their vested interests. At last, Shang Yang was sentenced to death by the ruler of Qin and was torn asunder by five carts. His tragedy manifested the tragically heroic fate of reformers and the great difficulty of reforms.

In the late Qing Dynasty, it was imperative for our nation to adopt reform in the face of aggression by the West and the danger of being subjugated. As the former Viceroy of Huguang, Zhang Zhidong was an innovator who advocated for reform. His Hanyang Steel Plant in Hubei Province was the largest steel plants in Asia at the time, and his Hubei Firearm Factory produced an average of nearly 10,000 guns per year during the ends of 1895 and 1909. Throughout modern and contemporary history, the Hanyang 88 Rifle was the rifle type used and manufactured most widely and serving the longest. It armed countless Chinese armed forces after 1896, which greatly promoted the modernization of the Chinese armies. Zhang Zhidong strongly advocated reform, thus he felt deep sorrow at the resistance to reform. Hence, the lament, "The traditionalists are tactless...while the innovators do not grasp the essence...."

At the Third Plenary Session of the 18th CPC Central Commission that deployed comprehensively continuing reform, Xi Jinping highlighted the importance of reaching a consensus on reform by discussing the difficulties encountered by ancient reformers. He expected to bolster and support the reformers, preventing them from feeling helpless under the converging attack from radical actors and conservatives. Reaching consensus on reform is what he firmly advocates. Since the 18th National Congress of the CPC, the Party Central Committee headed by Comrade Xi has spared no effort to push forward with reform, with the resolution of taking up our hammers and breaking the barriers, the bravery to advance through the rapids, the courage to make prompt and resolute decisions, and the wisdom to plan jointly to take into consideration every aspect of a matter. This magnificent feat raises hundreds of millions of Chinese people's expectation and confidence, making reform the most powerful driving force for China's modernization and the most distinctive spiritual totem of this era.

SCRAMBLE FOR THE "SHACKLES OF POVERTY"

I read from some material that in the beginning of 2012, the government of a county that was classified as "a national-level poverty-stricken county" posted "excellent news" on its official website—"Warm Congratulations on Our County Being Listed Among the Poorest Parts of China." Another case is the competition between two counties for the title of "the national-level poverty-stricken county". In tears, the mayor of the losing county said, "What made us lose the competition for the title of the poverty-stricken county was our extreme poverty." What is more, there is a county that had been listed in the Top 100 Counties in China since 2005, but retained its title as the key county in the national development-oriented poverty reduction programs until 2011, when this misconduct was exposed by the media. It is said that there were 17 national-level poverty-stricken counties on the 11th evaluation lists of the top 100 counties of China in basic economic competitiveness, the top 100 counties in Central China and the top 100 counties in West China. The relevant authorities should look into this phenomenon, cancel the titles of those that are not qualified, and give them to those who are in real need.

- Talks During the Inspection on the Work of Development-oriented Poverty Reduction in Fuping County, Hebei Province (December 29 to 30, 2012).

Commentary

At present, China's poverty alleviation movement is marching into the home stretch. We must ensure that all poverty-stricken people in rural areas get out of poverty by 2020. The task is difficult, and we are pressed for time. The cases of scrambling for the "shackles of poverty" told by Xi Jinping reveal the deep-seated issue in the process of poverty alleviation.

In the beginning of 2012, a large outdoor display screen in a county of Hunan Province displayed: "Warm congratulations on our county being listed among the poorest parts of China and becoming the main battlefield of the national poverty alleviation movement in the new era." This message of congratulations was inscribed "County Party Committee and County Government". The photo of this screen attracted widespread public concern immediately after it was exposed on the Internet. According to an article titled "xxx County Successfully Became Listed Among the Poorest Parts of China," on the official website of the county, the county government set a primary goal of its "Two Keys and Three Mains" working plan to be classified as a key area of the national poverty alleviation movement to take advantage of the policy of national development-oriented poverty reduction in the 12th Five-Year". "Undergoing innumerable hardships and difficulties and making every possible effort for two years," the county was ultimately included in the poorest parts of China. In this regard, many people noted sharply on the Internet that what this "poverty-stricken county" was actually congratulated on was their winning of the anti-poverty funds. They "flaunted poverty" for the purpose of garnering resources provided by the central government for poverty-stricken counties.

When Xi Jingping was heading the administration of Ningde, Fujian Province, he often emphasized that poverty alleviation requires a change of attitude. "The weak hatching bird can be the first to fly, and the poorest can be the first to become rich. However, to be the first to 'take flight' or to 'become rich', we must have such a concept in mind," he said repeatedly. To further poverty alleviation in Ningde, he emphasized many times that we should mentally wear away at the "poverty mentality", and he noted "It is entirely possible for impoverished regions to rely on their own efforts, policies, strengths, and advantages in certain areas to be the first to 'take flight' and make up for the disadvantages brought about by poverty."

The "shackles of poverty" not only mean large amounts of transfer payments from exchequer for the counties but it can also bring about policy support and special treatment. Essentially, the scrambling for the "shackles of poverty" is a consequence of the lack of morale to fight against poverty and to reflect the anaclisis of waiting for government aid, relying on financial grants, and requiring poverty allowances. Xi Jinping recited the cases of scrambling for the "shackles of poverty" to exhort us to change our attitude toward poverty, to equip ourselves with the wisdom of poverty alleviation, and not to lose our morale to fight against poverty or breed anaclisis. For the areas that scramble for the "shackles of poverty", to alleviate poverty is just like carrying faggots to put out a fire, which will indeed aggravate poverty.

We must eradicate the "poverty" that exists in our minds before we can eradicate it in our material lives. Xi has repeatedly stressed, "We should make a great attempt to bring into full play the pioneering spirit of the grassroots officials and masses and energize them to get out of poverty by hard work." To stimulate the initiative, enthusiasm, and creativity of the officials and the masses in impoverished areas, we should give them support so that they can convert external resources into steady streams of energy for poverty alleviation. Simply put, we cannot wait for all-around moderate prosperity but build it up with our hands.

"Are You Chinese?"

When I visited Sweden in 1979, I met a Malaysian Chinese in a square. He asked me in poor Chinese, "Are you Chinese?" Getting my answer "Yes", he turned excitedly and said, "I am so glad to see a Chinese here. Chinese are rarely seen in Sweden." Now, we can see Chinese people all over the world. In the Belgian capital Brussels, when I looked out from the seat of the city government, I found half of the people in a public square were Chinese. It would be totally out of the question for our nation to achieve present-day development if our Party did not carry out the historic decision of reform and opening up under the guidance of Comrade Deng Xiaoping.

– Speech During the Inspection in Guangdong Province (December 7–11, 2012).

Commentary

The situation of the Chinese overseas provides us with a global perspective for understanding China. Before reform and opening up, the Chinese rarely went abroad. Hence, the question "Are you Chinese?" Before the reform and opening up, there had even been influxes of illegal immigration in Guangdong Province, China. Some Chinese tried every means to go abroad. As the dividing line between Shenzhen and Hong Kong, Chung Ying Street in Shenzhen looked entirely different on both sides. In Hong Kong, the streets were lined with small-size villas, while in Shenzhen, the old and shabby huts spread across the village in confusion. These details reflected China's backwardness in economy and social development in those days.

"Are you Chinese?" In the year 1979, the world knew so little about China, and China was seriously isolated from the world. However, it was in that year that China embarked on the journey of reform and opening up. This is the reason why some overseas scholars believe that "The 21th century of human society began from China's year of 1978." More than

30 years later, the originally isolated China has already merged into the world. China's outbound tourism has been increasing rapidly. In 2015, the number of our outbound tourists reached 120 million, and overseas consumption amounted to 1.5 trillion yuan. By 2016, China was ranked as the world's top international tourism spender for four consecutive years, with an average annual contribution to global tourism revenues of over 13%. It was just at the time when China was going global in big strides and becoming the world's second largest economy when Xi was in Brussels and noted that "half of the people on a public square were Chinese."

We have more testaments to the influence of China's "go global" strategy. In Paris, France, many attendants of hotels, restaurants, and museums and even taxi drivers all receive a brochure. This was a manual especially issued by the Business Bureau and Regional Tourism Bureau of Paris to teach the French to speak simple Chinese and help them understand the preferences of Chinese tourists. In Seoul, Korea, Chinese advertisements can be seen everywhere in the airport, and many shop assistants can speak simple Chinese to attract Chinese tourists.

In Xi Jinping's first visit outside Beijing as the top CPC leader, he went to Guangdong—the cradle of China's reform and opening up, and he gave an account of what he saw and heard abroad. By comparing the present with the past, he opened a window before all people, with a clear view of the impact of China's development on the world. At the early stage of the reform and opening up, the Chinese people were rarely seen abroad. Nevertheless, more than 30 years later, half of the people on a square in Brussels are from China. Such details reflecting China's development can stir public feeling more easily than grand narratives.

Xi Jinping interpreted the impact of China's development on the world by citing his own experience. In doing so, he demonstrated that it was our insistence, Chinese characteristics and the efforts we made in pushing reform forward and opening up that made China the world's second largest economy. The "Chinese miracles" and "Chinese stories" have drawn the world's attention, and many have been touched and shocked by China. Xi has often said, "Reform and opening up was a great awakening in our Party's history. And it is this great awakening that has nurtured this new era and evolved this great creation of a new era from theory into practice." Standing at a new starting point, China will continue to follow this correct path, and it will take new measures and reach new levels.

No Unity, No Strength

A leading group is like a boat, and carrying out the work is like rowing the boat. As long as the group members work together with one heart and aim at a common goal, the boat will drive rapidly toward the goal. If the group members are divided over the goal and row the boat in different directions, the boat can only spin in situ, without any advance. What is more, if there is internal strife in the group, the boat will possibly capsize. To be together in the same boat is predestined good fortune. To work together is also predestined good fortune. Thus, the leading group member should cherish the chance to work together and achieve success hand in hand.

– No Unity, No Strength (January 19, 2007), from *Fresh Ideas of Zhejiang*.

Commentary

The Art of War is a military treatise attributed to Sun Tzu, a military strategist of the Spring and Autumn Period. Admired by later generations of strategists, it was honored as "the canon of war" and hailed as the lead text in the Seven Military Classics. As a world-famous military scripture, it has been translated and published into English, French, German, Japanese, and other languages.

There is a story about enemies sailing in the same boat in the chapter "The Nine Situations" in *The Art of War*: "The men of Wu and the men of Yue are enemies; yet, if they are crossing a river in the same boat and are caught by a storm, they will come to each other's assistance just as the left hand helps the right." Someone asked Sun Wu how to command troops. He answered that the troops should be deployed like a snake that strikes back during the hunt. The snake-shape battle formation could fight as a whole. When the enemy strikes at its head, it will attack back by its tail; when its tail, by its head; and when its middle, by head and tail both. The civilians of Wu and the civilians of Yue, who are enemies, could pull together in times of trouble, but doubly so the soldiers.

In truth, if we show mutual concern in the same boat and row the boat together, then the boat will cleave through the waves; however, if we row it in different directions and counteract each other, the boat will only spin in situ, without any advance. "A leading group is like a boat, and carrying out the work is like rowing the boat." Xi Jinping has often stressed that, as a leader, "you should be skilled at pooling the wisdom of the Party committee, other branches of county leadership, and officials at all levels. You should assume overall leadership but not take on every detail, divide duties but not undermine concerted efforts, and delegate duties but not totally let go." At the beginning of 2016, Xi Jinping made important instructions on the study of the article *Working Methods of Party Committees*. He demanded the leading groups of the Party committees (Party leadership groups) at all levels to review this classic work. The Organization Department of the Central Committee of the CPC issued a notice about including this article in the learning materials of the "Two Studies and One Actions" program. In the 67th year after the publication of the classic work, it once again attracted people's attention. This was because of its author, our founding leader Mao Zedong, but above all because of the methodology it reveals. This article begins, "The secretary of a Party committee must be good at being a 'squad leader'" and "good at handling his relationships with committee members." Then, it expounds, "If the 'squad members' do not march in step, they can never expect to lead tens of millions of people in fighting and construction," and "members of a Party committee should keep each other informed of and exchange views on the matters that have come to their attention." The classic text enunciates a single theme in less than 3000 Chinese characters—leading group members must unite. This is what Xi Jinping is driving at.

Xi Jinping illustrates abstract truth with concrete objects. He uses rowing a boat together as a metaphor for the solidarity and cooperation within the leading groups, which reveals that an important method for the leading groups of Party committees to carry out the work is to attain strength through unity. That is to say, they should work together with one heart.

A leading group's attainment of creativity, cohesiveness, and professional capabilities is determined by its unity. "The secretary of a Party committee should assume overall responsibility but not undertake everything. He is like a pianist; he should be able to play with both hands at once" "A good leading group must be good at cooperation." "Unity is an important matter in building the leading group. The pursuit of unity is a manifestation of the political mind and holistic view." Xi Jinping has repeatedly highlighted that unity can help to avert discord and incompatibility in the leading groups of the Party committees and prevent them from the absence of the cooperative spirit, to build them into "core teams" in the Party organizations. These "core teams" should bring their leadership into full play through clear-cut division of responsibilities as well as cooperation among the team members. Only in this way can our Party always maintain the position of strong leadership in the cause of socialism with Chinese characteristics.

BUILD UP "TWO MOUNTAINS"

We pursue harmony between man and nature, and between economy and society. In other words, we want "two mountains"—the green mountain and the gold treasure mountain. We can see the relationship of dialectical unity between these "two contradictory mountains." In fact, our understanding of the relationship between them has gone through three stages. At the first stage, we exchanged the green mountain for the gold treasure mountain, during which time we sought resources blindly without considering or while rarely considering the bearing capacity of the environment. At the second stage, we were importunate for both the mountains. At the same time, the contradictions among economic development, the lack of resources, and environmental degradation began to stand out, and we became aware that the environment is the foundation for our survival and development, for there is the mountain of ecological environment, there is the mountain of wealth. Then, at the third stage, we realized that the green mountain creates gold treasure unceasingly; that is to say, the green mountain is the gold treasure mountain itself. The green trees on it are money-spinners, and ecological advantages are economic advantages. The two mountains are harmonious, unified, and inseparable. The third stage is a higher realm, conforming to the requirements of the Scientific Outlook on Development and the concept of developing a circular economy and building a resource-saving and environment-friendly society. These three stages represent the process of transformation of an economic growth pattern, the process of improvement of conception development, and the process of harmonization of the relationship between man and nature.

– On the "Two Mountains" Concerning the Ecological Environment (March 23, 2006), from *Fresh Ideas of Zhejiang*.

Commentary

The "green mountain" and "gold treasure mountain" are two images that most vividly describe the relationship between economic development and environmental protection. The development concept implied by these "two mountains" not only directs the development of Zhejiang Province but also serves as a guide for national development.

In August 2005, as Party Secretary of Zhejiang Province, when he inspected Yu Village in Anji County, Zhejiang, Xi Jinping put forward the scientific judgment that "The green mountain is as valuable as the gold treasure mountain." The bamboo sea is the symbol of this village. It was where *Crouching Tiger, Hidden Dragon* was shot, a film directed by famous director Ang Lee. This film made Anji famous overnight, attracting a continuous stream of tourists to visit the grand bamboo sea. When Xi Jinping visited Yu Village, Anji, he highly praised the practice of the village of closing the mining area and taking the road of green development. The scene of Xi attending a symposium in the crude meeting room of the villager committee is still fresh in the memory of Pan Wenge, head of the villager committee of Yu Village. At the symposium, Xi exhorted the officials and villagers, "Do not cling to the development pattern of the past," and first proposed the thought "The green mountain is as valuable as the gold treasure mountain." Now, the annual tourism income of Yu Village has reached 15 million yuan, five times more than 10 years ago, when the mining industry was the major source of income for the village. Yu Village's green development is the most vivid evidence to support the important concept "The green mountain is as valuable as the gold treasure mountain."

This concept led the development of Zhejiang over the past dozen years. With regard to the strategy of "making full use of eight advantages and implementing eight major measures" that Xi Jinping put forward when heading the administration of Zhejiang, an important idea was to give full play to Zhejiang's ecological advantages and build a "Green Zhejiang". The green mountain not only is the "golden business card" of Zhejiang but it is also a "money-spinner" and a "treasure bowl" on its road of sustainable development. After assuming the post of General Secretary, Xi Jinping aired the view that "The green mountain is as valuable as the gold treasure mountain" on multiple occasions, making green development a consensus of the whole society.

The metaphor of the "green mountain" and the "gold treasure mountain" vividly illuminate the relationship between economic development and environmental protection. In Xi Jinping's view, the "green mountain" and the "gold treasure mountain" do not contradict one another; they are part of a harmonious and unified entity. Therefore, we cannot place importance on one of them while neglecting the other. To reach unification of the two mountains, we should avoid the wrong way of the first stage and get out of the cruel dilemma of the second stage. These three stages are the propositions that every government should thoroughly consider in the course of its development.

DONKEY AND HORSE THEORY

The primary fruit of modern democratic politics is the check-and-balance system on power. There is a famous "donkey and horse theory" with respect to this issue: A horse ran faster than a donkey. Upon comparison, people found that the horse's hoofs were better than the donkey's, so they replaced the hoofs of the donkey with the horse's. However, the donkey ran more slowly as a result. Then, the people made a second comparison. This time they found the horse had better legs. So they replaced the donkey legs with horse legs. To their surprise, the donkey could no longer run. Next, in the same way, they replaced the donkey's body, internal organs, etc., but the donkey did not run faster until the people replaced the whole donkey. This "donkey and horse theory" tells us that "democratic election" is simply a "horse hoof", and the practice of promoting democratic political construction only by installing a "horse hoof" is counterproductive. "Democratic management, democratic decision-making and democratic supervision" are as important and critical as "democratic elections". The democratic "dabbler" will make democracy a flash in the pan and even mess up the original system.

> – Talks During the Investigation in Jinhua (June 17, 2005), from Take the Lead, Take pragmatic Actions—Thoughts on and Practices in Promoting the New Development of Zhejiang Province.

Commentary

A donkey installed with a horse's hoofs is still a donkey, but it is a donkey that runs more slowly. If its legs, body, internal organs, and even the whole donkey are replaced with those of a horse, it would run faster, but totally become a horse. With an ingenious metaphor, vivid description, and interesting plot, this "Donkey and Horse Theory" expounded by Xi

Jinping elaborates on these theoretical problems clearly and thoroughly in a humorous way. He assumes a very easy manner to tackle complicated problems and explain profound theories in simple language.

In the talk, he also took the "Houchen Experience" as an example. The "Houchen Experience" originated from Wuyi County and was promoted in Jinhua. Houchen Village is in the suburb of Wuyi County. At the end of the twentieth century, with the advance of industrialization and urbanization, the collective funds of the village increased sharply in a short time, triggering discipline violations by some village officials, severe conflicts between the officials and the masses, constant petitions by the masses, and some other problems. In June 2004, the village found China's first Village Management Supervision Committee under the "rustic-style" innovation of grassroots democracy. It was set to supervise the implementation of a village management system and the village management itself as a third-party supervisory body independent of the village Party branch and villager committee. This was a prologue to China's exploration in the democratic management of villager affairs. From then on, Houchen Village set off on the innovative journey of improving the management system, promoting the construction of democracy, guaranteeing social harmony and achieving village prosperity through supervision, and finally finishing the transition from chaos to harmony.

After that, the *Organic Law of the Villager Committees of the People's Republic of China* stipulated the founding of the Village Management Supervision Committee, which defined this village management tactic as a national policy. This is a successful example of strengthening the construction of democracy at the grassroots level in rural areas.

Introducing the "donkey and horse theory" when he investigated Jinhua as Party Secretary of Zhejiang Province in 2005, Xi Jinping intended to elucidate that the construction of village-level democracy should cover "democratic elections, democratic decision-making, democratic management and democratic supervision." "The officials must have a comprehensive understanding of these four aspects," he said. Xi Jinping believes that democracy is not simply equal to democratic elections. If we promote democratic construction only by installing a "horse's hoof", it will surely ruin our original system because it is democratic "dabbling". Real democracy refers to a complete system that is strong in all four aspects. "The orange grown South of the Huaihe River is an orange, while that grown North of the river is a trifoliate orange." This is another old saying often quoted by Xi Jinping. The essential meaning he wishes to convey is that simply copying the political system of other countries will not work because the system might not become acclimatized, and this practice may even ruin the future of the country.

THE EMPEROR SHOULD GUARD THE GATE OF THE COUNTRY

What does official mean? To put it bluntly, the organization designates us as officials to send us to stand guard over our territory. That is to say, we are duty bound to defend our country. Liu Bang said in *Song of the Big Wind* that "A big wind rises, clouds are driven away. Home am I now the world is under my sway. Where are brave men to guard the four frontiers today?" It means that there is a group of people responsible for guarding the territory, so they should stand sentry. In the Ming Dynasty, Emperor Yongle moved the capital to Beijing. The fair-sounding reason he declared was "The emperor should guard the gate of the country." In other words, it is an unalterable principle that the emperor should not simply pursue a life of comfort but should guard the gate of the country. In the Qing Dynasty, the official guarding the embankment of the Qiantang River was set as Grade four, enjoying post-related benefits that were as good as those enjoyed by the governor. However, the official might take strict precautions against embankment breach. If he failed in this, he would drown himself in the river before the emperor called him to account for the accident. The imperial officials were this conscientious, and we present-day Party officials should have a stronger sense of responsibility and should understand responsibility and have the courage to bear responsibilities. We should safeguard the regions where we govern, promote their economic development and support the prosperity of the people there. This is the true meaning of being duty bound to defend our country.

– Officials Are Duty Bound to Defend Our Country (February 16, 2005), excerpted from Fresh Ideas in Zhejiang.

Commentary

Liu Bang was the Founding Emperor of the Han Dynasty and an outstanding statesman in ancient China. He was originally Village Constable of Sishui, Peixian County, from where he fled into Mangdang Mountain where he released captives without authorization. After Chen Sheng and Wu Guang started an uprising, Liu Bang also raised an army to fight the Qin government. In 206 BC, Liu Bang's troops marched into Bashang, and then Ziying, the emperor of Qin, surrendered to Liu Bang, and the Qin Dynasty collapsed. In the following Chu-Han Contention, Liu Bang won the final victory and thereafter unified China by establishing the Han Dynasty.

In 196 BC, on his triumphant return after crushing the rebellion raised by Ying Bu, King of Huainan, Liu Bang went back to his hometown in Peixian County and had a banquet with his old friends, elders and betters, and juniors. During the banquet, he improvised the *Song of the Big Wind* to express his desire to attract talented others and to make the best possible use of their talents.

Zhu Di, Emperor Yongle of Ming, was the fourth son of Zhu Yuanzhang, the founder of the Ming Dynasty, and the third Emperor of Ming. Zhu Di was named Prince of Yan on the founding of Ming. After settling in his fief Peiping (present-day Beijing), he was ordered many times to participate in military campaigns in the north and commanded the troops to march northward twice. Later, Emperor Jianwen ascended the throne and began taking back territory and power from imperial princes. In response to Emperor Jianwen's crackdown, Zhu Di launched the Jingnan Campaign and seized the reins of power in the capital Nanjing in 1402. In 1421, he reestablished Peiping as the new capital of Ming, a critical reason why those who remained from the Yuan Dynasty who had fled north threatened the security of Ming. Therefore, Zhu Di took the position that "the emperor guards the gate of the country" in consideration of national defense. This administrative measure meant the country's manpower and material resources were largely concentrated at the northern border.

In the Qing Dynasty, the officer in charge of the safety of the river embankment protected the life and family possessions of the people residing along the river. This was a highly responsible position. According to the *Chronicles of Haichang* and *Chronicles of Haining City*, "During Wuyue and the late Qing Dynasty, there have been hundreds of officials undertaking the position in charge of safety of the river embankment in Haining, Zhejiang Province. During the reign of Emperor Qianlong, once Qiantang River Tide breached the embankment of the city. Officer Zhao, who then was responsible for the construction and protection of the embankment, lamented on the breach, 'As the official responsible for protection of the embankment, I was discredited by His Majesty and among the people because I am incapable of performing my duties, that I can do nothing but apologize for the offence with my life.' Hardly had his voice faded away, he threw himself into the rushing river. The technicians, yamen runners, and civilians on the spot were all deeply moved." Officer Zhao's deed was a manifestation of the spirit of dedication until the end of life.

Liu Bang's *Song of the Big Wind*, Emperor Yongle's position that "the emperor guards the gate of the country" and Officer Zhao's spirit of dedication are all about responsibility and undertaking and emphasize that we should "understand responsibility and have the courage to bear responsibilities." As Xi Jinping has said, "If imperial officials had such a strong sense of responsibility, how can we proletarian officials evade responsibility or refuse to take responsibility?"

"Responsibility" is a word that is frequently used in Xi's speeches. In the speech at the press conference he attended for the first time as General Secretary of the CPC, he declared with an emphatic determination that "Our responsibility is weightier than mountains, our task arduous, and the road ahead long." In an exclusive interview with Russian Television, he made clear his philosophy of governance before the rest of the world: "I will govern by serving the people and fulfilling all my responsibilities." As it were, "responsibility" is the hallmark of his distinctive style of governing. Moreover, every leading official should reflect on his emphasis on "responsibility".

CANNIKIN LAW

We must realize that we are unable to achieve the all-around moderate prosperity of our province if we skip the moderate prosperity of the underdeveloped areas, and we are unable to realize the all-around modernization of our province if the underdeveloped areas are not modernized. It is like the Cannikin Law in economics—the capacity of a barrel is not determined by the longest stave but the shortest one. That is to say, whether our province can achieve the goal of building a moderately prosperous society in all respects and basically achieve modernization in advance is largely determined by our ability to narrow the gap between the regions of the province. This requires both the further development of developed regions and a great leap forward of development for underdeveloped regions.

– To Lengthen the Underdeveloped "Shorter Staves" (December 10, 2004), from *Fresh Ideas of Zhejiang*.

Commentary

According to the Cannikin Law, the capacity of a barrel is not determined by the longest stave but the shortest one. To fill a barrel with water, we must ensure that all of the staves are equally long and undamaged. If any stave is shorter than the others or has a hole in it, then the barrel will be unable to be filled. The Cannikin Law is often used to elucidate the development of a country or a region. The parts of a country or region are always prone to develop in an unbalanced manner. However, the elements that determine the overall development level of the country or region include not only the development level of its developed parts but also that of the underdeveloped parts. Therefore, as we advance our development, we should not only focus on our advantages and strong points but also pay more attention to our disadvantages and deficiencies. We must make up for the deficiencies to achieve coordinated development in a comprehensive and sustainable manner.

In 2002, to promote coordinated development across the province, Zhejiang launched the "Mountain Area—Coastal Area Coordination Program", which promoted project cooperation between the developed coastal areas and underdeveloped parts in the mountain areas of Southwest Zhejiang and on the islands in such fields as industrial development, new rural construction, labor training employment, and social undertaking development, so that the regions of the province could realize coordinated development and achieve modernization shoulder to shoulder. The aim of this program was to promote development toward the target through comprehensive cooperation between developed and underdeveloped regions and to lengthen the underdeveloped "shorter staves", so that all people of the province could share the fruits of economic and social development.

When heading the administration of Zhejiang, Xi Jinping integrated lengthening "shorter staves" and coordinated development into the practice of reform and development. One point in the strategy of "making full use of eight advantages and implementing eight major measures" that he proposed is that "To give full play to Zhejiang's advantages in coordinated rural-urban development and accelerate urban-rural integration." Since he assumed the post of General Secretary of the Party, Xi expanded his horizons and began to think about China's blueprint of coordinated development. In December 2012, having just taken office, he braved the snow and severe cold wind and traveled through the narrow and bumpy roads to get to the depth of Taihang Mountain, one of the poorest parts of China, with an annual per capital income of just 900 yuan. He said to the other officials, "It is absolutely worthwhile taking three and a half hours to get here from Beijing if we could visit those who are really poor today!" This showed his concern about narrowing the gaps between urban and rural areas and between the regions.

In an exclusive interview with Russian Television in February 2014, Xi made a figurative metaphor for coordinated development—"like playing the piano with all ten fingers." "Therefore, as a Chinese leader, I must take all factors into consideration based on a correct understanding of China's conditions, maintain an overall balance, and concentrate on priorities to promote the overall situation. I alternate my attention between major and minor issues," he said. Thus, the core thought is the promotion of coordinated development.

Utilizing the Cannikin Law, Xi Jinping gave a profound interpretation of the importance of coordinated development, which suggested that all-around moderate prosperity calls for the moderate prosperity of both developed and underdeveloped areas and calls for both material and spiritual civilization.

The thinking of coordinated and balanced development always dominates Xi's governance. "Coordinated development" is also a key element of the new development philosophy brought forward in the Fifth Plenary Session of the 18th CPC Central Commission. Uncoordinated development has been a long-standing problem in our country, especially reflected by relationships between regions, between urban and rural areas, between economy and society, between material and spiritual civilization, and between economic construction and national defense construction. For a country under the condition of backward economic development, the main task in a certain period may be to run faster. However, after running a certain distance, it should shift attention to relationship adjustment, specifically improving the overall efficiency of development. In this context, Xi Jinping emphasized, "Coordinated development is the key for China to coordinate all the activities of the nation in the 13th Five Year, like playing a chess game." This demands that we make a breakthrough in optimizing the structure and making up for deficiencies, strive to improve the coordination and balance of our development, and promote China's sustainable development in both economy and society.

SWEET POTATO THEORY

Someone proposed a "sweet potato theory", which figuratively described the phenomenon of "Jumping out of Zhejiang to develop Zhejiang." The vines of the sweet potato may stretch in all directions to absorb more sunlight, dew, and nutrients, so that the roots, from where they emerge, can become tougher and stronger. Similarly, our Zhejiang enterprises are now just branching out. They are integrating with Shanghai, taking part in our country's Western Development Drive and programs of revitalization of old industrial bases, such as Northeast China's old industrial bases, participating in international competition, and building up grain production bases, energy and raw material bases, and production and processing bases in other provinces and countries. This does not mean that our capital is flowing out and our enterprises are emigrating to other provinces or countries but that they are fulfilling the demand for resource allocation in wider regions and the demand for further development in a larger space, which is precisely in line with the strategy "To jump out of Zhejiang to develop Zhejiang and to develop Zhejiang from all over our country." We must have a correct understanding of this strategy, actively promote its implementation, and remain optimistic about the success to come.

> – Strive for Further Development in a Larger Space (August 10, 2004), from *Fresh Ideas of Zhejiang*.

Commentary

The vines of the sweet potato stretch in all directions to make the roots tougher and stronger. If the vines do not stretch, the roots have no access to nutrition; if the roots are not trained, the vines will lose their direction. The vines represent the methodology of furthering the opening up, while the roots represent the teleology of standing firm. It can be said that the "sweet potato theory" reveals the dialectical relationship between "standing firm" and "furthering the opening up."

Xi put forward the strategy "To jump out of Zhejiang to develop Zhejiang" when he was heading the administration of Zhejiang Province. "To jump out of Zhejiang" is like the vines of sweet potato stretching in all directions, the aim of which is to absorb more sunlight, dew, and nutrients. The expanding enterprises can help realize industrial gradient transfer and promote development transformation and upgrading, and its ultimate goal is "to develop Zhejiang." In Xi's view, "to jump out of Zhejiang" does not mean "flowing out" but represents "external expansion". He gave an example of the countless people from Wenzhou, Zhejiang Province who did business all over the country and even the world, and made contributions to the taxation there; however, they brought back up to 30 billion yuan to their hometown during the Chinese Spring Festival. This is powerful evidence to prove that the vines stretch in all directions to make the roots tougher and stronger.

After assuming the post of General Secretary of the Party, Xi integrated the "sweet potato theory" into his reflection on our country's future, based on which he designed the strategic blueprint "to jump out of China to develop China and to develop China from all over the world." In September 2013, he first put forward the initiative of jointly building a "Silk Road Economic Belt" in his speech at Nazarbayev University, Kazakhsta; in October, he launched the initiative of jointly building "the 21st Century Maritime Silk Road" in his speech to Indonesia's parliament. The strategic conception of the Belt and Road lays the foundation for Asia's boom and China's development.

With the relationship between vines and roots, Xi Jinping vividly interpreted the philosophy contained in the "sweet potato theory." Today, when China is comprehensively deepening its reform and is deeply integrating with the world, this theory is highly enlightening for us. Time and again Xi has stressed the fundamental strategy of taking root in China, absorbing the finest achievements of human civilization, and independently achieving national development, which the CPC and the Chinese people have employed and must be upheld and can never be doubted. In fact, it was the holistic application of both international and domestic markets, both international and domestic resources, and both international and domestic rules on the basis of independence and a firm foothold that drove China onto a unique road of development and enabled it to attain achievement that has amazed the world.

Today, as China's economy steps in the direction of a "new normal" and is faced with strategic opportunities, we should follow the prompting of Xi Jinping, "boasting a vast land of 9.6 million square kilometers, a rich cultural heritage and a strong bond among the 1.3 billion Chinese people, [to] unswervingly improve the open economy," we should "be resolved to improve the open economy." By doing so, we will infuse new energy into, invigorate and expand the market for our economic development.

WHY DID ARGENTINA LOSE ITS TITLE?

In high-level world soccer competition today, focusing only on personal skills and individual footwork is no longer the prevailing trend. Scoring mainly relies on the organic cooperation of the players, and coordination is now an important aspect of tactical awareness on the soccer field. A famous soccer commentator said with regard to Argentina's painful loss at the 12th World Cup final: "As a star player, Maradona focused only on the individual and not the collective. The individualistic style of the Argentine star ultimately resulted in their loss of this World Cup championship." Soccer fans often criticize some players for "dribbling too much" because they dislike it when players show off their own skills, which damages organic cooperation and misses opportunities to score. In local economic work, all departments at different levels—upper and lower, related and unrelated—must form an integrated whole. Each department has relative independence but is part of the whole and cannot be separated from the whole or cut off its relationships with other departments.

– "Economic Chorus" (September 1988), from *Up and Out of Poverty*.

Commentary

Maradona was an Argentine star player with excellent skills in footwork and dribbling. He was selected for the Argentine national football team at the early age of 17. He was always the key player, regardless of whether it was on the national team or on club teams. In a match against England, Maradona scored a goal by successively breaking through five defensive players, causing many people to gasp in admiration, "He is the greatest genius in football history."

Yet a football match is not a one-man show. It calls not only for the superior skills of the players but also for their spirit of teamwork and coordinating consciousness. If a team only pays attention to individual skills, without attaching importance to collective cooperation, it may present a wonderful one-man football show; however, it will be difficult for that team to win the match.

For instance, when the 12th FIFA World Cup was held in Spain, Maradona, who was under 22, wore the No. 10 shirt of the Argentine national team. In Argentina's 4–1 victory over Hungary, he scored two goals, making a showy display as a superstar. However, he paid no attention to teamwork but only to individual performance and was man-marked by all other teams thereafter and thus no longer scored. In the game against Brazil, he was red-carded for a foul on a Brazilian player who had fouled him before. This kept the Argentine team from reaching the final.

Victory and defeat on the football pitch have an enlightening significance beyond the football game. As a football amateur, Xi Jinping has a deep understanding of this. In the eyes of the British media, he is "a footballer on the diplomatic pitch." When he visited Ireland in 2012, the photo capturing the moment he played football was carried by all the major media around the world. This photo also attracted the attention of the media when he made a public New Year's greeting for 2014, as it was visible on his shelf; while visiting Germany in 2014, he visited the Chinese football players who were receiving training in Germany; in 2015, he paid a visit to the Manchester City football club in the UK. By showing his personal interest and building a congenial image, his "football diplomacy" brought China closer to the rest of the world. Xi once revealed that he has a "Chinese dream of football." Now the reform of football has already been included in the topics for discussion in comprehensively deepening reform.

The story about football told by Xi interprets the relationship between the whole and the parts: the integration of the parts will multiply the strength of the whole; the discord among the parts will cripple the whole. He has repeatedly emphasized the importance of coordination and cooperation in the governance of a country. "A soldier should always think and plan work from the perspective of the commander in chief," taking the whole situation into account.

CHOOSING AND APPOINTING TALENTED PEOPLE IS LIKE SELECTING AND USING A TOOL

A review of Chinese history shows that times of peace and prosperity have always accompanied the emergence of a great number of talents and wise minds. Almost without exception, historical personages of great achievements and attainments have attached great importance to talent. There are many much-told tales about this issue, such as "Xiao He pursued Han Xin in the moonlight" and "Liu Bei made three visits to the thatched cottage and invited Zhuge Liang to assist him in running the state." Let me share one more ancient story about recommending and employing people of virtue and talent, with the hope of arousing our reflection on this issue.

Li Shimin, Emperor Taizong of Tang, a great man known to all of us, has always been praised by later generations for his policy of personnel placement. After becoming emperor, he assigned the official Feng Deyi to recommend talents. However, after a few months had passed, Feng did not recommend any talent. Instead, he reported, "It was not because of me but there is no wizard available now." Emperor Taizong refuted him at once, "A man of noble character should choose and appoint talented people like he selects and uses a utensil. Every utensil has its strong point, and the man should make good use of this point. If we do not put it this way, do we have to borrow talent from other dynasties? The reason why you have not recommended any talent is that you do not have the capability to identify a talent. How can you say there is no talent? Are you belittling my people?" There is another story bearing witness to Emperor Taizong's practice of opening all avenues for people of talent by overriding all objections and acquiring and promoting talented people through different channels and by different methods. It tells of how he found Ma Zhou to be a bright person and trusted him with important positions. Born to a poverty-stricken family and springing from obscurity, Ma Zhou lived at the military officer Chang He's home as a hanger-on. One day, Emperor Taizong asked the officials for advice, and Ma Zhou wrote a memorandum containing more than 20 pieces of advice in the name of Chang He. This memorandum was greatly appreciated by the emperor. When the emperor was informed that it was produced by Ma, he immediately sent someone to invite Ma for a meeting with him. Eager to meet the bright person as soon as possible, he sent another subordinate to make Ma hurry. Emperor Taizong had a talk with Ma Zhou in person, who was only 29 years old at the time, and he deemed him talented, thus he appointed Ma as an official in the Chancellery. After that, Ma was promoted step by step. Helping the emperor handle many complex matters, Ma gradually became a famous official in the reign. It was the practice of acquiring talented people through different channels and by different methods, opening all avenues for people of talent and putting talents in important positions that helped Emperor Taizong achieve a prosperity seldom recorded in China's imperial society.

- Talents Play An Immeasurable Role in Economic Development (April 25, 1983), from *Know It Deeply, Love It Deeply.*

Commentary

During the reign of Li Shimin, Emperor Taizong of Tang, able men came forward in multitudes. He had the talented officials, Fang Xuanling, who did everything he could to serve his country; Li Jing, who had both civil and military abilities; Wei Zheng, who undertook the duty of criticizing the monarch's faults in the hope of pushing the monarch to surpass the legendary monarchs Yao and Shun; Wang Gui, who castigated the bad and extolled the good; and Dai Zhou, who had the ability to address various extremely onerous affairs. It was his strategy of making the best possible use of all talents and all things that assisted him in achieving the legendary "heyday of Zhenguan." This also reflects that his breadth of mind made him acquire the wisdom to choose and appoint talented people, which he compared to selecting and using a utensil, and his refutation against Feng Deyi's statement that "there is no wizard available today" reflected his thirst for talent and courteousness to the learned.

Another tale of Emperor Taizong shared by Xi Jinping was that Taizong found Ma Zhou to be a bright person and trusted him with important positions. Born in a poverty-stricken family and springing from obscurity, Ma Zhou lived at the military officer Chang He's home as a hanger-on. He won recognition from the emperor due to a memorandum containing more than 20 pieces of advice that he wrote in the name of Chang He. Ma once made the proposition that "Since ancient times, the rise or fall of a country was not determined by its hoard of money but by the monarch's awareness of the people's enjoyment and suffering." This memorial on politics by Ma Zhou was also spoken of highly by Mao Zedong, who was very fond of reading history, and was rated by him as "the remarkable paper second only to the *Countermeasure Against Public Security Issues* by Jia Yi." Emperor Taizong of Tang treasured Ma Zhou to the extent that he once stated, "If I do not see Ma Zhou for a while, I will always miss him." Cen Wenben, then Chancellor, also said that Ma Zhou's talents were comparable to those of Zhang Liang, a strategist of the Han Dynasty. In

644 AD, the 18th year of the Zhenguan Reign, Ma Zhou assumed the post of chancellor, and he also served as advisor of the Crown Prince Li Zhi. He instructed Li Zhi in earnest and taught him to manage state affairs, having a great influence on Li's ruling career. To commend Ma Zhou's great contribution to the country, Emperor Taizong wrote an inscription in person for him: "A phoenix intending to soar must flap its wings. A right-hand man cannot assist the ruler without loyalty and devotion." Such high praise was rare in the early Tang Dynasty, when famous officials and paragons of virtue and talent came out in succession.

By telling the story of Emperor Taizong of Tang, Xi Jinping made clear the vital function of the practice of opening all avenues for people of talent and putting talents in important positions in governance and putting forward the thinking that we should choose and appoint talented people like we select and use a utensil, and we should make good use of the strong point of each talent.

Xi Jinping always attaches great importance to talents, and he has repeatedly stressed, "China's success hinges on the CPC, on our officials, and on talent." He explained the extreme importance of talent from the perspective of overall strategy, "Without a large contingent of high-quality talent, the goal of building a moderately prosperous society in all respects and the Chinese dream of the great rejuvenation of the Chinese nation will not be realized smoothly." He expounded upon the importance of talent-involved work from the perspective of international competition, "The one who has the ability to cultivate and attract more talented people can dominate others in competition." He also elucidated the realistic path of deepening the reform of the talent mechanism from the perspective of respecting talent: "We should have a good sense of acquiring talented people through different channels and by different methods, treat them as treasures, and let them fully display their abilities." By expressing his eagerness for the talented, Xi gave officials at all levels a reminder and sent a sincere invitation to all talents.

BUYING A HORSE SKELETON FOR 500 TALES OF GOLD

In addressing issues concerning talent, we should have the attitude and spirit of "buying a horse skeleton for 500 tales of gold." After ascending the throne, King Zhao of Yan asked Chancellor Guo to recommend talented people in hope of taking his revenge on the state of Qi for the defeat of Yan. In this regard, Chancellor Guo told a story: there was once a king who wanted to buy a thoroughbred horse. However, his envoy bought the skeleton of a dead thoroughbred horse for 500 tales of gold. Afterward, his good reputation spread wide and far. People believed that the king treasured even the skeleton of a dead thoroughbred horse; thus, he would certainly treasure living thoroughbred horses still more. Before long, the king gained three thoroughbred horses that were alive. Chancellor Guo said, "Please consider treasuring me like the skeleton to attract more talents." Deeming the solution workable, King Zhao of Yan built a palace for Guo and bestowed special privileges on him. He also constructed a high platform piled with gold on the side of Yishui River, and he named it "The Platform for Talent". It was also called the "Gold Platform". Admiring King Zhao's fame, Ju Xin, Su Dai, Zou Yan, and other famous talents, in particular, Yue Yi, successively came to serve the state of Yan. Soon afterward, Yue Yi led troops to attack the state of Qi and defeated Qi utterly at one fell swoop, paying off old scores with Qi.

– Talents Play An Immeasurable Role in Economic Development (April 25, 1983), from *Know It Deeply, Love It Deeply.*

Commentary

"Buying a horse skeleton for 500 tales of gold" is a story that had spread through the ages since the time of ancient China. It is about how King Zhao of Yan accepted the advice of Guo Wei to vigorously attract talent to rejuvenate his state and utterly defeat the state of Qi on the strength of his talents. For thousands of years, "buying a horse skeleton for 500 tales of gold" was looked up to as a philosophy of respecting talent and remaining eager to find the most talented among the Chinese people.

Before King Zhao of Yan ascended the throne, the state of Qi took advantage of the political strife in Yan and invaded Yan. The state was almost ruined, and there was a large number of projects waiting to be completed. It was under such circumstances that King Zhao ascended the throne. In hope of rejuvenating his state through talented people, he showed a humble and generous attitude and consulted Guo Wei about tactics for attracting distinguished men. Thus, Guo Wei told him the story of "buying horse bones for 500 tales of gold." The story tells of a king who bid a thousand tales of gold for a thoroughbred horse. Three years had passed, and he failed to find such a horse. At this time, a person volunteered for the search and found one in 3 months, but unfortunately the horse was already dead. Beyond all expectations, he bought the skeleton of the dead horse for 500 tales of gold and brought it back to the king. The king flew into a rage when he saw the skeleton. "I need a living horse. Why did you buy me a dead one?" demanded the king. He answered with an easy, self-possessed mien, "Your majesty has earned the reputation that he treasured even the skeleton of a dead thorough-bred horse; thus, he would certainly treasure living thorough-bred horses still more. Once your majesty's reputation becomes known, the thorough-bred horses will come uninvited!" As expected, the owners of thoroughbred horses came in a continuous stream with their horses during the following year.

After King Zhao heard the story, he brightened Guo continued, "If your majesty really aims to win over talents, please consider treating me preferentially, then it will soon attract those who are more talented than I." In this way, Guo hoped to show others that King Zhao was courteous to the wise and condescending to talent. Following Guo's advice, King Zhao built up a palace for Guo, treated him as his teacher, and constructed the "Gold Platform" to attract talented people. Shocked by this measure, Yue Yi, Zou Yan, Ju Xin, and many other talents came to join King Zhao in droves, and it finally helped the state of Yan defeat Qi.

By telling the story of the relationship between King Zhao of Yan and Guo Wei, Xi Jinping introduced the methodology of attracting talent. Our leading officials must have a good sense of treasuring talented people. Only if we remain courteous to the learned and respect talent can we make the best use of all the talents in our country. Xi often stresses, "We should make good and flexible use of talents, establish a more flexible talent management mechanism, and eliminate the obstacles of the system and mechanism to open up the channel of talent flow and use." This requires leading officials at all levels to equip themselves with the awareness of seeking talent with eagerness and further optimize the mechanism of attracting talent. This is the inevitable course toward Xi's vision that the "employment of a competent person will attract more competent people, and all the others will take them as an example."

RESPECTING ELDERS IS A GREAT VIRTUE

The Chinese nation has a fine tradition of respecting elders. "Do reverence to the elders in your own family and extend it to those in other families." This thought was put forward by Mencius as early as 2000 years ago, when he answered King Xuan of Qi's questions about how to run a country. He elevated the tradition of "respecting elders" to the strategy of running the country. In the ruling classes of the past imperial dynasties, it was often seen that a father and his son fought against with each other for power and even appealed to arms. The proposition to respect the elder was their only means to present a false appearance of peace and prosperity and to win the people's support. Nevertheless, the working people under their dominion valued "respecting elders" as a great virtue that was necessary for them to conduct themselves in society, and they made it a custom through long usage. Today, this traditional virtue has evolved into a part of the socialist spiritual civilization by abandoning the original imperial elements and absorbing up-to-date social connotations. Our young- and middle-aged officials should practice what we preach and set an example.

– Young and Middle-aged Officials Should Respect the "Veterans"—A Signed Article on the *People's Daily* (December 7, 1984).

Commentary

It is a tradition for the Chinese people to conduct the funeral of their parents with meticulous care and to remember to make sacrifices to distant ancestors. "Respecting elders" is an emotional symbol shared by us, and it is a value-orientation that can strike a chord. In 1984, Xi Jinping published the article *Young and Middle-aged Officials Should Respect "Veterans"* in the *People's Daily* at the young age of 31, in which he quoted the verses of Zheng Banqiao to praise the value of elderly officials—"The new bamboo branches are taller than the old ones, and their growth is totally supported by the old branches." He noted that the succession of position within our Party and government neither represents the transfer of power between individual or opposing interest groups nor implies a power struggle, but it is rather a relay race aiming at a common goal and dedicated to a common cause.

Xi Jinping shows special respect for veteran comrades. When he worked in Zhengding County, Heibei Province, he always went out by bicycle unless he had to go outside the city gate. Instead, he assigned the BJ212, the only jeep of the county Party committee, to the veteran officials. When he found that there was no activity site for them, he emptied out the large meeting room shared by the county Party committee and the county government and set the room as the recreation room for elderly officials. Many elderly officials were reluctant to say goodbye to him when he was leaving Zhengding. One of them, Qi Yong, said, "Secretary Xi, we are really unwilling to have you transferred!" In the Hongruiyuan Shop of the Restaurant for the Aged in the Chengguan District, Lanzhou, Gansu Province, where he visited on February 4, 2013, he served a meal to the 72-year-old retired worker Yang Lintai in person. On November 3, 2013, he visited Shi Qiwen's family, a destitute household in Shibadong Village, Huayuan County, Xiangxi, Hunan Province. He held her hand and asked about her age. Informed that she was already 64, Xi said to her, "You are my senior." On December 28 of the same year, he participated in a reading activity at the Sijiqing Senior's Home in Beijing and patiently listened to the elder reciting the *Song of Health*.

Xi's proposition of "respecting the elder" is also embodied in his attention to family tradition and family education. When his father Xi Zhongxun's 88th birthday party was held in Shenzhen on October 15, 2001, the three generations of his family and many other relatives and friends all attended the party for the celebration, except Xi Jinping, then Provincial Governor of Fujian. This was not because he was unwilling to attend the party, but it was rather that he could not absent himself from the strains of office. He felt ashamed, and thus sent a letter of birthday felicitations to his father. He wrote affectionately in the letter that his perception of parents was like his affection for them, becoming deeper and deeper with the passing of time, and he hoped to inherit and learn the precious and noble qualities from his father.

Xi has treated the tradition of respecting the elder as a time-honored treasure. When he was transferred from Beijing to Zhengding, he stressed this tradition and stated, "Our young and middle-aged officials should practice what we preach and set an example." Decades later, he took this sentiment with him while being transferred back to Beijing. He repeatedly highlighted that "We should cultivate a healthy environment of respecting, caring and learning from the elders in our whole society," and he required that "Party committees and governments at all levels should conscientiously carry out work concerning veteran officials in the new situation from the perspective of inheriting our Party's fine work style and carrying forward the traditional virtues of the Chinese nation." As we enter the period of social transition, there is a risk of "getting old before getting rich" in the wake of population aging. Therefore, our traditional virtue of respecting elders will give us a leg up in coping with this risk. Xi's reaffirmation of this tradition is of distinctive epochal significance because it is about the inheritance of our culture; moreover, it concerns the complex issue of reform and development.

PART II

About Foreign Affairs

Stories of Friendship Between the People: "The Relationship Between Two Countries Is Based on the Friendship Between Their People"

"Great Brothers"

China and Chile are located far away from each other; however, the two peoples have enjoyed a long history of interactions and profound friendship. Pablo Neruda, a Nobel Prize laureate in literature and a major poet in Chile, referred to China affectionately as a "great brother." Even the names of our two countries, China and Chile, resemble those of two brothers, and our two people have indeed fostered a brotherly relationship.

The two people have a tradition of mutual understanding and affection. Although our two people are separated by the ocean, we admire each other. Neruda paid multiple visits to China and wrote poems such as *Cancion de la tierra China* and *El Viento de la Asia*, in which he expressed his love and best wishes for China. His works have been widely read in China, and they have influenced many Chinese poets. Jose Venturelli, a famous artist of Chile, lived in China for years. He learned from the technique of Chinese ink painting and created works such as the *Yangtze River*, which demonstrated his strong attachment to China. These poems and paintings reflect the profound friendship between the two peoples. These Chilean friends established the Chile–China Cultural Association, the first nongovernmental organization committed to developing friendly ties with China in Latin America. The organization has encouraged a great number of visionary people to join in the cause of cultivating the China–Chile friendship. In Santiago, there is a Yangtze River Primary School whose name signifies that the China–Chile friendship is as vibrant as the Yangtze River.

– Work Together for a More Promising Future of China–Chile Relations, a signed article on Chilean media (November 22, 2016).

Commentary

Pablo Neruda, who was born in Parral, Chile, in 1904, was a Chilean contemporary poet. He began to publish his poems at the age of 13. In 1923, his first volume of verse, *Crepusculario* (Book of Twilights), was published, followed the next year by *Veinte Poemas de Amor y una Canción Desesperada* (Twenty Love Poems and A Desperate Song). With keen interest in China and Chinese culture, Neruda visited China three times during his life. In 1951, he came to China to award the Lenin Peace Prize to Soong Ching-ling, and during this visit he met literary celebrities such as Mao Dun, Ding Ling, and Ai Qing. In an interview, when he learned that the traditional Chinese character "聶" in his Chinese name is composed of three "耳", which means ear, he said, "I have three ears, and the third ear is for listening to the sound of the sea."

Jose Venturelli, who was born in Santiago, Chile, in 1924 and died in Beijing in 1988, was a world-renowned master of painting, lithography, and mural painting, and he was also an "envoy" between China and Chile and between China and Latin America. In 1952, he visited Beijing with his wife and daughter by invitation. He was the first well-known Latin American artist to visit China after the founding of new China. As Deputy Secretary-General of the Asia and Pacific Ocean Peace Conference, Venturelli lived in China with his family for 8 years. During his stay in China, he developed deep friendships with Premier Zhou Enlai, artists Xu Beihong and Qi Baishi, and the poet Ai Qing. Venturelli also taught at the Central Academy of Fine Arts, bringing fresh artistic ideas to Chinese students. The Chinese culture also affected his artistic creations, arousing his pursuit of delicate lines and strokes, wide composition and a free use of colors. The paintings *Autumnal Rage*, *Lushan Mountain*, and *The Courtyard of Beijing* all employ traditional Chinese painting skills. The *Yangtze River* mentioned by Xi Jinping adopts the composition of traditional Chinese landscape painting. As his granddaughter Marva put it, "China was vital to Jose Venturelli because it shaped his mind, art and spirit."

China and Chile are located far away from each other; however, the two countries enjoy a long history of interactions and profound friendship. Early in 1952, Neruda, Venturelli, statesman Salvador Allende, and some other Chilean friends established the Chile–China Cultural Association, the first nongovernmental organization committed to developing friendly ties with China in Latin America. Today, Chile, which has a population of only approximately 16 million, has two Confucius Institutes and more than 20 Chinese language teaching centers. The Latin American Center of the Confucius Institute is located in Santiago, the capital of Chile. The Yangtze River Primary School, mentioned by Xi Jinping, is situated in La Reina, Santiago. The school was officially granted the name in 1987, and it began to pioneer the teaching of the Chinese language in primary school in 2008.

Xi had been to Chile in 2001. As he set foot on the beautiful soil of Chile again in 2016, he said, "I feel very much at home and begin my visit with great expectations." Just as he said in an article, "Even the names of our two countries, China and Chile, resemble those of two brothers and our two peoples have indeed fostered a brotherly relationship." He also recollected the "firsts" that have been achieved in the bilateral ties between the two countries: Chile is the first country in South America to establish diplomatic ties with new China, and it is the first Latin American country to sign a bilateral agreement with China on its WTO accession, to recognize China as a full market economy and to sign a bilateral Free Trade Agreement with China. Due to the concerted efforts of the two peoples, the two countries' bilateral ties have grown from strength to strength and yielded fruitful results that are "as vibrant as the Yangtze River." We also learn from the article that China Construction Bank opened a branch in Chile and became the first RMB settlement bank in Latin America, procuring another "first" for our relations, and China has become Chile's largest trading partner and its largest export market for products such as copper, cherries, blueberries, seafood, and wine. Former Chilean Ambassador to China, Fernando Reyes Matta said, "President Xi impressed us deeply with a string of firsts." In his visit to Chile, Xi cited this Latin American proverb: "A true friend can touch your heart from the other end of the world." This proverb aptly describes the "old-time" and "present-day" friendship between China and Chile.

"A Bond of Gold and Jade"

The Chinese people like to refer to a good relationship as "a bond of gold and jade." The gold medals for 2008 Olympic Games in Beijing were made of gold from Chile and jade from China. These medals are symbols of the brotherly relationship between the Chinese and Chilean people.

> – Work Together for a More Promising Future of China–Chile Relations, a signed article on Chilean media (November 22, 2016).

Commentary

In *A Dream of Red Mansions*, one of China's Four Great Classical Novels, Xue Baochai's gold lock and Jia Baoyu's Precious Jade of Spiritual Understanding were collectively referred to as the symbol of "a bond of gold and jade", which embodies predestined affinity.

The gold medals for the Beijing 2008 Olympic Games employ the design of "gold inlaid with jade" to express the Chinese people's tribute to the Olympic spirit and praise for the athletes. By integrating this element of Chinese culture, this pioneering and novel design broke through the tradition of a single material design for Olympic medals. The "gold inlaid with jade" medals linked China and Chile once again: the jade integrated by 6,000 gold, silver, and copper medals was Kunlun Jade, and the metals inlaid with the jade were all supplied by the world's largest mining giant BHP Billiton's mineral enterprise in Chile. The world's largest open-pit copper mine, the Escondida Copper Mine, provided the 13.04 kg of gold needed for the gold medals from its copper-bearing gold concentrate; Cannington Silver and Lead Mine provided 1.34 tons of silver to make the gold and silver medals; and Spence Copper Mine provided 6.93 tons of electrolytic copper for the copper and memorial medals. Chile is the world's largest copper exporter and China is the largest importer of Chilean copper, which imports 40% of its copper from Chile. The data from the Chilean Copper Commission suggests that, in 2014, China imported 2.2 million tons of copper from Chile, which is equivalent to 39% of Chile's copper exports.

Today, China and Chile are increasingly close in economic and trade activities. China has become Chile's largest trading partner and its largest export market, and Chile has become China's third largest trading partner in Latin America, second largest source of fresh fruit import, third largest wine importer, and seventh largest seafood importer. Since the bilateral Free Trade Agreement that was signed in 2006 entered into force, our bilateral trade has grown rapidly, with the bilateral trade volume reaching 31.8 billion US dollars in 2015, which is nearly fourfolds of 8 billion US dollars in 2005. Today, Chinese brands are at the top of the list in the Chilean market, and wine, salmon, and blueberries, cherries, grapes, and other edible fruits are now preferred by Chinese consumers.

In an article on the Chilean media, Xi Jinping took the medal of the Beijing Olympic Games as an example and expounded upon the "bond of gold and jade" between the Chinese and Chilean people. The medals made of Chilean gold and Chinese jade are a metaphor for Xi's profound assessment: China–Chile ties have enjoyed long-term stable growth because both sides are committed to treating each other as equals with mutual respect and trust and leveraging mutual complementarity for win-win outcomes. More importantly, both sides have kept up with the times and made pioneering efforts to push bilateral relations to new highs.

Geographically, Chile is farthest from China. However, Xi Jinping said, "If you have a friend afar who knows your heart, distance cannot keep you two apart." Now the Pacific Ocean can no longer keep China and Chile apart. Instead, the relationship serves as a bond or a bridge linking our two countries. In talks with Chilean President Michelle Bachelet, citing a high level of mutual political trust between our countries, our mutually beneficial and win-win economies, and increasingly closer multilateral cooperation, Xi said China–Chile ties have entered a new era of maturity and stability. During the visit, the two presidents agreed to lift the bilateral ties to a comprehensive strategic partnership, which marked the lift of the strategic coordination and the beginning of more in-depth and comprehensive development between the two countries.

The Century-Old Story of Sociedad Central de Beneficencia China

Peru and China are "neighbors" connected by the Pacific Ocean. The exchanges between our two peoples began more than 400 years ago. For years, the overseas Chinese living in Peru, together with the Peruvian people, shared weal and woe and strove for self-improvement by making arduous efforts, which made important contributions to the local economic and social development. Sociedad Central de Beneficencia China, which was established 130 years ago, also made a positive contribution in promoting the development of the relationship between China and Peru. As far as I know, at present, Peru has approximately 2.5 million Chinese Peruvians, who are of Chinese descent. The Spanish word "paisano" refers specifically to Chinese descendants in Peru, and "chifa", a word that originated from the Cantonese dialect for "having meals", has become the term the Peruvians use to refer to Chinese restaurants. The family-like friendship between our two nations has also taken root and sprouted in the heart of our two peoples.

> – Sailing Forward to Build A Bright Future of China–Latin America Relations—Speech at the Peruvian Congress (November 21, 2016).

Commentary

In 1884, the government of the Qing Dynasty sent Ambassador Zheng Zaoru, Director of the Imperial Entertainment Count, to the US, Spain, and Peru. After arriving in Peru, he learned that there were between 60,000 and 70,000 Chinese who had arrived in Peru approximately 40 years ago and who were distributed throughout Peru. In hope of establishing contact among all Chinese living in Peru, to protect their interests and carry out various charity efforts, he established Sociedad Central De Beneficencia China in 1886 in the hope of "promoting commercial intercourse and benefiting industrialists and businessmen, for the betterment of the Chinese people and Chinese association in Peru." Going through all kinds of hardships and difficulties over the past 130 years, Sociedad Central de Beneficencia China has become the oldest and most influential nation-wide overseas Chinese organization in Peru.

In adherence to the three aims of "promoting commercial intercourse and benefiting industrialists and businessmen, unselfishly helping other peers, and valuing comradeship," this organization has been making an important contribution in uniting the Chinese in Peru, promoting China–Peru friendship, and supporting the development of the motherland. In the mid-nineteenth century, a group of Chinese from Fujian, Guangdong and other places in China traveled across the sea to Peru. They undertook heavy tasks in railway construction and mining work and lived a tough life in Peru. This being the case, Sociedad Central de Beneficencia China raised funds in Peru to help them mitigate the difficulties and anxiety and provide financial assistance to the poor and old compatriots with no money to return home. At the same time, they established a Shelter for Chinese from Peru in Guangzhou to shelter older Chinese returning to China from Peru.

During the Chinese People's War of Resistance against Japanese Aggression, the Chinese in Peru were gripped by the warfare in their motherland. Sociedad Central de Beneficencia China set up the Fundraising Federation of Chinese in Peru for Resistance against Japanese aggression jointly with compatriots in Peru, with branches established throughout Peru. They organized the Chinese there to donate money and organize charity bazaars to give support to their homeland, raising 1 million US dollars for the fight within under 2 years. Zhou Enlai once praised them as follows: "The 6,000 Chinese 10,000 miles away, who contributed up to 2 million soles, are a good example for all overseas Chinese and a feather in our cap."

Today, Sociedad Central de Beneficencia China builds on past merits and forges ahead to keep their century-old "signboard" shining. It not only often assists and cooperates with the Chinese Embassy in Peru and the domestic units involved in overseas Chinese affairs in holding various seminars, celebrations, and galas but it also helps local police promote the relationship between the police and civilians and its fundraising committee organizes annually to donate to the nation-wide TV fundraising programs of Peru in the name of the Chinese. These benevolent actions have served as a bridge between the two peoples in promoting friendly exchanges and mutual understanding, which has been well received by those from all walks of life in the two nations. Due to the contributions it has made, Sociedad Central de Beneficencia China was honored with the title of "The Light of Overseas Chinese Associations" at The Eighth Conference for Friendship of Overseas Chinese Associations held in Beijing in June 2016.

The vast Pacific cannot block the deep friendship between the Chinese and Peruvian peoples. The year 2016 marked the 45th anniversary of the establishment of diplomatic relations between China and Peru. On such an important occasion, Xi Jinping related the history of Sociedad Central de Beneficencia China and the century-old friendship between the two peoples at the Peruvian Congress to demonstrate that "the family-like affinity between the two nations" is deeply rooted in history.

"Distance cannot separate true friends who feel so close even when they are thousands of miles apart." Peru, which is known as "the eagle of the Andes", was one of the first Latin American countries to have Chinese immigrants, establishing diplomatic relations with new China and carrying out economic and trade exchanges with China. Just 2 months before Xi Jinping's visit to Peru, Kuczynski, who had just assumed the presidency of Peru, made a state visit to China, which was his first official visit after his inauguration as president. The two heads of state exchanging visits within 2 months also set a new record in the history of bilateral exchanges between the two nations. Vice President Mercedes Aráoz of Peru noted with emotion that, "President Xi's visit to Peru is of great significance and will surely elevate the bilateral relations to a new height." Before the speech, Xi was awarded the Grand-Cross Medal of Honor of the Peruvian Congress. This indirectly proved that the bilateral relations between China and Peru have rapidly progressed in a positive direction.

"CHINESE PEOPLE'S TWO OLD FRIENDS" FROM PERU

We Chinese believe that "the pleasure of life lies in having close friends." Chinese and Peruvian people find it easy to connect and communicate. This calls to mind two Peruvian friends. One is Antonio Fernandez Arce, a late Peruvian writer and journalist who has had made frequent trips between China and Peru to present a real picture of China to the Latin American people since the 1960s. His daughter, Flor de Maria Fernandez, was born in Beijing in 1970; however, unfortunately, she suffered from severe blood poisoning. Learning this, then-Chinese-Premier Zhou Enlai immediately ordered medical experts to attend to the baby, and the People's Liberation Army responded immediately by organizing soldiers to donate blood to her. Eventually, Flor de Maria Fernandez made it through the crisis. After growing up, she followed in her father's footsteps, devoting her energy to the cause of friendship between the two nations in the long term.

Another friend, Mr. Guillermo Da Ino Ribatto, a Peruvian Sinologist and translator. He taught Spanish at China's Nanjing University and at the University of International Business and Economics from 1979 to 1991, producing works such as *Reports from China*, *Selected Poems of Li Bai*, and *Encyclopedia of Chinese Culture*. In addition, he took part in 25 movies in China, such as *The Great Decisive War* and *Chongqing Negotiations*, which was well received by Chinese audiences. Today, he is 87 years old. I heard that he still insists on visiting China every year. I pay high tribute to him.

– Sailing Forward to Build A Bright Future of China–Latin America Relations—Speech at the Peruvian Congress (November 21, 2016).

Commentary

Antonio Fernandez Arce, "an old friend of the Chinese people," was a Peruvian journalist and writer. Born in Trujillo, a city in northern Peru, in 1931, Arce was honored as president of the Journalists' Association of Peru at the age of 25, and he has successively served as editor in chief of several well-known newspapers in Peru.

Arce has long been concerned with the changes in and development of China, and he has published many articles on new China in newspapers and periodicals. He came to China with his wife in 1967 to work for the Beijing Broadcasting Station, and their daughter Flor de Maria Fernandez was born 3 years later. However, his newborn daughter suffered from severe blood poisoning and was soon in critical condition. Upon learning this, then-Chinese-Premier Zhou Enlai immediately ordered the best doctors in the People's Liberation Army to attend to the baby. At that time, Flor de Maria Fernandez had to be given a massive blood transfusion. However, the hospital did not have sufficient plasma that matched her blood type. In this urgent case, the medical authority quickly sought help from the garrison troops in Beijing, and soldiers rushed to the hospital to donate blood once after they were informed of the situation. Thanks to the Chinese soldiers who donated blood to help save her, Flor de Maria Fernandez eventually survived.

Arce also acted as a "special envoy" that promoted the establishment of the diplomatic relations between China and Peru. Around 1970, he conveyed China's willingness to further develop friendship with Peru and delivered China' concrete ideas of building diplomatic ties with Peru to Peru's authorities when he returned to Peru to visit his sick father. Later, the communication between China and Peru was facilitated through Arce's help, and China forged diplomatic relations with Peru on November 2, 1971. In 1983, he returned to China as a Spanish expert in the International Department of the Xinhua News Agency. He contributed many articles on China to the newspapers in Latin America and Spain.

Guillermo Da Ino Ribatto is a Peruvian Sinologist who is almost 90 years old but still sowing the seeds of Chinese culture. His predestined affinity with China took root in 1979 when he, as a Professor of linguistics and literature from the National University of San Marcos of Peru, gave lectures to 15 Spanish teachers at the invitation of Nanjing University. Beyond this, he also played the roles of "movie star" and "poet". He appeared in

25 Chinese movies, including *The Great Decisive War, Chongqing Negotiations* and *Mao Zedong and Snow*, during more than 20 years in China, and translated nine collections of poetry of the Tang Dynasty within 9 years, becoming one of the Latin American Sinologists who translated most poets of Tang. Additionally, he published multiple books on Chinese history and culture such as *Dragon Carving—Anthology of Ancient Chinese Poetry, Hard-working Bee—1000 Idioms, Proverbs, and Two-part Allegorical Sayings*, and *Encyclopedia of Chinese Culture*.

In a speech at the Congress of Peru, Xi Jinping told a touching story of two Peruvians, which illustrated that "the Chinese and Peruvian peoples are always connected emotionally, and they have always communicated well with each other" and that the two countries, whose hearts are closely linked, form a "community of common destiny." The friendship between countries definitely springs from the people and burgeons through communication. In the 1990s, Xi had visited Peru. When he revisited the land more than 20 years later, he expressed the China–Peru friendship in terms of three "goods"—"good brothers who trust each other," "good partners who pursue common development," and "good friends who shoulder responsibilities together." "The real happiness lies in the passion to keep expanding." He also quoted this famous saying of the Peruvian writer Rivero in his speech to express his hope that the people of the two countries would cooperate sincerely toward realizing their dreams. Peru is striving for "a just, fair and united Peru" by 2021, the 200th anniversary of its independence. By then, China will have built a moderately prosperous society in all respects, reaching the first goal of its "Two Centenary Goals". Xi Jinping combined the aims of the two countries precisely because he expects that the two people will "march forward shoulder-to-shoulder and reach their dreams hand in hand."

THE FREEDOM FIGHTERS SINGING REVOLUTIONARY SONGS

China and Zimbabwe, in spite of the vast distance between them, have maintained a traditional friendship that is deep and firm. During the struggle for national liberation in Zimbabwe, the Chinese people steadfastly stood behind the Zimbabwean people as comrades-in-arms. I was touched to learn that many Zimbabwean freedom fighters who received training from the Chinese side both in China and at the Nachingwea camp in Tanzania still sing songs such as the *Three Rules of Discipline and the Eight Points for Attention*.

- *Let the Sino-Zim Flower Bloom with New Splendor*, a signed article on Zimbabwe media (November 30, 2015).

Commentary

The song, *Three Rules of Discipline and the Eight Points for Attention*, is honored as "the best and most famous Red Song", which has been popular for a long time and can be heard on many occasions. The formulation and development of the Three Rules of Discipline and the Eight Points for Attention praised in the song span a total of 20 years, from October 1927, when the three rules of discipline were proposed in the Sanwan Reorganization, through the corresponding period of 1947, upon the issuing of *On the Reissue of the Three Main Rules of Discipline and Eight Points for Attention—Instruction of The General Headquarters of The Chinese People's Liberation Army*. The Three Rules of Discipline and the Eight Points for Attention were an important guarantee for the implementation of the party's agenda, guidelines, policies, and tasks, and they served as an important factor in maintaining the combat effectiveness of the army. They have played an important role in strengthening our armed forces, maintaining a close relationship between the army and the people, strengthening the unity between officers and soldiers, and securing the victory of the revolutionary war.

"Heighten our sense of discipline, and we will be invincible in the revolutionary war." As a famous military song of the people's army, the *Three Rules of Discipline and the Eight Points for Attention* was mentioned in the work of American journalists Snow, Smedley, and Salisbury. When Snow was conducting interviews in Yuwang County, Gansu Province, he heard the song sung by Xu Haidong and the Fifteenth Army of the Red Army headed by Xu, and from this song, he became aware of the critical reason why the Kuomintang army could not defeat the Red Army. The Red Army immediately triggered panic among the people when it arrived in northern Shaanxi. However, only a few months later, the local people began to affectionately refer to them as "our army". The "iron discipline, iron army and iron fighting strength" lodged itself in the public mind along with the song.

The Zimbabwean people are familiar with this Chinese military song because in the 1960s, China offered unselfish assistance to Zimbabwe during its struggle for national independence and liberation. There was a group of soldiers in Zimbabwe's "liberation army" who received Chinese military training, during which they not only acquired Chinese military strategies and tactics but also learned the Chinese revolutionary songs and caught the spirit of the Chinese revolutionaries. According to the Zimbabwean philologist Peng Weini, the *Three Rules of Discipline and the Eight Points for Attention* was the most widely circulated revolutionary song in the army, and it greatly bolstered military morale, enhanced the cohesion of the army, and broadly united the masses.

China and Zimbabwe established diplomatic relations on April 18, 1980, the day of independence of the Republic of Zimbabwe. Since then, the two countries have shown understanding and support for each other and helped each other; therefore, the friendly and cooperative relationship between them has developed smoothly and steadily, and fruitful results have been achieved in bilateral practical cooperation. This makes the China–Zimbabwe relationship a model of China–Africa solidarity and cooperation.

In December 2015, Xi Jinping paid his first state visit to Zimbabwe. In the article he published upon his departure, he mentioned that some Zimbabwean soldiers could still sing the song *Three Rules of Discipline and the Eight Points for Attention* and recalled that the Chinese people steadfastly stood behind the Zimbabwean people as comrades-in-arms during the national liberation struggle in Zimbabwe. His aim was to demonstrate that China and Zimbabwe enjoy a long-standing and strong friendship and to make clear that China would never forget its old friends.

To look back on history is to look toward the future. "China and Zimbabwe should not only be good friends in politics but also good partners in development," said Xi, adding that they, as "true all-weather friends," they should translate their time-honored friendship into a stronger impetus for bilateral practical cooperation to achieve common development and prosperity. As Xi noted, "Our friendship is rooted in the cultural traditions of our two countries that value sincerity and friendship, in the basic principles of independence and mutual respect to which we both adhere in conducting foreign relations, and in the common mission of our two countries to grow our economy and improve people's livelihood."

A CHINESE MOTHERS' GROUP—"LOVE OF AFRICA"

The China–Zimbabwe friendship has also taken root and sprouted in the heart of our two people. I know there is a Chinese mothers' group in Zimbabwe called "Love of Africa", and there is a "Father Cheng" from China who is so close with the local community that even his car's license plate number is remembered by the kids there. Over the years, they have brought care and warmth to local orphans. Such concrete actions are manifestations of the China–Zimbabwe friendship of the current generation and sow the seeds of friendship for future generations.

  – *Let the Sino-Zim Flower Bloom with New Splendor*, a signed article on Zimbabwe media (November 30, 2015).

Commentary

There is a Chinese mothers' group in Zimbabwe called "Love of Africa", which is known far and wide. The mothers donate money and supply to local orphanages, seek medicine from thousands of miles away for the orphans, and provide spiritual comfort for the orphans. Statistics show that the number of Zimbabwean orphans, which has continued to grow, now stands at approximately 1.8 million. They were abandoned by their parents, or their parents died early. Many even suffer from AIDS. Some lucky ones have been assigned to orphanages by the Social Welfare Bureau, and there are still many orphans who are homeless. Because of the country's limited economic and social development, most of the orphanages in Zimbabwe have a serious shortage of funds.

On April 10, 2014, to give aid to the orphans, Peng Yan and some other Chinese mothers living in Zimbabwe decided to establish a nonprofit organization. They gave the organization a positive name—"Love of Africa", and its Chinese name means "must love".

After its founding, "Love of Africa" selected a group of needy orphanages to which to provide assistance. In addition to making donations to them, they raise tuition fees for the orphans. Sowing the seeds of love on the continent of Africa, the mothers care for the orphans with selfless "Father Cheng". Their philanthropic actions have touched many people. Lindy, the Financial Manager of a local orphanage, expressed her gratitude to the members of "Love of Africa" for their unselfish help, saying, "I have never seen a kind person like them. Never before. They paid the children's tuition, brought them new mattresses, and bought food for them... It is hard for us to keep the orphanage running without the help from the Chinese mothers."

In an article published on the Zimbabwe media, Xi Jinping told the moving story of "Love of Africa". The local mainstream newspaper *The Sunday Mail* titled the article by Xi Jinping "From China, with Love". The editor of the newspaper later said in an interview that this title was derived from "my true feeling after reading the article."

In the article, Xi Jinping also included two sayings. One was from Zimbabwe, "Chikuni chimwe hachikodzi sadza," meaning that one is unable to cook corn porridge with only one piece of firewood and the other is a Chinese saying, "When everybody adds firewood, the flames will rise high." It can be said that the China–Africa friendship lays a solid foundation for the development of China–Africa relations. As Xi stated in the keynote speech delivered at the opening ceremony of the Second China–Africa People's Forum, "Now more and more ordinary people are becoming directly involved in China-Africa cooperation and exchanges, accompanied by higher and higher expectations of the development of China-Africa relations from both the Chinese and African people. Therefore, we should actively create conditions for more Chinese and African people to enjoy the increasingly fruitful results achieved in China-Africa cooperation to further consolidate public support for cooperation."

NEVER FORGET PROFESSOR COLIN MACKERRAS

I am delighted to see that Emeritus Professor Colin Mackerras of Griffith University is with us today. In 1964, Professor Mackerras went to China for the first time. Over the past five decades, he has visited China over 60 times, and he has made tireless efforts to present a real China to Australia and the world based on his personal experience of China's development and progress. It is worth mentioning that his son Stephen is the first Australian national born in China since the founding of the People's Republic in 1949. With his unremitting efforts and devotion, Professor Mackerras has built a bridge of mutual understanding and amity between our people. In September of this year, he was conferred the Friendship Award by the Chinese government. Professor Mackerras, I wish to express deep appreciation to both you and many other Australians for what you have done to enhance the friendship between our two nations.

– Jointly Pursue the Dream of Development for China and Australia and Realize Prosperity and Stability in Our Region—Speech at the Parliament of Australia (November 17, 2014).

Commentary

Colin Mackerras was born in Sydney in 1939. He started his Sinology research career during the 1950s and 1960s. After graduating from the University of Melbourne, he went on to study at the University of Cambridge in England. In 1964, when Australia had not yet established diplomatic relations with China, Mackerras, who had just graduated, along with his wife, offered to teach in China, and they had their eldest son Stephen in the country. The boy, who was born in February 1965, was the first Australian citizen born in the People's Republic of China. Today, that young scholar has now become a well-known China watcher, with many works to his credit. Professor Mackerras serves as an Emeritus Professor at Griffith University, the Australian-side Director of the Tourism Confucius Institute of Griffith University, and an Academician of the Australian Academy of the Humanities. With his love of China, he primarily focuses his research on the Chinese culture and China–Australia relations. Following Chinese drama with interest, he published *The Rise of the Peking Opera* and *Chinese Drama: A Historical Survey*. Studying China's ethnic minorities, he demonstrated profound knowledge and penetrating insight in *China's Ethnic Minorities and Globalization* as well as *China's Minority Cultures, Identities, and Integration Since 1912*. His works on Chinese history include *The New Cambridge Handbook of Contemporary China* and *China in My Eyes: Western Images of China Since 1949*. "It was my mother who influenced me to make the decision to come to China. But when I lived in China, it also influenced me like a mother," said Mackerras.

As an envoy for China–Australia friendship, Mackerras visited China over 60 times to attend academic conferences as a scholar or for tourism, communication or onsite investigation. He has also taught at Renmin University of China and Beijing Foreign Studies University many times. For decades, he traveled between China and Australia and made tireless efforts to present a real China to Australia and the world. In *China in My Eyes: Western Images of China Since 1949* published in 2013, he conducted a systematic review of the West's views and understandings of China since the founding of new China and forayed deeply into the political, economic, cultural, and other factors that have affected China's many images'. This book was well received by sinologists.

The stories of old friends should be passed down through generations, and the stories of making new friends should be told to the world. By telling the story of Professor Mackerras at the Parliament of Australia, Xi Jinping illustrated the idea in a vivid way—the bridge of mutual understanding and amity between countries must be developed jointly by a group of individuals who promote international friendship.

"The Chinese people will never forget any friend." Xi Jinping proved this with practical actions on diplomatic occasions. When more than 3,000 people from all walks of life from Japan and those friendly to China visited our country, he sat with them and discussed the old days with old friends to encourage China–Japan friendship; when he paid a state visit to India, he arranged a special meeting with the sister of Doctor Dwarkanath Kotnis, moving her to say that the Chinese government and the Chinese people still remember Dwarkanath Kotnis and his family; and in his visit to Egypt, he met with the Arab friends who received the Award for Outstanding Contribution to China–Arab Friendship, including Boutros-Ghali, the former United Nations Secretary-General. In June of 2014, Xi announced the Chinese government's decision to establish the Five Principles of Peaceful Coexistence Friendship Award, with the aim of engaging new friends to play an exemplary role in inheriting the spirit of the Five Principles of Peaceful Coexistence.

A Brazilian with a Chinese Heart

Carlos Tavares is an old man from Brazil. He has said that he is "a Brazilian with a Chinese heart." In the past 40 years, he has tirelessly engaged in studies in China, writing eight books and over 500 articles on China and delivering hundreds of speeches on the country. His writings guide many Brazilians to learn about China and to feel closer to China. When someone asked him what motivated him to do this, he said, "Nothing. I just want to introduce China to more people."

This touching story is a beautiful wave in the long river of China–Latin America friendship. Thanks to the contributions of a stream of Chinese and Latin American friends, the long river flows nonstop day and night like the Yangtze and Amazon Rivers.

- Carry Forward Traditional Friendship and Jointly Open up New Chapter of Cooperation—Speech at the National Congress of Brazil (July 16, 2014).

Commentary

When Chinese journalists assume a post in Brazil, many will be given the following advice: if you have questions about Brazil's past and present, go to the China scholar, Carlos Tavares; if you have questions about China's past and present, go to Carlos Tavares.

As an old man having reached 90, Tavares has been observing and studying China for more than 40 years. He began his career in 1971, when his first long report on China was published in *O Globo*, a Brazilian newspaper. In 1972, he risked his life to receive a delegation from China during the special period when China and Brazil had not yet established diplomatic relations and Brazil was under the dictatorship of the military government. In 1990, the Brazilian media released an exclusive interview with him in which he said that he was "a Brazilian with a Chinese heart." Having been awarded the China–Latin America and Caribbean Friendship Medal by the China–Latin America and Caribbean Friendship Association and the Brazilian National Federation of Commerce in 2010, he became one of the only two Brazilians to have received this honor thus far. He published an article entitled *The China-Latin America Relationship Is a Model of Mutual Benefit* in the *People's Daily* in July 2014, in which he stated, "China has established a close partnership with Latin America, although they are thousands of miles apart. This is of great referential value for promoting world peace and balanced development."

Shortly after his story was told by Xi Jinping in his speech, Carlos Tavares published his new book about China—*Dois Temas para Dilma: China e Portos*. This book shows the achievements of China's reform and development in recent years and introduces China's policy of opening up. At the publishing ceremony of the book, Carlos Tavares specially wore a tie covered with Chinese seal characters and stated, "China now is one of the most important economies in the world and is Brazil's largest trading partner. But most Brazilians do not understand China at all or have only a one-sided understanding of it, and some even have a prejudice against the country. In fact, China has been developing rapidly, and a lot the experience it has accumulated is worth learning by Brazil."

"China needs to know more about the world, and the world also needs to know more about China." This was what Xi wanted to express through the story of the "Brazilian with a Chinese heart." How can one really know China? In Xi's view, "It takes a good deal of effort to know China, and simply visiting a place or two is not really enough." To be open and inclusive, China should tell "Chinese stories" well, and it also needs more people to approach it, to know it, and to promote it. The "Chinese stories" need to be told not only by "me" but also by "you", and by everybody. Only in this way will we be able to help people remove their "blinders" and see the real China and enhance the understanding among the states and between the peoples.

The Arabian Restaurant in Yiwu

Due to the rapid development of China–Arab relations, the peoples of both nations are closely linked by their destinies. In Zhejiang Province where I used to work, there is a Jordanian businessman named Muhamad who runs a genuine Arabian restaurant in Yiwu City, where many Arab business people gather. Muhamad brings genuine Arabian cuisine to Yiwu, and in exchange he has achieved business success in this prosperous Chinese city, married a Chinese woman, and settled down in China. Integrating his own goals with the Chinese dream of happiness, this young Arabian man has attained a marvelous life for himself through his perseverance, which embodies a perfect combination of the Chinese and Arab dreams.

- – Promote the Silk Road Spirit, Strengthen China–Arab Cooperation—
Speech at the Opening Ceremony of the Sixth Ministerial Conference
of the China–Arab States Cooperation Forum
(June 5, 2014).

Commentary

The young Jordanian Muhamad enjoys a great reputation in Yiwu's foreign business circle. His wife Liu Fang is from Anhui Province, China. After coming to China for the first time and getting a job in an Arabian restaurant in Guangzhou, he began to appreciate China, and he was happy to have met Liu Fang, a sunny and open-hearted girl from Anhui who worked with him in the same restaurant. In 2001, Muhamad married Liu Fang and became a full-fledged son-in-law of China. He took over an Arabian restaurant that his uncle opened in Yiwu in 2002 and renamed it "花", the implied meaning of which is the flower of happiness and peace. He even designed a white flower as the logo of his restaurant.

As a world-renowned international trade city, Yiwu frequently trades with Arab countries, and its commodities attract a constant stream of Arabian businessman. In 2005, the Ministry of Public Security authorized Yiwu City to issue visas and residence permits directly to foreigners. As one of the more than 4,000 Arabian merchants who live in Yiwu, Muhamad now has his own trading company. His two sons are at primary school in Yiwu and can speak fluent Chinese. He says he lives happily and has made a lot of friends in China, and he intends to buy a house in Yiwu to settle down there.

So many Arabian businessmen gather in Yiwu because, as locals describe it, Yiwu has reconstructed the Silk Road, and its people are quite inclusive and enthusiastic. Traveling in Yiwu, one can come across foreigners speaking different languages, in the International Trade City or in the Huangyuan Garment Market or in Binwang Market. Yiwu's growth from a commodity distribution center to a trade base of businessmen can be attributed to its inclusiveness, and such inclusiveness pushes China to achieve one success after another.

"Gold lucky birds, silver lucky birds, fly here and there, and finally to Yiwu." These are lyrics from a ballad widely circulated in Yiwu. Having begun "exchanging sugar for chicken feathers," the open, market-oriented, and inclusive city of Yiwu has become a "world supermarket" that offers a wide range of products. In addition to "selling to the world", Yiwu also "buys from the world." Yiwu Import Commodity Pavilion has imported an accumulative total of over 55,000 categories of commodities from over 100 counties and regions all over the world. Since 2014, Yiwu's exports to Arab countries have accounted for more than half of its total exports. Every year, more than 100,000 Arabian businessmen come to Yiwu for procurement, and tens of thousands of Arabs want to settle down in Yiwu to realize their dream of life.

Dreams are universal language without barriers. Xi Jinping has noted on many occasions that the Chinese dream is intrinsically interlinked with the world's dreams and the dreams of people around the world: "The dream is also about having more economic vibrancy, free trade and investment facilitation, better roads, and closer people-to-people exchanges. Moreover, the dream is about ensuring greater security and prosperity for the people and giving children a better environment in which to grow, work and live." At the Opening Ceremony of the Sixth Ministerial Conference of the China–Arab States Cooperation Forum, through the story about the Arabian restaurant in Yiwu, Xi Jinping demonstrated that the realization of the Chinese dream will bring the world peace, not turmoil, and that it will bring opportunities, not threats.

Proposing the Chinese dream, Xi Jinping looks forward to the Asian dream and the Asia-Pacific dream, which echo the American dream and the European dream. According to Xi, the Chinese dream is never closed or isolated, but it is interlinked with dreams of people around the world such as the American dream. Dreams are "like seeds under the ground. They must grow and sprout to embrace the sunshine." Muhamad's Chinese story is just a link in the interlinked dream that arises from openness and inclusiveness, mutual learning and mutual benefit.

A HALF-CENTURY JOURNEY SEEKING HIS MOTHER

Back in the late 1940s, a young Chinese man working in Xinjiang met a pretty girl named Valentina at a local hospital. They fell in love, got married, and had a child. However, due to the political climate and for other reasons, Valentina returned to her home country when their son was only 6 years old. When the boy grew up, he tried all means to find his mother but to no avail. In 2009, at the age of 61, he finally found out that his mother was living in Almaty. He visited his 80-year-old mother there and took her to China for a sightseeing tour. This happy family reunion, although overdue for half a century, is a strong testament to the friendship between our people.

- – Promote Friendship Between Our People and Work Together to Build a Bright Future—Speech at Nazarbayev University (September 7, 2013).

Commentary

This transnational love story began toward the end of the 1940s when Li Yuankang's father, Li Huaiyu, who worked in Xianjiang, met his mother, Valentina, who worked at a local hospital. The young boy and young girl from different counties fell in love and then married and had a child. In 1954, due to social and political pressures, Valentina returned to her home country with their daughter, leaving 6-year-old Li Yuankang in China. Li Yuankang said, "Mom, sister, don't cry. Dad and I will be back in a week." The parting scene lingered in his memory for more than a half-century.

The flavors of the bread, milk, and sausage that his mother prepared for him in his childhood and the old watch and toy carriage he asked for from his mother on parting became the one and only refuge for him to bear his yearning for her.

In the 1980s, with the death of his father, Li missed his mother even more. Every time an acquaintance was going to Russia or a nearby commonwealth of independent states, he asked the acquaintance to take the information he had to help him find his mother to the destination. In the winter of 2007, one of his friends sent his information to a relative-seeking TV program called "Wait for Me", which was produced by RUTV, the Russian state TV station. Fortunately, the staff of the program found a piece of information from Kazakhstan that highly corresponded with Li's. It turned out that his mother Valentina was also seeking her son.

In September 2009, the program "сколько лет сколько зим" (Long Time Ago) of the CCTV Russian International Channel and "Wait for Me" jointly provided a cross-border live video broadcast. On December 27, Li Yuankang participated in the program arranged by CCTV in Moscow, and at the same time, his mother and sister, who were living in Almaty, Kazakhstan, also attended it on invitation. In the telestudio, as his mother came into his view, although she no longer looked as young as she was on their parting day, he immediately dropped to his knees, knelt before her, and embraced her legs, with tears coursing down his cheeks. His mother was stooped with age, and her skin was now wrinkled by time.

This touching ending was attributed to the increasingly closer people-to-people and cultural exchange between China and Kazakhstan. People-to-people exchange now results in 500,000 visits per year, and it includes 12 pairs of sister provinces. Prefectures and cities have been connected, and our peoples connect with each other like "relatives". After learning about Li Yuankang's story from Xi Jinping, almost all Li Yuankang's relatives and friends called him to congratulate him. He said he felt glad and warmed by the fact that President Xi referred to him in the speech: "It can be said that the family affection between me and my mother and sister who live in Kazakhstan symbolizes the friendship between our two nations."

"The history of a land is the history of its people." In the speech at Nazarbayev University, through the reunion story of the long-separated family, Xi Jinping showed the profound China–Kazakhstan friendship, family-like affection between the two peoples, and the cultural heritages of the two counties, making the two peoples closer.

China and Kazakhstan are neighbors as close as lips to teeth. Their exchange can be traced to the ancient Silk Road, and on the exchange will be continued in the Belt and Road Initiative. Before coming to the story of "a half-century journey of seeking his mother", Xi stated, "Shaanxi, my home province, is at the starting point of the ancient Silk Road. Today, as I stand here and look back at that episode of history, I can almost hear the camel bells echoing in the mountains and see the wisps of smoke rising from the desert. It has brought me close to the place I am visiting." From the perspectives of history and reality, respectively, the memory of Xi's home-town at the starting point of the ancient Silk Road and Xi's sympathy for Li Yuankang's half-century journey of seeking his mother are combined to communicate that Xi sincerely cherishes the China–Kazakhstan friendship.

"PANDA BLOOD" DONATED TO CHINESE FRIENDS

You may know that the Rh-negative blood type is called "panda blood" in China because it is as scarce as a panda. It is very hard for Rh-negative patients to find a compatible blood source. Ruslan, who studied at Hainan University in China, happens to be Rh-negative. Since 2009, he has been donating blood twice a year, helping to save Chinese patients of his same blood type. When praised by his Chinese friends, he simply said, "I feel this is what I should do. It is my duty to help others."

> – Promote Friendship Between Our People and Work Together to Build a Bright Future—Speech at Nazarbayev University (September 7, 2013).

Commentary

"Panda blood" refers to the Rh-negative blood type, which is as scarce as a panda. It is very difficult for Rh-negative patients to find compatible blood sources in China. The RH blood group system is the second most important blood group system of human beings, after the ABO blood group system. It is usually indicated by an Rh-positive or Rh-negative suffix to the ABO blood type. Most of the people among us are Rh-positive. Among Europeans and Americans, 15% of the people are Rh-negative, while among Asians, only 0.3–0.4% are.

The protagonist in this story, Ruslan, who studied at Hainan University in China, is one of them. He enrolled at Hainan University in 2009. He said, before going to the university, he rarely donated blood in his home country because he was young then, and he did not realize that he had a scarce blood type until he came to China. In China, he became involved in voluntary blood donation following the lead of his classmates. He donates blood twice per year so that his "panda blood" can help meet the urgent needs of Chinese patients. Because of this, he was acclaimed by the Chinese President as an envoy of friendship between the two countries. Ruslan said it was a great honor and stated, "I am very happy to further contribute to the friendly exchanges between China and Kazakhstan!"

Ruslan's story in China is the epitome of China–Kazakhstan friendship. According to Kazakhstan statistics, the number of Kazakhstan students studying in China has already reached 11,200, and many of them are the "envoys of friendship between China and Kazakhstan" praised by Xi Jinping. Kazakhstan sisters Myra and Naia are students of Xi'an Jiaotong University. When they had just arrived in China from Kazakhstan, they "did not understand Chinese at all." However, today they are "familiar with Xi'an even more than the cities in their homeland, so that sometimes they have to ask for directions when they return to their hometown." There is another "senior Kazakhstan student" who studied in China and can speak Chinese fluently—Karim Masimov, who was appointed by the Prime Minister of Kazakhstan 2014. Similarly, an increasing number of Chinese are now traveling to Kazakhstan. With superb skills and a conscientious attitude, Wang Kun and Lan Zhixue, two technicians from Ningxia, China overcame obstacles one by one and solved major technical problems for the Atyrau Refinery, one of Kazakhstan's top three refineries. This has become a favorite local tale. When they returned to their homeland, the Kazakhstan party organized a grand farewell ceremony at the airport. In today's interconnected world, such "envoys of friendship" between China and Kazakhstan can be compared to scenic sights that move between the two nations.

Young people are the mainstay of friendship between our people. The common interest and ideals they hold for life bring them together in true friendship. The story of "panda blood" not only manifested the mutual affinity and friendship between the Chinese people and the Kazakhstan people but it also expressed Xi Jinping's expectation that the young people of the two countries would undertake the responsibility of the envoy of friendship and contribute their youth and strength toward the development of the comprehensive strategic partnership between their home countries.

In the speech, Xi Jinping presented to the young people the words of the great Kazak poet and philosopher Abay Qunanbayev: "The world is like an ocean and our time is like strong wind. The waves in the front are the elder brother while those behind are the younger brother. Driven by wind, the waves from behind constantly press on those in the front. This has been the case since ancient times." From Li Yuankang's "half-century journey of seeking his mother" to "donating panda blood", the two touching stories involving the Chinese and Kazakhstan people reveal a truth: "The key to sound relations between states lies in amity between the people," while the key to amity between the people is based on friendly exchanges between the nations' young people.

THE FEELING OF TAKING ALL THE GOLD MEDALS

I am a football fan myself. Chinese football players have worked very hard, but so far, our national team has qualified for the World Cup only once. It was Mr. Bora Milutinovic who led the Chinese football team to the World Cup and who also happened to be the head coach of Mexico's national football team.

I have heard an anecdote: A Mexican sports official once asked the head of the Chinese diving team, how do you feel taking all the gold medals? Two years ago, our Mexican friends had a taste of such success. With the help of Chinese coaches, Paola Espinosa, known as the "princess of diving" in Mexico, and her teammates swept all titles in the eight diving events of the 2011 Pan-American Games. We hope that the Mexican diving team will get more gold medals in the future and that our two countries will win even more "gold medals" in cooperation.

– Seek Common Development to Create a Better Future—Speech at the Senate of Mexico (June 5, 2013).

Commentary

The "magic football coach" Bora Milutinovic is a man who lives in the memory of both Chinese and Mexican football fans because of the miracles he created.

At the 1986 Mexico World Cup held in Mexico, Milutinovic led the "straw hat legion" of Mexico to the quarterfinals, and his "Team 1986" gave a classic performance in the football history of Mexico. In addition, at the 2002 FIFA World Cup that took place in South Korea and Japan, he led his "Team 2002" to a classic record of Chinese football. On October 7, 2001, scoring a goal through team member Yu Genwei, the Chinese football team defeated Oman at Shenyang Wuli River Stadium, qualifying China for its first appearance at the World Cup. As the only coach who has led five different teams to the World Cup, Milutinovic, a Serbian, was rated by the *Global Times* as one of 60 foreigners who have influenced China. The Mexicans gave praise: "This is another miracle created by Milutinovic," who first made a name for himself in Mexico, and believe that "It is of great significance to the World Cup itself" that China, as the world's most populous country, made its first appearance in the World Cup finals.

With regard to diving, few people in China know that, in addition to China's "Dream Team", there is also a "Mexican Dream Team"—the Mexican diving team. This team swept all eight gold medals for diving events at the 2011 Pan-American Games, with its "princess of diving" Paola Espinosa taking half the medals. The person who led Mexico to taste the success of taking all the gold metals was Ma Jin, a sports coach designated by the Chinese government. As a member of the Chinese coaching team to aid Mexico, she understood the responsibilities of managing the divers' training in her spare time, equipment deployment, contest arrangement, and even the divers' daily lives. The mentoring relationship between Ma and Espinosa began with Espinosa's defiance against Ma. However, with her improvement in performance, she later treated the coach as someone she greatly trusted. The "princess of diving" and her boyfriend even presented a birthday gift to Ma—a necklace pendant with a pattern of a boy and a girl. They hoped that Ma would regard them as her own children. As Ma became famous in Mexico, she was honored as an envoy of friendship between China and Mexico. She was met by the former Mexican presidents many times, and the Mexican government even awarded her the Order of the Aztec Eagle, the highest honor Mexico awards foreigners in the country, in recognition of her contribution to the Mexican diving cause and the promotion of friendship between China and Mexico. Ma believes that diving is one of the highlights of the sports exchange between China and Mexico and that the development of the friendship between the two countries will provide a better environment for and further facilitates her sports exchange activities in Mexico.

Sharing the stories of Milutinovic leading the Chinese football team to the World Cup and the Chinese diving coach helping the Mexican divers win gold medals, Xi Jinping conveyed the idea that "unity means strength, while isolation means weakness." In today's world, no country can develop without interdependence, and only cooperation can push us to mutual benefit and win-win results.

After telling this story, Xi Jinping shared an old Chinese saying: "A single flower doesn't make spring, while one hundred flowers in full blossom bring spring to the garden." Xi then quoted the Mexican poet, Alfonso Reyes: "The only way to be successfully national is to be generously universal." What does taking all the gold medals feel like? We can all obtain a sense of that through win-win cooperation. Developing together is much better than developing by oneself. By relaying these sports stories, Xi Jinping illustrated this idea. As he said, "By working closely together, the countries will gain far more than what their combined strengths could produce."

A Young Chinese Couple's African Honeymoon

Let me tell you a story of a young Chinese couple. When they were kids, both the boy and the girl got to know Africa from Chinese TV programs and have since been captivated by this continent. Later, they got married and chose Tanzania as their honeymoon destination. So, on their first Valentine's Day after the wedding, they went there and backpacked across this country. They were overwhelmed by the hospitality and friendship of the local people and the magnificent savanna of the Serengeti. After the couple went back to China, they posted what they saw and heard in Tanzania on their blog, which received tens of thousands of hits and several hundred comments. This is what they wrote in their blog: "We have completely fallen in love with Africa, and our hearts will always be with this fascinating land." This story speaks to the natural feeling of kinship between the Chinese and African people. As long as we keep expanding people-to-people exchanges, the friendship between our peoples will take root deeply and continue to flourish.

– Trustworthy Friends and Sincere Partners Forever—Speech at the Julius Nyerere International Convention Center (March 25, 2013).

Commentary

The young couple, Mr. Chen and Ms. Li, in President Xi's speech, is fellow travel enthusiasts. They both yearn for "poetry and the far afield" and met each other on a trip. Their trip to Africa adds an exotic color to their honeymoon. On February 14, 2010, the Lunar New Year's Day in China, they embraced their second morning in Africa, and the day was also the first Valentine's Day after their wedding.

Why did they select Africa as their honeymoon destination? Mrs. Li said that she had enjoyed watching CCTV's program *Animal World* in her childhood, and Africa impressed her as a pure land where man and nature live in harmony in a way that could purify one's soul. The films *Lion King, Madagascar* and *Out of Africa* as well as documentary films about Africa produced by the BBC conjured images of rambling across the continent. Coincidentally, her husband had the same dream. Thus, they decided to make their long-standing dream come true in Tanzania during their honeymoon.

Mrs. Li shared with the media the amazing and moving moments they experienced on the trip. They ran with the animals in the Great Migrations, they searched for lions and cheetahs at the craters, they witnessed the beauty of the equatorial snow mountains from the "roof of Africa", and they even swam with dolphins in the Indian Ocean. However, what impressed them most were the African friends with whom they became acquainted on the road. For example, there was a taxi driver who not only patiently helped them to find a hotel but also helped them carry their baggage in the rain until he was drenched. There was a tour guide who led them on a walk a great distance so that they could appreciate the wild animals without invading the animals' territories or disturbing them. With their simplicity, kindness, and love for nature, the African people build a bridge to the heart of the Chinese people.

Tourism is an important link in the friendship and cooperation between countries and Africa is the destination of China's outbound tourism with the fastest growing market share. According to the *Annual Report of China Outboard Tourism Development 2015* issued by the China Tourism Academy, Africa seized 9.4% of the Chinese outbound tourism market in 2014, showing a year-on-year growth of 80.9% as the fastest growing destination in recent years. Meanwhile, statistics show that the number of Chinese tourists visiting Kenya to watch the Great Migrations of animals during August and October each year has already surpassed tourists from Europe and the US.

Tanzania was the first stop of Xi Jinping's state visit to Africa as Chinese President. One hearing this, Tanzanian President Kikwete said, "I could hardly believe my ears." When talking about China's "affinity" for Africa, Xi shared the Chinese young people's story of yearning for, exploring in, and falling in love with Africa. This is a convincing demonstration of ordinary Chinese people's pure affection for Africa, and it is also a contemporary episode in the continuing epic of friendly China–Africa exchanges.

Xi is also an important witness of China–Africa friendship. As early as his youth, he knew well the sincere exchanges between the first-generation leaders of new China—Mao Zedong, Zhou Enlai, and others—and the African statesmen of the older generation, and he has paid seven visits to Africa. Through the young couple's story, he hoped to communicate that there is natural feeling of kinship between the Chinese and African peoples; as long as we continue to expand people-to-people exchanges, the friendship between our peoples will grow deep roots and continue to flourish.

CHAPTER 6

Stories of Relationship Between the Countries: "Harmony Is Most Important in the Implementing of Regulations"

THE CHINA–IRAN FRIENDSHIP ON THE SILK ROAD

This will be my first trip to Iran, yet like many other Chinese, I do not feel like a stranger in your ancient and beautiful country, thanks to the Silk Road that linked our two great nations for centuries and to the many legendary stories of our friendly exchanges recorded in history books.

Over 2,000 years ago, during the Western Han Dynasty in China, the Chinese envoy Zhang Qian's deputy came to Iran and received a warm welcome. Seven centuries later, during the Tang and Song dynasties, many Iranians came to China's Xi'an and Guangzhou to study, practice medicine and conduct business. In the thirteenth century, the famous Iranian poet Saadi wrote about his unforgettable travel to Kashgar, Xinjiang. In the fifteenth century, a renowned Chinese navigator, Zheng He, from the Ming Dynasty led seven maritime expeditions that took him to Hormuz in southern Iran three times. The much-prized Persian carpet is woven out of a fusion of China's silk and Iran's sophisticated techniques, and the exquisite blue and white porcelain is produced—thanks to a mixture of Iran's "smaltum" (a type of material containing cobalt, unique to Iran) and China's advanced skills. Via Iran, China's lacquerware and pottery as well as papermaking, metallurgy, printing, and gunpowder-making skills were spread to the west end of Asia and further on to Europe. From Iran and Europe,

© People's Publishing House 2020
People's Daily, Department of Commentary,
Narrating China's Governance,
https://doi.org/10.1007/978-981-32-9178-2_6

pomegranates, grapes, olives as well as glass, gold, and silverware were introduced to China.

- Work Together for the Bright Future of China-Iran Relations, a signed article on Iranian media (January 21, 2016).

Commentary

Like China, Iran is also an ancient civilization with a history of over 5,000 years. Ancient Iran was a place that had to be passed through on both the Silk Road and the Maritime Silk Road. Today, with a territory spreading all the way to the Caspian Sea in the north and to the Persian Gulf in the south, Iran stands by the Hormuz Strait—the intersection of "The Belt and Road", holding the "throat" of the maritime traffic artery of the Middle East.

The exchanges between China and Iran date back to the second century BC. According to *Records of the Historian—Biography of Ferghana*, Zhang Qian was dispatched to the Western Regions as an envoy twice, in 138 BC and 119 BC, pioneering the Silk Road. On his second trip to the Western Regions, he dispatched his deputy Gan Ying and a team to the Parthian Empire (now Iran) from Quici (now Kuqa, Xijiang) via the Seleucid Empire (now Iraq), and the envoy from the Han court received a warm welcome from the Parthian King, who led a 20,000-people cavalry lined up to greet him. Due to the unceasing exploration from the Eastern Han Dynasty through the Tang Dynasty, the "Silk Road" eventually reached the Mediterranean coast in Europe, with the part within the territory of Tang stretching westward from Chang'an, the capital of Tang, to Yangguan by way of Hexi Corridor and the region outside the territory of Tang spanning Iran.

It almost seemed that our two countries were simply a camel ride or a boat trip away from each other. Indeed, the thousand-mile-long land and Maritime Silk Roads made it possible for China and Iran, two ancient civilizations, and their peoples, to embrace and befriend each other. As Saadi wrote, "Those who are far away and are of times long past deserve to be cherished more." Saadi is to Iran what Du Fu is to China. As "the greatest classical writer of Persia", Saadi has been a model of Persian literature for hundreds of years. Due to the China–Iran exchanges, people created works of art like the Persian carpet and blue and white porcelain. They gave poets inspiration while promoting cultural and people-to-people exchanges between the two countries.

The Middle East tour was Xi Jinping's first state visit in 2016, which confirmed that Xi had already left his diplomatic footprints all over the world since the 18th National Congress of the Communist Party of China. All three countries to which he paid state visits at this time are China's important partners and ardent supporters in the "The Belt and Road" initiative. As Xi said, today the relationship between China and the Middle Eastern countries is having a new start that features the spirit of peace, cooperation, openness, inclusiveness, mutual learning, and mutual benefit; thus, we should draw on our past progress and chart a new course for the future. The historical story shared by Xi in his speech set the tone for the renewed embrace of the two ancient civilizations.

In ancient times, our two countries maintained a friendship through the exchange of needed goods; today, we share one vision on "The Belt and Road". In the past, China and Iran made important contributions to opening of the Silk Road and by promoting exchanges between Eastern and Western civilizations. The China–Iran friendly exchanges for more than 40 years of diplomatic relations have continued to embody the Silk Road's spirit of peace, cooperation, openness, inclusiveness, mutual learning, and mutual benefit. Hassan Rouhani, the Iranian President, said, "President Xi is the first foreign state head to visit Iran after the settlement of the Iranian nuclear issue. This reflects the high level of positive relations and friendship between Iran and China." In the speech, Xi Jinping, taking the pomegranate introduced from Iran to China as an example, expressed his new expectations for China–Iran relations and his hope for even more fruitful cooperation between our two countries.

A MEMORIAL STATUE OF DENG XIAOPING

How time flies! As we look back on the history of China–Singapore relations, we cherish all the more the memory of two great statesmen who forged this relationship, Mr. Deng Xiaoping and Mr. Lee Kuan Yew. Five years ago, on another visit to Singapore, I joined Mr. Lee Kuan Yew in unveiling a commemorative marker in honor of Mr. Deng Xiaoping on the bank of the Singapore River. Although both of them are no longer with us, their great achievements will always be remembered.

– Forging a Strong Partnership to Enhance Prosperity of Asia—Speech at the National University of Singapore (November 7, 2015).

Commentary

On the banks of Singapore, there is a memorial statue of Deng Xiaoping. It is a half-length statue produced by the famous sculptor Li Xiangqun. While gazing at the statue, we can see fortitude from Deng Xiaoping's amiable face, the impression that he is musing on something or is somewhere far away. His well-known saying, "Development is of overriding importance," is displayed on the back of the statue.

Deng Xiaoping first set foot in Singapore and stayed there for 2 days more than 90 years ago on his way to France to study and work. He formed lasting ties with Singapore in those 2 days. In 1978, when the surge of China's reform and opening up was brewing, Deng Xiaoping once again stepped on that soil. During his visit, he congratulated Lee Kuan Yew on "the changes of Singapore", and he received Lee's recognition that China undoubtedly had the ability to catch up with and even surpass Singapore. "We came from the later generations of peasantry from Fujian, Guangdong and other provinces in China, those who neither knew a single word nor had any farmland. However, they (the Chinese) have countless compatriots who were the dignitaries and scholars who remained to guard the Central Plains," Lee explained. After hearing that, Deng did not speak. In the famous South Talks in 1992, Deng Xiaoping further proposed, "We should learn from Singapore's experience."

With the consent of the governments of both countries, the epigraph outlines Deng's life story, the relationship between him and China's reform and the special role he played in the relationship between China and Singapore. "In his famous 1992 South Talks, Deng Xiaoping spoke of Singapore's well-managed and orderly society. Since then, many Chinese officials have been sent to Singapore for training. Over the years, the two countries have frequently exchanged high-level visits, enhancing economic cooperation, expanding people-to-people and cultural exchanges, and further deepening bilateral relations," the epigraph states.

On November 14, 2010, when the evening lights were lit, Xi Jinping, China's then Vice-President, and Lee Kuan Yew ended the talks and walked along the verdant lane of rain trees to attend the unveiling ceremony of the statue that was being held on the riverbank.

On November 7, 2015, Xi Jinping visited Singapore on the occasion of the 25th anniversary of the establishment of diplomatic relations between China and Singapore. In his speech at the National University of Singapore, he recalled the two great men, Deng Xiaoping and Lee Kuan Yew, and he recollected the scene when he unveiled the memorial statue of Deng Xiaoping 5 years before. His affectionate words recall to our minds the road to China–Singapore cooperation, which has advanced with the times. "China has drawn on the Singaporean practices in addressing tough challenges encountered in its reform and development endeavors. For its part, China's development has also created tremendous opportunities for Singapore's development." Xi added that with the concerted efforts of our two peoples as well as increasing political mutual trust and deepening practical cooperation between the two countries, the China–Singapore relationship will surely make even greater progress, and our two countries will surely enter a new era.

How Faithful Are China and Pakistan to Each Other

In 2008, when the devastating earthquake struck Wenchuan, China, Pakistan responded immediately and sent all its transport aircrafts to ship its entire reserve of tents to China. The Pakistani medical team on the transport plane had to remove all of the seats to make room for the tents, and they sat on the floor all the way to China. Today, thousands of Pakistanis are working side-by-side with Chinese engineers and workers on projects undertaken by China in Pakistan, and there are many moving stories about their cooperation.

Similarly, whenever Pakistan has been in need, China has come to its help. China firmly supports Pakistan's efforts to uphold the sovereignty, independence, and territorial integrity. When Pakistan was hit by a severe flood in 2010, China provided immediate relief assistance via air and land routes. We dispatched the largest ever medical team and sent a large convoy of vehicles and helicopters to carry out rescue operations, the first time that such an operation was undertaken in the history of China's rescue assistance. Following the terrorist attack in Peshawar at the end of 2014, China invited the students who had been injured in the attack and their families to spend some time in China to recuperate so the trauma those kids had experienced could be healed with the care and love of the Chinese people.

In the most recent evacuation mission in Yemen, the Chinese navy evacuated 176 Pakistanis from the Port of Aden, and the Pakistani navy evacuated eight Chinese students from Mukalla Port. The Pakistani commander gave the order that the ship would not leave until all the Chinese students were on board. His stirring words again show that the China–Pakistan friendship is indeed deeper than the sea.

- Building a China-Pakistan Community of Shared Destiny to Pursue Closer Win-Win Cooperation—Speech at the Parliament of Pakistan (April 21, 2015).

Commentary

China and Pakistan are close to each other in both geography and emotion, and they have close ties in their interests. Pakistan was the first Islamic state to establish diplomatic relations with new China, with the diplomatic relations being established as early as May 21, 1951. Chinese leaders have described the unswerving friendship between China and Pakistan as "higher than mountains and deeper than oceans", and our Pakistani friends further enrich the description with two more "thans"—"sweeter than honey and stronger than steel".

"It is better to give up gold than betray the China–Pakistan friendship." This is a famous saying in Pakistan. Following the devastating earthquake that struck Wenchuan on May 12, 2008, the then Pakistani President Pervez Musharraf visited the Chinese embassy in Pakistan and expressed his sincere condolences to the Chinese people. As "China's staunch ally", Pakistan exhausted almost all it had to help China. It "sent all its transport aircrafts to ship its entire reserve of tents to China", and it kept the cost of the tents secret from China—"The aid should not be measured in terms of money. Did our Chinese brother charge us for the help they had provided for us?"

As a Chinese saying goes, "Strong wind reveals the strength of the grass, and genuine gold withstands the test of fire." When Pakistan is in need, China has also come to its help. In July 2010, a severe flood hit Pakistan, with one-fifth of the country, a population of 20 million, being affected for nearly 3 months and the economic losses reaching more than 10 billion US dollars. As a quick response to the disaster, China dispatched its largest ever medical team. Braving the heat, the medical personnel waded through the water to treat the injured people. Some of them even got sunstroke, yet they again threw themselves into the relief work having barely finished receiving fluid infusions. Some medical personnel drank up to 15 bottles of water per day because of the heat. In December 2014, the Pakistani Taliban waged a terrorist attack in the Peshawar Army Public School, causing 141 deaths among the teachers and students. "The coffins are too distressing to lift up, even the smallest one." China immediately condemned the attack and provided immediate assistance for Pakistanis, and it even invited two groups of injured students and their families to spend some time in China to recuperate. Under the arrangement of China, they visited Beijing, Shenzhen, Hong Kong, Guangzhou, and some other Chinese cities, enabling them to "get a taste of Chinese history, culture and development and feel the profound friendship between the Chinese and Pakistani peoples."

Chinese people call their true friends "faithful friend" and Pakistan has always been such a "faithful friend" of China. A Pakistani leader once said, "If anyone wonders how friendly two countries can be with each other, he should learn from the relationship between China and Pakistan." Pakistan is a country whose primary school textbook includes the words, "China is a staunch ally of Pakistan", and Pakistan is known as the one and only "all-weather strategic cooperative partner" of China.

"Meeting a good friend for the first time is like having a reunion with an old friend." This was what Xi Jinping said about his first visit to Pakistan. He also said, "Although this is my first visit to your country, Pakistan is not at all unfamiliar to me." "The moment we arrived in your beautiful country, my colleagues and I have been overwhelmed by your warm hospitality. It is just like coming to the home of dear brothers," he added. During the visit, Xi, President Hussain, as well as Prime Minister Sharif, agreed to elevate China–Pakistan relations to "an all-weather strategic cooperative partnership".

In Pakistan's parliament, Xi gave an affectionate account of the governmental intercourse and people-to-people exchanges between China and Pakistan, which demonstrated that the friendship between China and Pakistan is based on trust and mutual support, and we are devoted friends going through both good and hard times. His words also showed that our two countries will always move ahead together, rain or shine. Meanwhile, he asserted that China will always maintain its relationship with Pakistan from a strategic and long-term perspective, and he gives Pakistan high priority on its diplomatic agenda. He also substantiated the China–Pakistan community's shared destiny through five positions. In his speech, Xi also expressed his expectation by citing what the former Chinese Ambassador to Pakistan, Geng Biao, for whom he had once worked, has said, "The traditional friendship between China and Pakistan will spread far and wide, just like the Karakoram Highway."

NEWTONIAN MECHANICS

I know Ms. Chancellor is a Doctor of Physics. Thus, I have thought about how to better promote China–Germany relations on the basis of Newton's three laws of motion. First, we should firmly capitalize on the "inertia" of China–Germany cooperation. Cooperation is the main theme of the relationship between China and Germany, and it is what our two countries should unwaveringly strive for. We should continue to strengthen high-level exchanges and give full play to the mechanisms of government consultation and strategic dialog to continuously enhance strategic mutual trust. Second, we should deepen the practical cooperation between the two countries to promote the "acceleration" of the development of China–Germany relations. Today, China is carrying out the policy of promoting adjustment through reform to promote development through adjustment. We are confident that we will achieve sustained and sound economic development, thus creating more opportunities for China–Germany cooperation. Our two countries should strengthen our sense of partnership and opportunity, and in the spirit of mutual benefit and joint development, we should continue to expand our intertwined interests and deepen practical cooperation in an all-round way. Third, we should reduce the "reactive force"in the development of our bilateral relations. We should focus on common interests, seek common interests while reserving minor differences, and reduce resistance to the development of bilateral relations.

- Talk with German Chancellor Merkel in Saint Petersburg (September 6, 2013).

Commentary

Born in 1643, Newton was a famous English physicist who was regarded as an "encyclopedic genius". His book *Philosophiæ Naturalis Principia Mathematica* published in 1687 was a masterpiece that epitomized the first scientific revolution. The explanation of universal gravitation and the three laws of motion was the basis on which all scientific views in physics were proposed during the following three centuries, and it is the foundation of modern engineering science.

During the Eighth Leaders' Summit of the G20 held in Saint Petersburg, Russia, in September 2013, Xi Jinping met German Chancellor Merkel and used Newton's three laws of motion to illustrate the general direction of as well as the new opportunities and potential problems facing China–Germany relations.

Obtaining a doctorate in physics from the University of Leipzig, Merkel worked as a science researcher before entering politics. Xi's use of Newtonian mechanics as a metaphor not only was a reasonable application of Western culture but it also represented his respect for Merkel's learning and cultivation. Xi offered another metaphor: "Developing the relationship between China and Germany is like driving a car. We must look ahead to make the trip safe and smooth. As long as our two countries enrich the fuel and hold the steering wheel properly, the car of China–Germany cooperation will certainly run fast and steady and head for a bright future." Only if we make a blueprint for the development of our bilateral relations in a more macro- and long-term perspective can we drive the car faster and better.

"A River Runs Deep Because of Its Source"

As an African saying goes, "A river runs deep because of its source." The friendly exchanges between China and Africa date back a long time. In the 1950s and 60s, the first-generation leaders of new China—Mao Zedong, Zhou Enlai, and others—and African statesmen of the older generation ushered in a new epoch in China–Africa relations. Since then, the Chinese and African people have sincerely supported and closely cooperated with each other to fight against colonialism and imperialism and achieve national independence and liberation in the pursuit of development and national revival. A fraternal bond has been formed in this process, which has seen us through thick and thin.

– Trustworthy Friends and Sincere Partners Forever—Speech at the Julius Nyerere International Convention Center (March 25, 2013).

Commentary

Although China and Africa are far apart, the friendly exchanges between them date back a long time and appear high-powered, with similar historical experiences, China and Africa have always shown compassion for and supported each other to achieve national liberation, during which time they have built a deep friendship and became good friends in good times and bad.

During the African people's struggle for national independence in the 1950s and 1960s, China stood firmly by them and fully supported their righteous struggle against colonialism and imperialism and for national independence. Mao Zedong once made it clear that, "to do our jobs and to make friends", we should focus on "three continents: Asia, Africa and Latin America".

From December 1963 to February 1965, Zhou Enlai paid three state visits to Africa with his visiting delegations, leaving his footprints in ten African countries. These visits began the construction of a new type of China–Africa relationship and laid the groundwork for China–Africa friendship that has lasted for over 50 years. During the visits to Egypt and Algeria, Zhou Enlai put forward the five principles for developing China's relations with African and Arab countries. These principles laid the foundations for China–Africa exchanges, based on which the two sides built a new type of relationship that advocated mutual understanding and mutual support. The exchanges between China and Africa can be described as equal and sincere, setting a good example in the history of international relations.

The African people have also given strong support and selfless assistance to the Chinese people. In October 1971, the 26th Session of the UN General Assembly passed a resolution to restore the lawful seat of the People's Republic of China in the UN. Eleven of the 23 sponsor countries were African countries, and 26 among the 76 affirmative votes were from Africa. China has also received strong support from the overwhelming majority of African countries on a number of major issues. For example, they helped China defeat anti-China bills on the human rights situation in China and proposals for Taiwan's participation in the UN, and they supported China's accession to the WTO and China's bid for the Olympic Games.

Over the past half-century and thereafter, the friendly and cooperative relationship between China and Africa has been tested by the years and has continuously been consolidated and developed. Currently, 52 of Africa's 54 countries have established diplomatic relations with China.

On March 24, 2013, Xi Jinping arrived at Julius Nyerere International Airport, Tanzania, and began his 26-hour state visit to the East African country. This was Xi Jinping's first trip to Africa as Chinese President, and it was his sixth trip to Africa. In the important speech at the Julius Nyerere International Convention Center, Tanzania, he described the long-standing China–Africa friendship to demonstrate that China–Africa relations did not develop overnight. Neither are they a gift from someone else. They have been nurtured and built, step by step, by our two sides over the years.

"Friends are as good as their word; they travel a thousand li to keep a rendezvous." In this important speech, Xi also made a concise proposition to further develop the China–Africa relationship: first, in treating African friends, we stress the importance of "sincerity"; second, in conducting cooperation with Africa, we stress the importance of "real results"; third, in strengthening the China–Africa friendship, we stress the importance of "affinity"; fourth, in resolving problems that may arise in cooperation, we stress the importance of "good faith". This proposition vividly illustrated the essence of China–Africa relations: sincerity, friendship, mutual respect, equality, mutual benefit, and common development. Although separated by vast oceans, China and Africa share a strong empathy with each other.

The TAZARA Was Constructed by Friendship

More than 40 years ago, over 50,000 Chinese brothers and sisters came to Africa with their devotion to the African people. They fought side-by-side with the brothers and sisters of the people of Tanzania and Zambia, overcoming various difficulties and completed the construction of the Tanzania–Zambia Railway (TAZARA), known as the railway of friendship and the railway of freedom, with their sweat, their blood, and even their lives. More than 60 of them sacrificed their precious lives on this piece of land far away from home. They translated the great spirit of internationalism with their lives. They are the heroes who cast the monument of China–Tanzania and China–Africa friendship. Their names, just like TAZARA, will always be remembered in the hearts of the Chinese, Tanzanian and Zambian people.

– Speech During the Visit to the Cemetery for Memorable Deceased Chinese Experts Assisting Tanzania (March 25, 2013).

Commentary

At a cemetery in the southwestern suburb of Dar es Salaam, literally, "The residence of peace", 69 Chinese compatriots who sacrificed their lives while assisting Tanzania in its construction were buried. At the cemetery, the grass looks like a green carpet, the green pine trees and Delonix regia stand high and straight. A huge stela is inscribed with red lettering: "Cemetery for Memorable Deceased Chinese Experts Assisting Tanzania" in both Chinese and English.

Since the 1960s, China has sent tens of thousands of experts to Tanzania and made selfless contributions to the economic construction of this African country in various fields. Among the 69 sacrificed compatriots, some helped the Tanzanian people build coal mines, develop agriculture, or cultivate water conservancy; however, most of them sacrificed their lives constructing the Tanzania–Zambia Railway (TAZARA).

TAZARA is an outstanding symbol of China–Africa friendship. From May 1968, when the first Chinese exploring team stepped into the boundless wilderness overgrown with grass to route the railway, to July 1976, when TAZARA was officially open to traffic, more than 50,000 Chinese engineering technicians made enduring contributions to the construction of the railway. Going through hardships and dangers, engineering technicians from China, Tanzania, and Zambia opened up a 1,860-kilometer railway that crossed the towering mountains. As the economic artery connecting Tanzania and Zambia as well as other African countries, this railway has created favorable conditions for the economic development of the two countries and supported the struggle for national liberation in southern Africa, thus being honored as "the road of freedom" and "the road of liberation" by the two peoples.

Zhang Mincai, a hydraulic expert buried in the Cemetery for Memorable Deceased Chinese Experts Assisting Tanzania, was the first Chinese expert to sacrifice his life in assisting Tanzania. In the search and exploration for drinking water for the local people in the bush, in October 1967, Zhang Mincai was attacked by a swarm of wild bees. After being informed of this, Premier Zhou Enlai immediately sent a doctor from China to rescue him; however, the doctor was unable to save his life, and Zhang Mincai died at the age of 35.

By paying a tribute to the memory of the late Chinese experts assisting Tanzania and telling the stories of the friendly cooperation between China and Africa with deep emotion, Xi Jinping expressed his wish to carry forward the spirit of the TAZARA and to treasure and cherish the tradition of friendship between China and Africa. In Xi's first overseas trip as Chinese President, he paid a visit to Africa, which he described as "a continent full of promise". This reflected China's consistent brotherhood with developing countries. In strengthening the China–Africa friendship, we stress the importance of "affinity". Through the story, Xi proclaimed to the world that the friendly exchanges between China and Africa are not based on certain conditions, but rather, they are supported by their thick-and-thin friendship. As Charles Sanga, Tanzania's former ambassador to China, said, "Xi Jinping's sheer joy stirred by the continuous development of the African continent is so sincere and moving. It is love from the bottom of his heart."

"GOLDEN KEYS" FROM MUSCATINE

This afternoon, I will go to visit Iowa, which will be my second visit to the state in 27 years. I am going to tell my old friends there that the "golden keys" that the representative of Muscatine City Hall presented to us 27 years ago symbolized the opening of local exchanges and cooperation between our two countries. And today, there are already 38 sister province/state relationships and 176 pairs of sister cities between our two countries. 47 out of the 50 American states have seen their exports to China grow several or even dozens of times over the past 10 years. This shows that once open, the door to local exchange and cooperation between China and the United States cannot be closed by any force. On the contrary, it will only open wider and wider.

- Work Together for a Bright Future of China-US Cooperative Partnership—Speech at Welcoming Luncheon Hosted by Friendly Organizations in the United States (15 February 2012).

Commentary

Muscatine is the county seat of Muscatine County, Iowa, in the United States. It is located along the Mississippi River. Agriculture and animal husbandry are its economic backbone, and it is especially famous for growing watermelons and producing mother of pearl buttons.

In 1985, Xi Jinping, the then County Party Secretary of Zhengding, Hebei Province, led a delegation to Iowa and visited the small town of Muscatine to conduct an on-the-spot investigation of local agriculture and animal husbandry. When he visited the farms, he asked the farmers to demonstrate how to cultivate sweet potato seedlings in a greenhouse; when he lived with a local family, he took every opportunity to learn about America; after returning to China, he wrote a detailed report, which cited many comments by local Americans and made reference to the development of agriculture and animal husbandry in Zhengding. In the eyes of the American locals, Xi was a "very capable leader, always clear with what he wanted to know, always punctual and neatly dressed, and always showing burning curiosity." No matter where he went, he asked questions and consulted with those he met.

In February 2012, Xi Jinping, the then Chinese Vice President, revisited Muscatine. During his visit, US Iowa Governor Branstad and his wife; Vice Governor Reynolds and his wife; Muscatine's Mayor; the Dvorchaks, the landlords who had received Xi Jinping in 1985; and local high school student representatives gave Xi Jinping and his delegation a warm reception. The old friends said that Xi's visit bridged the past and future, renewed the special affinity and friendship established 27 years ago, and set an example for both the American and Chinese people. They hoped and believed that Xi's visit would provide an impetus to a better partnership between our two countries. During this visit, the Mayor of Muscatine presented another "golden key" to Xi; Xi was the first person to receive two "golden keys" in Muscatine's history.

"To me, you are America." These words of Xi will be forever in the minds of the Muscatine people. On September 17, 2015, Muscatine's Mayor Dwayne Hopkins named the house where Xi had stayed 30 years ago, the "Sino–US Friendship House", which is now open to the public in honor of China–US local cooperation and friendship. "This house is a symbol of friendship between China and the US," said Gary Dvorchak, son of the Dvorchaks. As one enters the "Sino–US Friendship House", one is embraced by a warm "Chinese flavor". One can also appreciate the group photos of Xi and his Muscatine friends on the walls and over the fireplace.

There is an old Chinese saying that "A new dress is better than an old one, but an old friend is more intimate than a new one." On February 15, 2012, Xi revisited the city of Muscatine, and he used this saying to describe his friendship with his former landlords, the Dvorchaks. Xi went on to say, "The American people are as simple, industrious, enthusiastic, and friendly as the Chinese people. There are many common interests between the two peoples, and they can surely become good friends and good partners in mutually beneficial cooperation." The story of the "golden keys", which he told at the welcome luncheon, not only reflects China's way of making friends—maintaining old friendship while renewing it—but it also highlights the importance of local exchange and cooperation between China and the United States.

Xi Jinping, who came up from the grassroots level, attaches great importance to cooperation and exchange with foreign countries. At the Third China–US Governors' Forum held in Seattle on September 22, 2015, he stressed that "state-to-state relations ultimately rely on the support of the people and serve the people" and that "provinces and states are closest to the people".

CHAPTER 7

Stories of Cultural Fusion: "Diversity of All Things on Earth Is Natural Law"

A LITTLE MOLE FROM CZECH REPUBLIC

Czech Republic is one of the first countries to recognize and establish diplomatic relations with the People's Republic of China. Since the establishment of diplomatic ties 67 years ago, the traditional friendship between our countries and peoples has gone from strength to strength. In the 1950s, a well-known Czech painter, Zdenek Sklenar, came to China and became good friends with Wu Zuoren, Qi Baishi and other renowned Chinese painters. After returning to his country, Zdenek Sklenar drew many illustrations of the Monkey King, which is fondly regarded as a unique variation of the image of this popular character. *Krtekis* was the first foreign cartoon series introduced to China. The chubby, kind-hearted and courageous little mole became immensely popular among China's young audience. Bedrich Smetana's symphonic cycle, *Ma Vlast* and Jaroslav Hasek's *The Good Soldier Svejkare* are also masterpieces that are familiar to the Chinese public.

– Time to Renew and Energize China–Czech Ties, a signed article on Czech media (March 26, 2016).

Commentary

The well-known Czech painter Zdenek Sklenar was born in 1910. In the 1950s, when Sklenar held an exhibition in China, he was fascinated by

214 PEOPLE'S DAILY, DEPARTMENT OF COMMENTARY

the story of Sun Wukong, the Monkey King of China. From then on, through his painting, he began to introduce the Monkey King and the story *Journey to the West* to the Czech people. Sklenar created his Czech "Monkey King" with perfect integration of Chinese traditional cultural elements and Czech national characteristics, which are brightly colored and diverse in terms of image. He redesigned the more than 500 characters in the *Journey to the West* and created an even more unique "metamorphosis" for the "Monkey King", who embodies 72 metamorphoses. Because of this, Sklenar is honored as the "Czech Monkey King".

"Little Mole" is a national cartoon character valued by the Czech people as a national treasure. It stems from *Krtekis*, a classic story by Zdenek Miller, a famous illustrator and film director from Czech Republic. In the production of the cartoon, to help the mole break through boundaries and language barriers, Miller created a rich array of movements, facial expressions and simple sounds to communicate information, avoiding verbal communication. In the 1980s, *Krtekis* was introduced to China and later became a classic memory of a generation. In March 2016, *Krtek a Panda* (Panda and Little Mole), a cartoon series produced jointly by China and Czech Republic, began to be shown. Integrated with the Chinese elements, the little mole continues to sow the seeds of friendship in the hearts of the children of both countries

Born in 1824, Bedrich Smetana was the founder of Czech classical music, a pioneer in the Czech national opera, and father of Czech national music. Unfortunately, he went deaf in 1874, however, he never stopped creating and presented many works thereafter. The symphonic cycle *Ma Vlast* referred to by Xi Jinping is Smetana's representative work. Jaroslav Hasek, a famous Czech writer born in 1883, was known for works that were characterized by humor and satire. His representative work *The Good Soldier Svejkare* described an ordinary Czech soldier, Svejkare's, experience in the First World War, exposing the tyrannies of the Austro-Hungarian Empire and the corruption of its army. Many commentators have compared Svejkare to Cervantes's Don Quixote. *The Good Soldier Svejkare* has been translated into nearly 30 languages, including Chinese, and it is much loved by people all over the world.

In March 2016, Xi Jinping visited Czech Republic. This was his first visit to Central and Eastern Europe as the Chinese President. Before discussing

China–Czech cultural exchange, he made a point of praising Czech's "picturesque landscape, rich cultural heritage and talented people". Recollecting his visit to this country in the 1990s, he said he was deeply impressed by the hard work and ingenuity of the Czech people, their dynamic economic and social progress and Bohemian culture nourished by the Vltava River.

The Czech artist created the paintings of the "Monkey King" according to the image of Sun Wukong, and *Krtekis* was immensely popular among the Chinese children. Such anecdotes presented in articles published by the Czech media not only reveal the historical friendship between China and Czech Republic, but they also prove the significance of cultural exchange. With these references, Xi showed that the Chinese and Czech peoples have long admired and appreciated each other's civilization and culture. Such exchanges have greatly increased in recent years; thus, there is hope that the two countries will further encourage people-to-people and cultural exchanges in the future.

China as Seen by Singaporean Students

Last July, several Singaporean college students in their early 20s joined a "See China 2015" program to learn about China by taking photographs. This was a program that took them to Northwest China. There, they captured images of modern China through the camera lens and experienced and shared Chinese culture with others by watching the local Qinqiang Opera, eating Lanzhou hand-pulled noodles and taking a river trip on sheepskin rafts. Two Chinese students studying at the National University of Singapore spent an entire year filming the personal stories and dreams of 50 Singaporeans. I am sure you know many similar anecdotes of such people-to-people exchanges.

– Forging a Strong Partnership to Enhance Prosperity of Asia—Speech at the National University of Singapore (November 7, 2015).

Commentary

"See China" is a cultural experience program co-organized by the Academy for International Communication of Chinese Culture (AICCC), Beijing Normal University and the Huilin Foundation. It invites young foreigners to observe China through their own eyes. By taking pictures with their own cameras and working on their own videos, they can tell Chinese stories, record Chinese scenes and display the Chinese spirit. The 2015 "See China" project attracted the participation of 100 young college students from 20 countries. They produced a total of 100 short documentary films under the theme "People, Home and Nation". The work *Chopsticks: Yin and Yang in Qingdao* explores the philosophy of the equilibrium between yin and yang in the Chinese culture through chopsticks; *A Bowl of Lanzhou Beef Noodles* reflects on the "home" culture based on beef noodles; *Together* records the daily life of an old couple who have workedin a university as logistical staff for many years. Through close contact, continuous tracking, and in-depth observation, the participants in this program "saw a different China". One participant said that the 17-day process of shooting in Lanzhou, Gansu Province, changed her impression of China's western cities and showed her a city in Northwest China that interweaves tradition with modernity.

The anecdote about the two college students from China who observed 50 Singaporean people through their camera lenses also shows us the "great strength of dreams" from the perspective of "the other". Among the 50 characters in their photos, the youngest was just a few days old, while the oldest had already reached 97. Their stories pieced together a colorful pictorial scroll of the Singapore era. The first exhibition of the photos was held in a shopping center, and the people who visited were mostly local people passing by. After seeing the exhibition, they noted with surprise and emotion that in their Lion City, there is not only a member of the Flying Tigers, who fought against Japanese aggressors, but also a xylographer who created countless works by constantly striving for perfection for decades, and there is even the "watchman of the luxuriant cultural protection forest"—the founder of the Grassroots Book Room. Their emotion was evoked by so many touching stories, and they were surprised because these stories were all around them, but they had never recognized them.

As a Chinese saying goes, "Instead of complaining that one's talents go unrecognized, one should learn to appreciate the wisdom of others." In a speech at the National University of Singapore on November 7, 2015, Xi Jinping shared these stories about how the college students of China and Singapore, respectively, explored and discovered anecdotes in each other's country. This shows that the baton of friendship between the two countries is being taken up by their younger generations, and it further proves that only if young people in both China and Singapore learn more about both countries and learn from each other can they deepen our friendship.

Every exploration of civilization and every journey of in-depth communication is an opportunity to open our hearts. Xi Jinping has often warmly invited people from all over the world to China to experience and learn about it. He has emphasized that "when trying to learn about China, one must guard against drawing conclusions based on partial information," and "we also hope that the world will view China in an objective, historical and multi-dimensional light and see the true and full picture of a dynamic China." In his view, "If political, economic and security cooperation is the rigid force to promote the development of national relations, then people to people communication is the soft force to improve the relationship between the peoples and promote spiritual communication between them. Only when the two forces converge can we better promote the sincerity and compatibility among all countries."

In Search of Shakespeare

"To be, or not to be, that is the question." This line from *Hamlet* has left a lasting impression on me. When I was barely 16 years old, I left Beijing for a small village in northern Shaanxi province to be a farmer and spent seven years of my youth there. Back in those days, I tried every means to lay my hands on William Shakespeare's works, reading *A Midsummer Night's Dream*, *The Merchant of Venice*, *Twelfth Night*, *Romeo and Juliet*, *Hamlet*, *Othello*, *King Lear* and *Macbeth*. I was captivated by their dramatic plots, vivid characters and emotional intensity. Standing on the barren loessland of Shaanxi as a young man, I often pondered the question of to be or not to be. Eventually I made up my mind that I shall dedicate myself to serving my country and my people. I am sure that Shakespeare not only appeals to readers with his literary talents, but he also inspires people's lives in profound ways.

Chinese playwright Tang Xianzu of the Ming Dynasty (1368–1644) was acclaimed as the "Shakespeare of the East". He produced a number of world-famous works, such as the *Peony Pavilion*, *Purple Hairpin*, *A Dream under the Southern Bough* and *Handan Dream*. Tang was a contemporary of Shakespeare, both of whom died in 1616. Next year will be the 400th anniversary of their passing. China and the UK could jointly celebrate the legacy of the two literary giants to promote people-to-people exchanges and deepen the mutual understanding between our two countries.

– Work Together to Promote Openness, Inclusiveness and Peaceful Development—Speech at a Dinner Hosted by the Lord Mayor of the City of London at the Guildhall in London (October 21, 2015).

Commentary

William Shakespeare and Tang Xianzu were contemporary dramatists who, respectively, lived in the West and the East. The two masters died in 1616, and they were both listed among the Top 100 Historical Cultural Celebrities by UNESCO in 2000.

As the most important British writer in the European Renaissance, Shakespeare wrote many dramas and sonnets, being honored as "Zeus on the Olympus of human literature". From his works, we not only feel the exquisite art of language, but we can also discover ideas and themes that are freighted with meaning. From his works, we know the melancholy and irresolute prince Hamlet, the evil and ruthless conspirator Macbeth, the opinionated general Osero, the muddleheaded and tyrannical King Lear, and many other unforgettable characters. In his work, we read of love and forgiveness, revenge and betrayal, death and destruction, and "the emotions of humanity and the brilliance of life". The themes of the works are broad and profound. The Argentine writer Jorge Luis Borges once effused: "All rivers of consciousness lead to Shakespeare. They flow circuitously, ceaselessly day and night." The poet Ben Jonson, Shakespeare's best friend, even asserted, "He was not of an age, but for all time." In addition to the four great tragedies *Hamlet, Othello, King Lear* and *Macbeth,* he also produced many other classic works, including *Romeo and Juliet, A Midsummer Night's Dream, The Merchant of Venice, Twelfth Night,* and *As You Like It.*

Tang Xianzu was a Chinese playwright and litterateur in the Ming Dynasty who created many works throughout his life. His *Peony Pavilion, Purple Hairpin, A Dream under the Southern Bough* and *Handan Dream* are collectively called the "Four Dreams of Linchuan". Like Shakespeare's great works, these works show the breadth and depth of life. Many lines and characters from them have long been widely known and shared through the ages. From his works, we came to know Du Liniang, who believes that "The origin of love is elusive, yet in it we fall head over heels"; we know the scholar Lu Sheng, who reached a high position and enjoyed great wealth in an unrealizable dream; and we also know the traveler Chun Yufen, who also had an illusory dream in which he was appointed Governor of Nanke by the king of the Great Kingdom of Ashendon. Tang Xianzu was a master in using the dream as a metaphor for human life. His romantic literary imagination, gorgeous style of writing and profound humanistic spirit were all unsurpassed in the dramatic writing circles of his time.

Both Shakespeare and Tang Xianzu were "epoch-making giants" in an "epoch of giants". Eulogizing human dignity, value and power, they, respectively, represented the souls of the Western renaissance and Eastern humanistic enlightenment. Endowed with the gift of art, they were not of a country but for the whole world.

After Xi Jinping's visit to the UK, Fuzhou, Jiangxi Province, China presented a bronze statue depicting the meeting of Tang Xianzu and Shakespeare to Shakespeare's Birthplace Trust. The bronze statue is now standing in Shakespeare's Birthplace, while its twin is in Tang Xianzu Memorial Hall in Fuzhou, China. They bear witness to the cultural exchanges between China and the UK.

In a speech at a dinner hosted by the Lord Mayor of the City of London at the Guildhall in London on October 21, 2015, Xi Jinping described the spiritual communication across time between him and Shakespeare and the resonance across borders between Tang Xianzu and Shakespeare. In doing so, he vividly illustrated his assessment that "In today's world, openness, inclusiveness and mutual learning is a defining feature of our times." By using storytelling, he expressed his hope that China and the UK will shorten their "cultural distance" through culture exchanges, allowing "the essence of the culture of both countries" to produce a magic "chemical reaction" in "the way of thinking and way of life of the two peoples".

I'd Like a Glass of Hemingway's Mojito

The Chinese people have always held American entrepreneurship and creativity in high regard. In my younger years, I read the *Federalist Papers* and Thomas Paine's *Common Sense*. I was interested in the life stories and thought of George Washington, Abraham Lincoln, Franklin Roosevelt and other American statesmen. I also read the works of Henry David Thoreau, Walt Whitman, Mark Twain and Jack London. I was most captivated by Ernest Hemingway's *The Old Man and the Sea* and its descriptions of the howling wind, driving rain, roaring waves, small boat, the old man and the sharks. So, when I visited Cuba for the first time, I paid a special visit to the breakwater in Cojimar where Hemingway wrote the book. In my second visit to Cuba, I dropped by the bar Hemingway frequented and ordered a mojito, his favorite rum drink with mint leaves and ice. I wanted to sense for myself what was on his mind and what the place was like as he wrote those stories. I believe that it is always important to make an effort to get a deep understanding of the cultures and civilizations that are different from our own.

– Speech at the Welcoming Dinner Hosted by Washington Local Governments and Friendly Organizations in the United States (September 22, 2015).

Commentary

Born in 1899, the famous American writer Hemingway was referred to as a "tough guy in the literary arena" and was praised as the spiritual guide of the American nation. After the outbreak of World War I, he threw himself onto the Italian battlefield as a driver of the Red Cross. It was during that period that he was promoted to the rank of Lieutenant and awarded three military meritorious medals. It was also during that time that he received 237 scarring shrapnel wounds and nightmarish memories. After recovering, while working as a journalist in Paris, he began to write novels. In 1926, his first novel, *The Sun Also Rises*, was published, a novel that mirrors the physical and psychological damages of the war to the younger generation. Hemingway and the writers he represented were thus known as the "lost generation".

The novella *The Old Man and The Sea*, published in 1952, is one of Hemingway's most famous and influential works. It is about an old fisherman named Santiago who fights a giant marlin and a shoal of sharks, and it extolls the indestructible spiritual strength of human beings in the face of hardships. "Man is not made for defeat. A man can be destroyed but not defeated." This often-quoted saying comes from *The Old Man and The Sea*. In his 62 years of life, Hemingway also created many other masterpieces such as *A Farewell to Arms, The Snows of Kilimanjaro*, and *Across the River and into the Trees*. In 1954, Hemingway won the Nobel Prize in Literature.

Hemingway spent more than one-third of his life in Havana, Cuba. He once spoke of the place this way: "I love this country and I feel at home. A place that makes one feel like home, except his birthplace, is where he shapes his destiny." In Havana, there is a restaurant-bar called La Bodeguita

Del Medio, whose best-known drink is the Mojito, a cocktail prepared by adding mint leaves to a mix of Cuban specialty rum and lemon juice. The Mojito was Hemingway's favorite drink.

Like Hemingway, *The Federalist Papers* also represents the American spirit. In May 1787, at the invitation of the Confederate States Congress of America, the Constitutional Convention was held in Philadelphia under the auspices of George Washington. The convention vetoed the *Articles of Confederation* and instead produced a new constitution. For the new constitution, the states of the US produced two diametrically opposed views: some states supported it, while the others opposed it. Hence a most heated debate took place in American history. The *Federalist Papers* was a direct outcome of the debate. It is a collection of articles and essays written under the pseudonym "Publius" by Alexander Hamilton, James Madison and John Jay and published in New York newspapers to promote the ratification of the new constitution.

Thomas Paine was one of the founding fathers of the United States, and the country's name "the United States of America" was given by him. During the American War of Independence, he wrote the popular pamphlet *Common Sense*, which encouraged the people of North America to strive for independence and to establish a republic.

As an old Chinese saying goes, "It is the very nature of things to be unequal in quality." Every culture has its own unique value. Xi Jinping enumerated the American classics he had read and his visit to the bar in honor of Hemingway to demonstrate that civilizations come in different colors; civilizations are equal, and civilizations are inclusive. "It is always important to make an effort to obtain a deep understanding of the cultures and civilizations that are different from our own," Xi said.

From the speech excerpt, we can find that Xi is no stranger to majestic Mount Rainier and charming Lake Washington. He also mentioned the impact of the film *Sleepless in Seattle* on the Chinese people in the speech. This classic film about loving and being loved has shaped Chinese audiences' initial impression of Seattle as the Romantic City. Even today, the words on the film posters are still mentioned: "What if someone you never met, someone you never saw, someone you never knew; was the only one for you? This is Seattle, a city that believes in enchanted love." Xi cited this example to illustrate a point, "Greater exchanges and mutual learning among civilizations can further enrich the colors of various civilizations, heighten people's enjoyment of cultural life, and open up a future with more options."

THE WHITE HORSE CARRIED BUDDHIST SCRIPTURES TO CHINA AND MONK XUANZANG WENT ON A PILGRIMAGE TO THE WEST

In 67 AD, Kasyapa Matanga and Dharmaraksa, two eminent monks from India, arrived in Luoyang, China. There, they translated the Sutra of Forty-two Chapters, the first Chinese translation of Buddhist scriptures. We have stories of the white horse carrying Buddhist scriptures to China and Monk Xuanzang's pilgrimage to the west. They brought Indian culture as well as Buddhist scriptures to China. During his seven expeditions, the great Chinese navigator Zheng He visited India six times and brought with him neighborly friendship from China. Indian dance, astronomy, a calendar, literature, architecture and sugar-making techniques were introduced to China, while Chinese paper-making, silk, porcelain, tea and music were spread to India. All these bear witness to a long-running history of exchanges and mutual learning between our two peoples.

– In Joint Pursuit of a Dream of National Renewal—Speech at the Indian Council of World Affairs (September 18, 2014).

More than a week ago, the Indian Prime Minister, Narendra Modi, visited my hometown in Shaanxi Province, China. I joined him in Xi'an, the capital of Shaanxi, to trace the history of cultural exchanges between China and India. During the Sui and Tang dynasties, Xi'an was also an important gateway for friendly exchanges between China and Japan, which attracted many envoys, students and monks to study and live. Abe no Nakamaro was a representative of them. He forged a deep friendship with the great poets of the Tang Dynasty Li Bai and Wang Wei, leaving behind a touching tale.

– Speech at China–Japan Friendship Exchange Meeting (May 23, 2015).

Commentary

Buddhism was introduced eastward to China from its cradle in India. In the Eastern Han Dynasty, Emperor Ming of Han sent envoys to the Western Regions to seek the Buddha dharma. The envoys travelled westward to the Greater Yuezhi (now the region that spreads from Afghanistan to

Central Asia), where they came across Kasyapa Matanga and Dharmaraksa, two eminent monks who were preaching the Buddha dharma in the region. At the invitation of the envoys, the eminent monks joined the envoys to have a white horse carry Buddhist scriptures to Luoyang, China in 67 AD. Hence the story "the white horse carrying Buddhist scriptures to China". Emperor Ming even ordered the construction of the White Horse Temple in Luoyang. There, the eminent monks translated the Sutra of Forty-two Chapters. It was said in *A Record of Buddhist Monasteries in Luo-Yang*, a book of Buddhist records produced in the Southern and Northern Dynasties, that, "The White Horse Temple was built by Emperor Ming of Han, from where Buddhism was introduced to China."

Compared to "the white horse carrying Buddhist scriptures to China", Monk Xuanzang's pilgrimage to the west may be more widely known. *The Journey to the West*, one of the well-known Four Great Classical Novels of Chinese literature, was actually created on the basis of the story of Monk Xuanzang. According to historical records, in the Tang Dynasty, the eminent monk Xuanzang began his pilgrimage to the west from Chang'an. By way of the Western Regions, he finally reached India after all types of hardship and danger. After his study in India, he returned to Chang'an with Buddhist scriptures, and he translated the scriptures in Dacien Temple, Hongfu Temple, Ximing Temple and other places in succession. Xuanzang "concentrated on translation and was unwilling to trifle away any second" to the extent that he refused the request of Emperor Tai of Tang that he resume secular life and assist the emperor in the affairs of state as a minister. Given that the original Buddhist scriptures written in Sanskrit on which he based his translations were scattered and lost, his translations were regarded as "the secondary Sanskrit scriptures" or "quasi-Sanskrit scriptures". In addition to translating the Buddhist Scriptures, Xuanzang also composed the *Buddhist Records of the Western World* according to his experience in India. This book vividly describes the local customs and practices of India, and it serves as an important resource for studying the travels between China and the Western Regions and Buddhist history. More than that, Xuanzang even translated Lao-Tzu's *Tao Te Ching* into Sanskrit and introduced it to India according to the *Old Book of Tang*.

Abe no Nakamaro was a Japanese student sent to Tang China in the Japanese Nara period. In the Kaiyuan era, he passed the civil-service examination. He was a gifted poet who was not only knowledgeable and brilliant but also emotional and forthright. He even formed a close friendship with the Chinese poets Li Bai and Wang Wei. Before returning to his homeland, he composed a poem entitled *Written Before Returning to the Home Country Under Orders* as a farewell present to his Chinese friends. This poem was also included in Finest Blossoms in the Garden of Literature (Wen Yuan Ying Hua), a fine poem collection compiled in the Song Dynasty, as the only work produced by a foreigner in the collection. Wang Wei also composed a poem for seeing off him: *To See off the Directorate of the Palace Library, Zhao Heng, upon his Return to Japan.* From the line in this poem "After this departure, we will be far away from each other, and how can we receive each others' message", we can feel the deep friendship between them.

All these stories of exchanges and mutual learning in history formed the bridges connecting China and neighboring countries. Xi Jinping told the anecdotes of the white horse carrying Buddhist scriptures to China, Monk Xuanzang's pilgrimage to the west and the close friendship between Abe no Nakamaro and the great poets of Tang to illustrate the unbreakable cultural kinship and historical connections between China and neighboring countries.

Xi has a penetrating viewpoint on neighboring countries: We cannot move a neighbor who is at enmity with us; however, we can strive for new neighbors with whom we get along well. However, we cannot move our country; therefore, we can do nothing but live amicably with neighboring countries. China and its neighboring countries conducted exchanges and mutual learning in ancient times and has gone through hardships together in modern history. We live side-by-side, we have similar cultures, and our friendship was formed in ancient times. Hence, the best choice for us is to establish a good-neighborly relationship. As Xi stressed, the very purpose of China "is to express our genuine desire to live in harmony with our neighbors and concentrate on common development. We want to work together with our neighbors to make the pie of cooperation even bigger so that we can all share the fruits of development".

TAGORE'S CHINESE HOMETOWN

Ninety years ago, Rabindranath Tagore, the great Indian poet admired by the Chinese people, visited China and was warmly received there. Upon setting foot on China's soil, Tagore said, "I don't know why, but coming to China is like coming home." Upon leaving China, he said quite sadly, "My heart stays."

- In Joint Pursuit of a Dream of National Renewal—Speech at the Indian Council of World Affairs (September 18, 2014).

I have had a keen interest in Indian civilization since childhood. The fascinating history of India held me deeply captivated when I read books about the Ganges civilization, Veda culture, Maurya Dynasty, Kushan Dynasty, Gupta Dynasty and Mughal Empire. In particular, I have read a lot about the colonial history of India when the Indian people fought arduously for national independence and when Mahatma Gandhi lived and conceived his ideas. By so doing, I was hoping to gain insights into the evolution and character-making of this great nation. I have read Tagore's poetry, such as *Gitanjali, Stray Bird, Gardener and Crescent Moon*, many lines of which remain fresh in my mind. He wrote, "If you shed tears when you miss the sun, you also miss the stars", "We come nearest to the great when we are great in humility", "Wrong cannot afford defeat but Right can", "We read the world wrong and say that it deceives us", "Let life be beautiful like summer flowers and death like autumn leaves." Such beautiful and philosophical lines have inspired me deeply in my outlook on life.

- In Joint Pursuit of a Dream of National Renewal—Speech at the Indian Council of World Affairs (September 18, 2014).

Commentary

Rabindranath Tagore was the first Asian winner of the Nobel Prize in Literature, and he was also regarded as the "international spokesman" of the Indian civilization. Throughout his 60-year literary career, he produced more than 50 collections of poems, including the masterpieces *Gitanjali, Crescent Moon, Gardener* and *Stray Bird*, as well as 12 novels and novellas, nearly 100 short stories, and more than 20 dramas. With a huge influence in India, Tagore and Gandhi, two great men of India who were contemporaries, were collectively referred to as the two great sages of Indian literature and politics. Tagore gave Gandhi the title of "Mahatma", while Gandhi hailed Tagore as a "Great Mind".

For China, Tagore was an old friend. During the Chinese New Culture Movement, Many of Tagore's works were introduced to China, and they have influenced Chinese readers generation after generation. In March

1924, at the invitation of Liang Qichao and Cai Yuanpei, a six-person delegation headed by Tagore came to visit China. During his visit to Hangzhou, China, Tagore delivered a speech titled "Look for the Way to Light through Friendship" at the Department of Education of Zhejiang Province before an audience of over 3,000. He even composed a poem at the scene as a tribute to the beauty of Hangzhou: "The hills are shrouded in mist and embraced by the lake at the foot, the water is waving gently with the breeze as if asking the hills to move, but the proud hills stand still."

During Tagore's visit to China, Liang Qichao presented him with a Chinese name— 竺震旦—on the occasion of Tagore's 64th birthday. " 竺" was derived from " 天竺", the name of India in ancient China, and " 震旦" was the name of China in ancient India. Tagore accepted the Chinese name with pleasure. The name, which was generated from a perfect combination, also conveyed the Chinese people's expectation of Tagore's great role in a cultural exchange between China and India.

In return, Tagore made unremitting effort to advance Chinese studies. In 1937, he established a Chinese institute at Visva-Bharati University, pioneering the study of China in India. The institute has hosted the Chinese writer Xu Dishan, the painter Xu Beihong and the education scholar Tao Xingzhi, all of whom have given lectures there. The portrait of Tagore that we often see today was painted by Xu Beihong when he lectured in India. In 1941, on his last birthday, Tagore dictated the poem, *I Have Ever Set Foot on the Land of China,* in which he recalled the good times he had spent in China.

Literary classics are the cultural treasures of a nation and an effective carrier of state-to-state exchange. The classical texts and wise thoughts often strike a chord with people of different cultural backgrounds. In the speech delivered at the Indian Council of World Affairs on September 18, 2014, Xi Jinping narrated his story of reading Tagore, and he quoted Tagore's famous lines, narrowing the distance between him and his audience. He told the audience that he "had a keen interest in Indian civilization since childhood"; he recounted the history of India as if sharing family treasures; and he read Tagore's famous lines in a clear voice. His storytelling was just like a chat with an old friend, reflecting deep friendship and profound significance.

In 1990, Xi was transferred to Fuzhou from Ningde to serve as prefectural Party secretary. On departing from Ningde, where he had worked for nearly two years, he gave the local leaders some parting words, which were derived from Tagore's story after visiting China and returning to his country. A friend asked Tagore, "What have you lost in China?" "Nothing, but my heart," he answered. Xi took this as a metaphor when he said, "Although I am about to leave East Fujian, I leave behind my heart, which sincerely loves this place."It is human nature that those who understand each other cherish the friendship between them; and such understanding can warm their hearts. As long as you warm the heart of another and touch that friend with a sincere heart, the friendship between you will be ever deeper.

The Colored Glaze Under Famen Temple

In 1987, 20 exquisite pieces of glazed ceramic were excavated at the underground chamber of Famen Temple in China's Shaanxi Province. These East Roman and Islamic relics were brought into China during the Tang Dynasty. Marveling at these exotic relics, I thought hard and concluded that as we approach the world's different civilizations, we should not limit ourselves to simply admiring the exquisiteness of the objects involved. Rather, we should try to learn and appreciate the cultural significance behind them. Instead of satisfying ourselves with their artistic presentation of people's life in the past, we should do our best to recognize the objects' inherent spirit.

– Speech at UNESCO Headquarters (March 27, 2014).

Commentary

Located in Famen town, Fufeng County, 120 km west of Xi'an, Shaanxi province, China, and established in the late Eastern Han Dynasty, Famen Temple was widely regarded as the "ancestor of pagoda temples in Guanzhong". Famen Temple Pagoda, the pagoda standing in Famen Temple, was named "Grand True Relic Pagoda" due to the discovery of a finger bone of the Sakyamuni Buddha in its underground palace. In 1569, the third year of the reign of Emperor Longqing of the Ming Dynasty, the four-storied wooden Famen Temple Pagoda, which had been reconstructed during the Zhenguan period in the Tang Dynasty, collapsed because of an earthquake. Thus it was rebuilt again and became a spectacular 47-m-high 13-storied pagoda with eight sides.

In the 54th year after the reconstruction, the pagoda began to tilt towards the southwest after another earthquake. The pagoda body was overweight due to its top-heavy structure, and there was an underground palace under the footing of the pagoda. In 1981, the west half side of Famen Temple Pagoda collapsed in heavy rain, followed by the fall of the pagoda spire. In 1987, the underground palace of Famen Temple Pagoda was opened when the footing was being cleared up in preparation for the rebuilding of the pagoda. A large quantity of precious historical relics were unearthed, including more than 20 pieces of colored glaze as well as four pieces of Buddhist relics, 121 pieces of gold and silverware and 14 pieces of secret color ware.

Since it was introduced into China in the third century, the colored glaze ware has long been regarded as a category of treasure more precious than gold and silverware. The more than 20 pieces of unearthed colored glaze ware included not only bottles and dishes but also teacups and saucers, which were made in East Rome, West Asia and China, respectively. Most of them were fashioned in the Islamic style, and the colored glaze relics bear witness to the transportation and cultural exchanges between China and the Western Regions and possess extreme value as cultural relics.

Although imported from abroad, the colored glaze had long been utilized in people's daily life in the Tang Dynasty, playing an important role in the material culture of Tang. Wei Yingwu, a poet of Tang, once composed a poem entitled "The Colored Glaze" to praise it: "The glaze is colored, but as transparent as ice; the glaze seems devoid of content but can obstruct tiny dust. If the tableware made of colored glaze is absent from a luxurious banquet, it is a thorough betrayal of the beauty-like glaze." Li He, another poet of Tang, who was dubbed the "Ghost of Poetry", once described the colored glaze in this way: "The colored glaze wine glass is glittering, the good wine is amber, and the wine drops lying on the rim of the cup are just like some red pearls."

The exchanges and mutual learning among civilizations have helped the spread of Chinese culture to the rest of the world and the introduction into China of cultures and products from other countries. Recounting the anecdote about when he marveled at the exotic colored glaze, Xi asserted the truth: "Civilizations have become richer and more colorful through exchanges and mutual learning."

For the first time, the leader of China gave a comprehensive exposition of his deep understanding of the development of world civilization, as well as its expansion and principles, on the podium of the UN. Also for the first time, the Chinese leader presented in a systematic way the viewpoint that it is exchanges and mutual learning among civilizations that form a bridge of friendship among peoples, a driving force behind human society, and a strong bond for world peace. During the speech, Xi Jinping categorized the philosophy of "exchanges and mutual learning among civilizations" into three dimensions: first, civilizations come in different colors, and such diversity has made exchanges and mutual learning among civilizations relevant and valuable; second, civilizations are equal, and such equality has made exchanges and mutual learning among civilizations possible; third, civilizations are inclusive, and such inclusiveness has given exchanges and mutual learning among civilizations the needed drive to move forward. He provided an ingenious metaphor: "The Chinese people are fond of tea, and the Belgians love beer. To me, the moderate tea drinker and the passionate beer lover represent two ways of understanding life and knowing the world, and I find them equally rewarding. When good friends get together, they may want to drink to their heart's content to show their friendship. They may also choose to sit down quietly and drink tea while chatting about their lives." If all civilizations can uphold inclusiveness, the so-called "clash of civilizations" will no longer be relevant. This is what he highlighted in this speech.

THE HISTORY OF CHINA-WEST EXCHANGES ON THE SILK ROAD

In the second-century BC, China began working on the Silk Road leading to the Western Regions. In 138 BC and 119 BC, Envoy Zhang Qian of the Han Dynasty made two trips to those regions, spreading Chinese culture there and bringing into China grape, alfalfa, pomegranate, flax, sesame and other products. In the Western Han Dynasty, China's merchant fleets sailed as far as India and Sri Lanka where they traded China's silk for colored glaze, pearls and other products. The Tang Dynasty saw dynamic interactions between China and other countries. According to historical documents, the dynasty exchanged envoys with over 70 countries, and Chang'an, the capital of Tang, bustled with envoys, merchants and students from other countries. Exchanges of such a magnitude helped the spread of the Chinese culture to the rest of the world and introduced into China cultures and products from other countries. In the early fifteenth century, Zheng He, the famous navigator of China's Ming Dynasty, made seven expeditions to the Western Seas, reaching many Southeast Asian countries and even Kenya on the east coast of Africa. These trips left behind many good stories of friendly exchanges between the people of China and countries along the route. In the late Ming and early Qing Dynasties, the Chinese people began to learn modern science and technology with great zeal, as European knowledge of astronomy, medicine, mathematics, geometry and geography were being introduced into China, which helped broaden the horizon of the Chinese people. Thereafter, exchanges and mutual learning between Chinese civilization and other civilizations became more frequent. There were indeed conflicts, frictions, bewilderment and denial in this process. But the more dominant features of the period were learning, digestion, integration and innovation.

– Speech at UNESCO Headquarters (March 27, 2014).

Commentary

"Walking along the ancient Silk Road, I seem to hear the camel bells of the caravan; hearing the neigh of horses, I seem to enjoy the prosperity of the Han and Tang dynasties." Since the Western Han Dynasty, there has been a great trade route linking China, Central Asia, Western Asia and Europe and traversing Eurasia, on which silk and porcelain were carried westwards, while fine horses and gems streamed eastwards. This route led a magnificent chapter of the history of Chinese–Western communication. In the late nineteenth century, the German geographer Ferdinand von Richthofen coined the name "Silk Road" for this route in his book *China*, following with wide recognition of the name.

"The ships of our fleet all hoisted high sails, like the clouds blot out the sky. Day and night, we galloped ahead like shooting stars. We crossed over the raging billows as if we were rambling on the road." This is a narrative about a scene on a maritime channel of trade and cultural communication, which stretched from the southeast coastal region in China to East Africa and Europe via the Indo-China Peninsula, and states in the South Sea, Indian Ocean and Red Sea. This channel was the "Maritime Silk Road", named by Édouard Chavannes, a French Sinologist. After the Song Dynasty, porcelain took over the position of silk as the staple export commodity of China. Therefore, the Maritime Silk Road was also called "the porcelain road".

There were two Chinese who made outstanding contributions along the Silk Road and the Maritime Silk Road. One was Zhang Qian of Western Han. In 138 BC and 119 BC, Emperor Wu of Han twice sent Envoy Zhang

Qian for trips to the Western Regions. Because of the trips, the main line of the Maritime Silk Road took shape, starting from Chang'an (now Xi'an) to the countries in those regions via the Hexi Corridor. Zhang Qian spread Chinese culture in the regions while bringing grape, alfalfa, pomegranate, flax, sesame and other products into China. The places he passed were all without Chinese footprints; thus, it was said that it was Zhang Qian who opened the road.

Another great contributor was Zheng He of the Ming Dynasty. He was ordered to lead a fleet of up to 200 ships carrying over 27,000 people to sail the western Pacific and the Indian Ocean. They visited more than 30 countries and regions during the voyage, travelling as far as East Africa and the Red Sea. Zheng He's voyages to the West were the largest scale, most ship-borne and longest lasting sea voyages with most seafarers in ancient China, which were more than half a century earlier than the voyages by the European countries, directly reflecting the strength and prosperity of Ming.

As pioneering works in the history of human civilization, the Silk Road and the Maritime Silk Road formed the longest international transport route linking the East and the West in ancient times. They were the achievements co-accomplished by various ethnic groups along the route, which were truly the roads of communication and friendship. The Silk Road and the Maritime Silk Road were not only the ties of economy but also the "blood vessels" where civilizations blended. The great contributions from them could be seen in scientific and technological progress, cultural communication, species introduction, spiritual, emotional and political exchanges among various nations as well as the creation of new human civilizations.

Looking back to the days a millennium ago, the Silk Road showed mankind a means of mutual exchange of needed goods, a means of building understanding between peoples, and even a means of mutual learning between civilians. Sharing the stories of ancient China's promotion of exchange with the western countries along the Silk road, Xi Jinping made clear, "The Chinese civilization, although born on the soil of China, has come to its present form through constant exchanges and mutual learning with other civilizations", and he stressed, "Only through exchanges and mutual learning can a civilization be filled with vitality." To look back on history is to embrace a brighter future. In his speech, Xi also cited two western quotes. One was from Victor Hugo: "There is a prospect greater than the sea, and it is the sky; there is a prospect greater than the sky, and it is the human soul." The other was given by Napoleon Bonaparte: "There are only two forces in the world, the sword and the spirit. In the long run the sword will always be conquered by the spirit." Through these quotes, he told the world that, on the one hand, we need a mind that is broader than the sky as we approach different civilizations; on the other hand, we should seek wisdom and nourishment from various civilizations to provide support and consolation for people's minds, and we should work together to tackle the challenges facing mankind.

PRESIDENT YUDHOYONO COMPOSED A SONG

In this connection, I recall the song *Hening (Silence)* composed by President Yudhoyono. In October 2006, he came to Guangxi, China, for the commemorative summit marking the 15th anniversary of China-ASEAN dialogue relations. On the Lijiang River, Yudhoyono was overwhelmed by inspiration and wrote these beautiful lyrics. "The beautiful days I spend with my friends have kept recurring in my life." The mountains and rivers in China deeply touched President Yudhoyono and reminded him of his childhood and hometown. This shows just how strong the bond and affinity are between our two peoples.

- Make Joint Efforts to Build China-ASEAN Community of Common Destiny—Speech at Indonesian Parliament (October 3, 2013).

Commentary

Susilo Bambang Yudhoyono was the sixth President of Indonesia. He was born in a poor military family in Pacitan, East Java, Indonesia, in 1949 and won the Indonesian presidential election in 2004. During his presidency, he established a campaign against the corruption sweeping through Indonesia with "stand by the people" and "preserve political integrity" as slogans, punishing a large number of corrupt officials and thus being praised by his people as "Mr. Clean".

Not only did he make a difference in politics, but he also made a contribution to music by authoring three music albums between 2007 and 2010. He put his patriotic emotion into his songs and called on the people of the whole country to hang together, love their country and create a better future for the country.

On October 29, 2006, Yudhoyono visited Guilin when he came to Guangxi, China, for the commemorative summit marking the 15th anniversary of China–ASEAN dialogue relations. He did some sightseeing on the Lijiang River and in the Reed Flute Cave. In October, the scent of osmanthus wafts across Guilin, and the Lijiang River, like a green silk ribbon, wraps around the mountains. If you travel by boat on the river, you will seem to be in a gallery. Fascinated by the beauty of the Lijiang River, Yudhoyono praised it in poetic words, "God endowed the Lijiang River with such unique beauty, and I am very privileged to enjoy her beauty. I will bring my whole family here at a certain proper time to share the beautiful scenery with them." The landscape scenery on the Lijiang River stirred President Yudhoyono's memories of childhood and hometown and inspired him to compose the song *Hening (Silence)*: "In the silent night, standing outdoors in the beautiful village, I thought to myself, over and over. The beautiful days I spend with my friends have kept recurring in my life. The village is quiet and silent, where the flowers of love are in full blossom. And I am farming and weaving, on and on. I pray silently in my heart: God bless my nation. Please vouchsafe its eternal peace and eternal harmony."

In his speech at the Indonesian parliament, Xi Jinping told the story of Yudhoyono composing his song to show that, "It is through the efforts of these envoys of friendship that we have built bridges of friendship and opened windows to sincere understanding that the friendship between our two peoples has been everlasting and has grown stronger and more robust as time goes by."

In this speech, Xi quoted a proverb from Indonesia: "It is easy to make money but difficult to make friends." A history of world civilization is largely a history of people-to-people exchanges and intertwining. Those heart-stirring cultural exchanges are the most simple and solid emotional ties to sustain and develop state-to-state relations. The friendship between countries requires mutual understanding, mutual support and cooperation. It is also necessary for the people of insight in both nations to further develop it in a down-to-earth way.

XIAN XINGHAI BOULEVARD

The ancient city of Almaty is also on the ancient Silk Road. In Almaty, there is Xian Xinghai Boulevard, which got its name from a true story. At the outset of the Great Patriotic War in 1941, Xian, a renowned Chinese composer, arrived in Almaty after much travail. By then, he was worn down by poverty and illness, and had no one to turn to. Fortunately, the Kazakh composer Bakhitzhan Baykadamov took care of Xian and provided him with the comfort of a home.

It was in Almaty that Xian composed his famous works, *Liberation of the Nation, Sacred War* and *Red All over the River*. He also wrote the symphony Amangeldy based on the exploits of the Kazakh national hero. These pieces served as a rallying call to fight fascism and proved immensely popular with the local people.

– Promote Friendship Between Our People and Work Together to Build a Bright Future—Speech at Nazarbayev University (September 7, 2013).

Commentary

Throughout millennia, people of various countries along the ancient Silk Road have jointly written a chapter of friendship that has been passed on to this very day. The story of the Chinese composer Xian Xinghai contributed a page to this chapter.

In 1940, Xian was ordered to go to the Soviet Union to compose the score of the documentary film *Yan'an and the Eighth Route Army* and participate in post-production. However, the outbreak of the German-Soviet war in 1941 not only brought film production to a standstill but also blocked his way back to China. Therefore, after much travail, he travelled to Almaty. By then, Xian was worn down by poverty and illness and had no one to turn to, nor a fixed abode. Fortunately, the Kazakh composer Bakhitzhan Baykadamov took care of him and provided him with the comfort of a home. Remaining true to the ideals of their music, both composers in the hard days composed music under each other's encouragement and forged a deep friendship.

As an admirer of Xian's talent in music, Baykadamov recommended Xian to a newly started concert hall in Kostanay, a city in northern Kazakhstan, as a music instructor. There, Xian made tireless efforts to inspire the local people with music. Upon his efforts, the concert hall opened successfully and held the first concert after the outbreak of the Great Patriotic War. In addition to acting as a commander, he played instruments in some performances. The local people therefore presented him with a Kazakh name, which means happy. He often went on performance tours to mountain villages with peers and studied the folk music of Kazakhstan, upon which he acquired the skills of playing a tambura and collected, adapted and composed many works in the local style. His famous works *Liberation of the Nation, Sacred War* and the orchestral suites *Red All over the River* were produced there. His symphony *Amangeldy*, which was composed based on the exploits of the Kazakh national hero, even served as a rallying call to fight fascism and proved immensely popular with the local people. After the death of Xian, Almaty named a street near the house of the Baykadamovs "Xian Xinghai Boulevard" and erected a monument for him.

With the surge of various cultures on the Silk Road, people felt connected by spiritual ties, which, like water, served to refresh them and thus deepened the mutual understanding among the peoples along the road. Looking back on the history of the Silk Road, it can be seen that the exchanges and mutual learning contributed to the progress of human civilization. This is the meaning of Xi's speech at Nazarbayev University.

Although Xian's story is merely a single page in the chapter of mutual learning and friendly exchanges written jointly by the people of various countries, it irrefutably proves that, "On the basis of solidarity, mutual trust, equality, inclusiveness, mutual learning and win-win cooperation, countries of different races, beliefs and cultural backgrounds are fully capable of sharing peace and development." Xi'Jinping's statement effectively translated the valuable inspiration intended by the story of "Xian Xinghai Boulevard."

CHAPTER 8

Stories of Historical Emotions: "Distance Can Never Separate Real Friends"

THE TREASURE BOAT OF ZHENG HE IN SINGAPORE

In the early fifteenth century, China's great navigator, Zheng He, visited Singapore several times on his ocean voyages. A full-size replica of the treasure boat of Zheng He is on display in the maritime museum of Singapore to honor this historic event. In the late Ming and early Qing dynasties, many people from China's Guangdong and Fujian provinces migrated to Southeast Asia, bringing with them Chinese culture and skills, and sowing the seeds of China–Singapore friendship.

– Forging a Strong Partnership to Enhance Prosperity of Asia—Speech at the National University of Singapore (November 7, 2015).

Commentary

In the early fifteenth century, more than 600 years ago, a huge fleet organized by the government of the Ming Dynasty and headed by Eunuch Grand Director Sanbao, Zheng He, set sail from Liujiagang Port in Taicang, China. Over the next 28 years, Zheng He headed this fleet to conduct seven voyages, travelling by sea to more than 30 countries and regions in Asia and Africa. These were the world-renowned Zheng He' voyages to the West. This heroic undertaking by Zheng He occurred more

© People's Publishing House 2020
People's Daily, Department of Commentary,
Narrating China's Governance,
https://doi.org/10.1007/978-981-32-9178-2_8

than half a century before Columbus discovered the New World, and it is regarded as the harbinger of the age of exploration.

As people marvel at Zheng He's seven voyages, they focus their attention on the majestic treasure boat. Liang Qichao, a famous modern scholar who once emphasized that "People will never have another Zheng He" and noted that "There are two matters concerning Zheng He's voyages that are worthy of particular attention." One matter is "the development level of the navigation facilities in the Ming Dynasty". According to historical records, Zheng He's treasure boat was "148 meters long and 26.6 meters wide." That is approximately 125 meters long, 50 meters wide, with a draught of nine meters and a displacement of more than 17,000 tons. Compared to this "colossus", the flagship of Columbus's fleet (25.9 m long) was a "tiny boat", and even the wooden warship Victoria built four centuries later by means of the British mobilizing the whole nation's capability and taking 6 years to build "lagged behind it". This is historical evidence of the national strength of Ming.

Despite having the world's largest fleet, Zheng He aimed at neither invading nor plundering other countries, nor playing the role of the "maritime hegemon"—quite the contrary. He served as an "envoy of peace" promoting exchanges between the East and the West throughout his voyages. Every time he arrived in a country, the first thing he did was to declare the imperial edict and express Ming's hope of sharing the joy of peace with the world; the second was to convey Ming's will to establish and develop friendly exchanges with the country by presenting gifts to the King and officials; and the third was to conduct trade negotiations. During the seven voyages, Zheng He did not seize a single inch of land in other countries, nor did he pillage any country. Instead, he treated all nations with courtesy and equality, and he even brought them a large number of exquisite articles such as silk and porcelain. Because of this, the treasure boat of Zheng He is still praised by many countries and regions as a symbol of "peace", "friendship" and "communication."

Today, a full-size replica of Zheng He's treasure boat is on display at the Singapore Maritime Experiential Museum, which is situated on Sentosa Island, Singapore, to honor this historic event. The treasure boat is as high as a three-story building and extremely majestic. An open theater is set at the bow of the boat, where visitors can recapture Zheng He's stories of his voyages by watching animated short films on a large screen.

"Harmonious" and "new" were the words most frequently expressed in the news reports on Xi Jinping's visit to Singapore. Narrating the story about the replica of the treasure boat of Zheng He, Xi illustrated the "close bonds among our peoples" and expressed his expectations of China–Singapore cooperation in making progress in our respective endeavors toward development.

With regard to Xi's visit to Singapore, citizen groups throughout the country extended to him a warm welcome as though they were receiving a "relative". The local people said with emotion that, "President Xi has worked in Fujian for many years, and the vast majority of us Singaporean Chinese are from Fujian and Guangdong, China, so we have a deep sense of kinship with him." In fact, Xi came to Singapore three times as early as the 1980s and 1990s. As an old friend of President Chen Qingyan and Premier Li Xianlong, he met them many times. In terms of China–Singapore friendship, Xi is a witness as well as a facilitator. "Looking ahead, I believe that Asia is once again taking the lead in promoting the development of history. Asia is our homeland, and it is where our future lies." He concluded the speech with these sincere words. Words that are spoken from the heart often become more deeply rooted in the hearts of others. This is an important reason why Xi has repeatedly set off a whirlwind of charisma with his "Xi-Style Diplomacy" in his state visits.

The "Friendly Past" of China and the US

Some 230 years ago, Empress of China, a US merchant ship, sailed across vast oceans to the shores of China. Some 150 years ago, tens of thousands of Chinese workers joined their American counterparts in building the trans-continental Pacific Railway. Some 70 years ago, China and the United States, as allies in World War II, fought shoulder-to-shoulder to defend world peace and justice. In that war, thousands of American soldiers lay down their precious lives for the just cause of the Chinese people. We will never forget the moral support and invaluable assistance the American people gave to our just resistance against aggression and our struggle for freedom and independence.

- Speech at the Welcoming Dinner Hosted by Washington Local Governments and Friendly Organizations in the United States (September 22, 2015).

Commentary

On February 22, 1784, a cargo ship with a carrying capacity of 360 tons sailed from New York, US, to Guangzhou, China. At that time, the US, which has just gained independence and was being aggressed by the British trade blockade, urgently sought to communicate with the outside world. The American merchants thus extended an olive branch to China, a nation on the other side of the Pacific Ocean, and gave the ship a name of respect and beauty—Empress of China. On May 11, 1785, the Empress of China returned home fully supplied from its first voyage between China and the US carrying a great quantity of Chinese commodities back to the US including pottery, porcelain, silk and sandalwood fans. The so-called father of the US, and its first president, George Washington appreciated the porcelain brought by the ship and selected and bought more than 300 pieces. Today, these antiques, which were created two centuries ago, are preserved at Mount Vernon, Washington's former residence and at the Museum of Pennsylvania. An "old China hand" from the US once commented that, "To a crazy ship all winds are contrary. It is gratifying that the Empress of China was not such a crazy ship because it brought splendid and brilliant Chinese culture, which much benefits America."

The Pacific Railroad, the great artery of America traversing the continent from east to west, was also branded with "Chinese impressions". In 1863, it broke ground. Compared with the eastern section that stretched across the broad plains, the western section had to cope with poorer construction conditions brought about by the complex terrain. Nevertheless, the Chinese workers were said to "have achieved what other people could not achieve". The then-governor of California reported to Andrew Johnson, then-President of the US, "They are composed and silent. Additionally, they were very industrious and peace-loving, with much higher endurance then other nationals. These Chinese people have amazing learning ability. They soon learned the expertise needed in future railway construction and could become skilled in the shortest possible time in any kind of work." As a result, Chinese workers quickly became the main force in the construction of the western section, with up to more than 6,000 Chinese workers fighting on the front line of the Pacific Railroad.

Furthermore, China and the US share an "indelible national memory" that the two peoples stood side by side to fight against fascism. The

Flying Tigers, established by American pilot Claire Lee Chennault, delivered 800,000 tons of war reserves to China's battlefield and shot down and destroyed more than 2,600 enemy aircraft on this battlefield, achieving brilliant victories, one after another. The opening of the Hump route further ensured the transport of strategic supplies in China at the critical moment when the Burma Road was cut off. In the years we fought together, every American pilot in China carried a blood chit with him. The main text of the blood chit read "This foreign person has come to China to help in the war effort. Soldiers and civilians, one and all, should rescue, protect, and provide him medical care." As long as the Chinese civilians came across an injured pilot wearing this blood chit, they treated him with all their capabilities.

In 2015, Xi Jinping visited Seattle, Washington, as the first stop of his state visit to the US Meeting old and new friends, Xi responded to some people's doubts by retelling the stories about the American merchant ship—the Empress of China, the Pacific Railroad constructed jointly by the Chinese people and the American people, and the two people's fighting against fascism, making clear that, the vast Pacific Ocean has ample space to accommodate our two great nations, and we have a deep foundation of public opinion and historical origin upon which to build a new model of major-country relationship.

In this speech, Xi also noted that a number of things are particularly important for our efforts in advancing the new model of the major-country relationship between China and the US from a new starting point: we must read each other's strategic intentions correctly; we must firmly advance win–win cooperation; we must manage our differences properly and effectively; and we must foster friendly sentiment among our peoples. The above-mentioned three stories were told by Xi after his proposal of the latter, which served as a support for the following point: "Although geographically far apart, our peoples boast a long history of friendly exchanges."

"The Foreign Soldiers of the Eighth Route Army" on the Battle of Resistance Against Japanese Aggression

We the Chinese will never forget the invaluable support given by peace-loving and justice-upholding countries, peoples and international organizations in our fight against Japanese aggressors. The Soviet Union provided tremendous material support to our war of resistance. The American "Flying Tigers" took great risks in opening the Hump route. A large number of anti-fascist fighters from Korea, Viet Nam, Canada, India, New Zealand, Poland, Denmark, as well as from Germany, Austria, Romania, Bulgaria and Japan, participated directly in our war of resistance. Dr. Norman Bethune of Canada and Dr. Dwarkanath Kotnis of India came all the way to China to treat the wounded and rescue the dying. Dr. Jean Bussiere of France opened his own "Hump" route to transport medicine with bicycles. John Rabe of Germany and Dr. Bernhard Arp Sindberg of Denmark worked courageously and resourcefully to protect Chinese refugees from harm in the Rape of Nanjing. Michael Lindsay of Britain, internationalist fighter Hans Schippe, and other journalists covered China's war of resistance and told the rest of the world stories of China's heroism. Toward the end of the war, the Soviet Red Army moved into China's Northeast, sweeping the Japanese aggressors there together with the Chinese military and people, which hastened the Japanese defeat. All these stories remain popular among the Chinese people.

- Speech at the Reception Commemorating The 70th Anniversary of the Victory of The Chinese People's War of Resistance Against Japanese Aggression And the World Anti-Fascist War (September 3, 2015).

Commentary

During the war, more than 70 years ago, the common cry for justice brought anti-fascist allies together to stop the scourge of the evil from spreading. To this day, some moving stories still circulate.

Norman Bethune was a doctor from Canada. In January 1938, he led a medical team to travel across the sea to China. He spent the following two years in China in healing the wounded and rescuing the dying on the battlefield. In the famous Battle of Qihui, Bethune set up an operating table in a temple 3.5 km from the battlefront, where he working continuously for 69 h and performed surgery on 115 wounded soldiers, despite the fact that the walls had been blasted down by the enemy. At that time, he was nearly 50 years old, yet he donated 300 ml of blood to the sick and wounded twice. He often said, "You should allow me to serve as a machine gun." On November 12, 1939, Bethune died of blood poisoning, which he got during an emergency surgery on an injured soldier at the age of 49 in Huangshikou Village, Tangxian County, Hebei Province.

Dwarkanath Kotnis was a doctor from India. His Chinese name was "柯棣华", in which "柯棣" was transliterated from this family name "Kotnis". To express his determination to struggle in China, he selected the Chinese character "华" (meaning "China") as his given name, hence came the Chinese name " 柯棣华". He came to China with a five-person medical team after the outbreak of World War II. In February 1939, he joined the medical team of the Eighth Route Army in Yan'an, and in July 1942 he joined the CPC. During more than two years in the Shanxi–Chahar–Hebei border area, he always followed the example of Bethune, sparing no effort to treat and rescue the wounded from the battles against the Japanese army. He stated, "I am unwilling to leave my post for even one minute" even when he suffered a serious disease. In December 1942, he died of an epileptic seizure at the battlefront at the early age of 32.

Jean Bussiere was a doctor from France. During the Chinese People's War of Resistance against Japanese Aggression, doctors and medics were in short supply in the anti-Japanese base areas of the Eighth Route Army. Under the circumstances, he took advantage of his identity as a foreign doctor to cross the Japanese army's blockade and took on the task of transporting medicine, bandages and other medical supplies for the Eighth Route Army. At first, he transported the supplies by car. However, as the Japanese army carried out the policy on rationing of gasoline, he opened his own "Hump" route to transport medicine with bicycles.

Our British friend Michael Lindsay, who served as a communications technology consultant, not only trained radio talents for our revolutionary bases but also designed and built antennas and transmitters for the Eighth Route Army, enabling the rest of the world to hear the "voice of Yan'an".

The German friend Hans Schippe risked hardships and dangers to interview the Eighth Route Army and the New Fourth Army in Yan'an, southern Anhui and northern Jiangsu in wartime. Writing a great number of reports to disclose the true situation of heroic resistance by the Chinese's people to the rest of the world, he was called "the foreign soldier of the Eighth Route Army".

September 3 is a day worth being forever etched in the memory of people all over the world. On this day in 1945, the Chinese people, having fought tenaciously for 14 years, won the great victory of their War of Resistance against Japanese Aggression, marking the full victory of the World Anti-Fascist War. On that day, the world was once again blessed by the sunshine of peace. On such a special day, Xi Jinping affectionately told the stories of foreign friends fighting with the Chinese people to stress that peace is not easily come by, and it must be resolutely defended.

Success in creating a better future hinges on correctly understanding history. In his speech, Xi Jinping explained the Chinese people's view of history from two positive and negative perspectives. From the negative perspective, forgetting history is tantamount to betrayal, and denying past aggression is to make a mockery of history and constitutes an insult to the human conscience. Such behavior can only lead to a loss of credibility in the eyes of people all over the world. From a positive perspective, history's lessons are a valuable asset that belongs to all mankind. We should draw wisdom and strength from history, pursue peaceful development and work together to create a more promising future for world peace. At the Commemoration of the 70th Anniversary of the Victory of the Chinese People's War of Resistance Against Japanese Aggression and The World Anti-Fascist celebration held on the same day, Xi not only reaffirmed China's diplomatic philosophy, "China will never seek hegemony or expansion," but also announced that China will cut the number of its troops by 300,000. This action is an embodiment of China's dedication to peace.

MARSHAL'S DAUGHTER IN THE NAZI CONCENTRATION CAMP

Fighting shoulder to shoulder against the common enemy, the Chinese people and the Belarusian people paid a huge sacrifice for and made splendid contributions to the victory of the World Anti-Fascist War. In a Nazi concentration camp in Minsk, Zhu Min, the daughter of Zhu De, one of the founding fathers of new China, fought against German fascists with her friends in Belarus. General Tang Duo extended a helping hand to Minsk in its war of liberation. The Belarusian pilots from the Red Army of the Soviet Union set foot on Chinese soil to help the Chinese pilots fight Japanese aggressors in air combat, and they took part in important battles for the liberation of Northeast China. The "Heroes of the Soviet Union" such as Air Marshal Aleksej Sergejevič Blagoveščenski, Air Marshal Nikolajenko and Major General Zdanovic were outstanding representatives of these heroes.

– Let the Symphony of the Friendly China-Belarus Cooperation Struck up a More Lively Beat—A Signed Article on Belarus Media (May 8, 2015).

Commentary

Zhu Min was the only daughter of Marshal Zhu De. In February 1941, Zhu Min was sent to The First International Children's School in Moscow, Soviet Union, under the alias of "Chi Ying" to avoid exposing her identity. The family name "Chi" alluded to "Zhu" (both of these two Chinese characters mean "red"). The cold climate in Moscow caused Zhu Min, who had suffered from asthma since she was very young, to have a relapse. Therefore, the Children's School sent her to the Young Pioneers' Summer Camp set in a suburb of Minsk, the capital of Belarus, to recuperate. Unfortunately, however, the night Zhu Min arrived at the camp, the German-Soviet war broke out. The enemy occupied Minsk before the children could retreat, whereafter they transported the children to a Nazi concentration camp. In the concentration camp, Zhu Min and her companions insisted on "fighting against" fascism despite torment from the enemy. They either took advantage of the enemy's inattention and poured water into the cartridge boxes to make the bullets damp, or they spit into or mixed elements such as sand with gunpowder while making bullets. Zhu Min and her companions did not escape from the Nazi concentration camp until early 1945, when they were liberated by the Soviet army.

"The Flying General" Tang Duo was the only Chinese pilot who fought with the Luftwaffe in the Soviet Union, Poland and Germany. He joined a fighter company of the Soviet Air Force during the Great Patriotic War. As deputy commander of the fighter company, he once led four attack planes flying at a very low altitude to destroy dozens of enemy planes, distinguishing himself and leading him to be praised as the "Chinese eagle" in the Soviet Union's Great Patriotic War. He also set a record of six times take-offs within a single day in the battle of liberation of East Prussia in the spring of 1945. Due to his brilliant achievements in war, he was awarded by the government of the Soviet Union the Order of Lenin, the Order of the Red Banner, the Order of the Red Star, the Order of the Patriotic War and many other orders and medals.

The Chinese people will never forget the assistance from the "old friends". Upon the outbreak of the Chinese People's War of Resistance

Against Japanese Aggression, the China Aid Volunteer Air Force from the Soviet Union composed of a large number of Soviet pilots came to China. Air Marshal Aleksej Sergejevič Blagoveščenski commanded a fighter plane company composed of Chinese and Soviet pilots in several aerial combats in China during the period from 1937 to 1938. When the Chinese city of Wuhan was hit by an air raid initiated by the Japanese army in May 1938, Blagoveščenski's company destroyed a total of 36 enemy planes, seven among which were shot down by him. Another air marshal, Nikola-jenko, once successfully undermined the Japanese army's plan of a dense bombardment in Hankou leading a team of pilots equal to only one-third of the enemy forces. During more than four years, the China Aid Volunteer Air Force from the Soviet Union produced 14 "Heroes of the Soviet Union".

In his articles published in the Belarus media, Xi Jinping shared the time-honored China-Belarus friendship with the world in an impressive and memorable way by telling the story of Marshal Zhu De's daughter, Zhu Min, and the stories of the pilots of the two countries who fought side by side.

In the eyes of Chinese readers, Zhu Min was the daughter of Marshal Zhu De; however, few of them know that she had experience fighting against German fascists with her friends in Belarus. In the memories of Belarusian readers, Blagoveščenski was their air marshal; however, they are unaware that he was "Captain Zhang Fei" in the Chinese people's hearts because he traveled to China to participate in air combat against Japanese aggressors. Skobelev, the curator of the Belarusian Great Patriotic War Museum, noted with emotion that, "In his article, President Xi told the story of how the Chinese people and the Belarusian people fought side-by-side in World War II and established a strong friendship, which was very useful for the Belarusians to gain an understanding of the history of the Chinese People's War of Resistance Against Japanese Aggression."

THE HUMANITARIAN SPIRIT LIGHTING UP THE DARKNESS

On July 7, 1937, the Japanese aggressors launched a brutal war of aggression against China, bringing an unprecedentedly dreadful disaster to the Chinese people. China was flooded with the flames of war and the smoke of gunpowder, and the Chinese people were plunged into an abyss of misery. It was a scene of utter desolation, full of the dead bodies of the starved and the murdered.

Japanese troops captured Nanjing on December 13, 1937, and they began the extremely brutal Nanjing Massacre. More than 300,000 Chinese compatriots were murdered, including a large number of children dying unnatural deaths and innumerable women who were raped. A third of the buildings in the city were damaged, and large quantities of property were looted. The Nanjing Massacre, committed by Japanese aggressors, was one of three major massacres during World War II. It was an atrocious crime against humanity, and it was a dark page in human history.

Nevertheless, what touches us is that during those days of bloody slaughter, Chinese compatriots helped and supported one another in defending their homeland, and many foreign friends protected the Nanjing residents and recorded the atrocities of the Japanese aggressors, despite the risks. German businessman John Rabe, Bernhard Arp Sindberg from Denmark, and American priest John Magee were among the foreign friends. The Chinese people will never forget their humanitarian spirit and brave and righteous acts.

– Speech at the National Memorial Day for Nanjing Massacre Victims (December 13, 2014).

Commentary

Even the dark night cannot cover a glimmer of light. On December 13, 1937, Japanese troops captured Nanjing and began the extremely brutal Nanjing Massacre. At the critical moment when the time-honored city of Nanjing was reduced to a "sea of death", the German friend John Rabe called together dozens of foreigners in China to establish the "NanKing Safety Zone", which sheltered approximately 200,000 Chinese people from slaughter during the massacre. He was therefore called the "Schindler of China". Despite the bombing by the Japanese army, Rabe not only resolutely stayed in Nanjing to protect the unarmed Chinese civilians, but he also composed *The Good Man of Nanking*, which devotes more than 2,400 pages to record the atrocities of the Japanese aggressors, and it has been rated as one of the most important and most detailed and accurate historical materials of the Nanjing Massacre.

It was also during that period, when Nanjing was stormed and captured, that the Danish friend Bernhard Arp Sindberg sheltered Chinese civilians in the Nanjing Jiangnan Cement Plant where he lived. In an effort to prevent the Japanese from entering the factory, Sindberg deliberately placed the flags of Denmark and Germany around the plant, and he also had a flag of Denmark of nearly 1,350 square meters painted on the roof of the workshop, "raising the biggest flag of Denmark in China". From mid-February 1938 through mid-March, he, together with his fellows, provided shelter for more than 15,000 civilians.

When the American friend John Magee, who regarded China as his "home", was in Nanjing, he secretly filmed the Japanese atrocities using a home video camera, leaving four reels of film that contain 105-min records of the atrocities. In 1946, he bravely took the seat of a witness in the international tribunal for the trial of Japanese war criminals in Tokyo, accusing the Japanese army of the bloody brutalities in Nanjing. Today, the precious video taken by Magee is still played continuously in the Memorial Hall of the Victims in Nanjing Massacre by Japanese Invaders.

Justice will never be evaded, and the humanitarian light will never be extinguished by darkness because it is the eternal hope of mankind. At China's first National Memorial Day for the Nanjing Massacre Victims, Xi Jinping, by reviewing the stories about how the Chinese people and the international friends stood side-by-side to defend Nanjing from aggression, he proclaimed to the world that we Chinese will never forget the invaluable support given by the peace-loving and justice-upholding countries, the peoples and international organizations in our fight against Japanese aggressors, much less forget the glory of their humanity.

At the state memorial ceremony, Xi Jinping stepped onto the memorial platform with Xia Shuqin, an 85-year-old massacre survivor, and Yuan Zeyu, a 13-year-old descendant of Nanjing Massacre victims, with his hand supporting Xia Shuqin. Together they unveiled a "ding" (a type of ancient Chinese cauldron symbolizing state power and prosperity) dedicated to the victims. The moral of the ding is that "we all should remember the bitter lessons of war," and we "should cherish and safeguard peace". The reason to remember history is not to prolong hatred, but to call upon every good-hearted person to stand on guard for peace.

THE CLOSE CONNECTION BETWEEN BRAZIL AND CHINESE TEA

"If you have a friend afar who knows your heart, distance cannot keep you two apart." You cannot find a verse more appropriate than this to describe the relationship between China and Brazil. Although the two countries are separated by oceans, the vast Pacific Ocean could not stop the process of friendly exchanges between the two peoples. Two hundred years ago, the first Chinese tea growers traveled across great geographical distance to Brazil to plant tea and teach their skills. At the Vienna International Exhibition held in 1873, the tea produced in Brazil was widely praised. The Chinese and Brazilian peoples have forged a sincere friendship over the years, which is like the hard work of the Chinese tea growers who plant hope, harvest pleasure and taste friendship. The Chinese painting master Zhang Daqian lived in Brazil for 17 years. His masterpiece *Ten Thousand Miles of the Yangtze River*, *Mount Huang*, and *Homesickness* were produced in the Bade Garden, his residence in Brazil.

- Carry Forward Traditional Friendship and Jointly Open up a New Chapter of Cooperation—Speech at the National Congress of Brazil (July 16, 2014).

Commentary

Many people associate the "Kingdom of Samba", Brazil, with coffee. However, few people know that as the world's largest coffee producer, Brazil, has "Chinese tea" as its first national drink. Here, Chinese tea is also an imported good, the same as coffee.

Brazil's tea planting history can be traced back to long ago. During the period from 1812 to 1819, a group of tea farmers, who had rich experience in tea planting, came to Rio de Janeiro, Brazil, from China via Macao, and they began to plant Chinese tea in a well-cultivated manner on a specially authorized field in Tijuca, Rio de Janeiro. Not only did they successfully plant tea in Brazil, they also taught the Brazilian people the skills of tea planting and production, making Brazil the third largest tea-producing country in the world, following China and Japan. This phase of history was even reproduced as a performance at the opening ceremony of the 2016 Rio Olympic Games.

With the help of Chinese tea farmers, Brazil's tea-planting industry boomed, with several other regions following Rio and becoming engaged in tea planting. In those days, the tea produced in Brazil not only met domestic demand, but it also successfully entered the global market. At that time, drinking tea was fashionable in Brazilian high society, and tea was once the national drink of Brazil. At the Vienna International Exhibition held in 1873, tea produced in Brazil won second place to Chinese tea.

Now, there is a sightseeing stand called the "Pavilion of China" in Tijuca Forest National Park in Rio. There visitors can experience a famous view of the city, which was built to commemorate the Chinese tea farmers who used to grow tea there. The "Pavilion of China" even appears in *Rio*, a film that is popular around the world.

The famous Chinese painter Zhang Daqian, who lived in Brazil for 17 years, built a celebrated garden—the Bade Garden—in a suburb of Sao Paulo. When he had just arrived in Brazil in early 1953, one day Zhang Daqian strolled along a hillside near his friend's home, where at that time was living temporarily, and he came up a scene that resembled his hometown of Chengdu Plain. As a result, he bought the land and took three years to build a Chinese-style garden covering an area of 145,200 square meters. There are many persimmon trees planted in the garden, and it is said in China that the persimmon tree has eight virtues. "Eight virtues" refers to "八德" (Ba De) in Chinese characters, hence the name Bade Garden. According to the *Miscellaneous Morsels from Youyang* by Duan Chengshi, a writer in the Tang Dynasty, the persimmon tree has seven virtues: first, it can live long; second, it provides shade; third, there is no bird's nest; fourth, it is not wormy; fifth, its autumn leaf can be used for play; sixth, it can give joy to guests; and seventh, its fallen leaf is big and can be used to write on. Zhang Daqian added the eighth virtue: its leaves can be decocted for treating gastric diseases (another version suggests that Zhang deemed the persimmon tree a subject worth painting).

As a Brazilian proverb goes, friendship is like wine, the mellower it is, the more aromatic it smells. The friendly exchanges between China and Brazil confirm this idea. "Nothing, not even mountains and oceans, can separate people with shared goals and vision." This point was vividly conveyed by Xi Jinping in his speech, during which he reviewed the history of friendly exchanges between the two peoples, and he used the industrious cultivation by the Chinese tea farmers as a metaphor for the sincere friendship between the peoples in their long history.

To look back on history is to embrace a brighter future. During Xi's visit to Brazil, there was an episode that reflected the increasingly intimate relationship between China and Brazil: after arriving in Brazil, Xi attended the welcoming ceremony under the escort of Brazil's cavalry. Such a high level of official welcoming was not been seen in Brazil for years. The Latin America tour in 2014 was Xi's second trip to Latin America and the Caribbean as Chinese President. Receiving great attention from China, Brazil is the first leg of Xi's ongoing Latin America tour. In the speech, he shared touching stories and showed sincerity, making him a foreign leader who won the most applause at the National Congress of Brazil.

CHAPTER 9

Personal Experiences: "Eternal Belief"

"The Most Memorable Is Hangzhou"

Hangzhou is a renowned historical and cultural city and a center of business and trade in China. Famous for Bai Juyi, a leading Chinese poet in the Tang Dynasty, and Su Dongpo, a popular poet in the Song Dynasty who spent time in Hangzhou, as well as the West Lake and the Grand Canal, Hangzhou has a fascinating history and rich and enchanting cultural heritage. Hangzhou is also an innovative and vibrant city with booming e-commerce. Just click the mouse in Hangzhou, and you connect the whole world. Hangzhou is also a leader in ecological conservation. Its green hills and clear lakes and rivers delight the eye on sunny days and present a special view on rainy days. Hangzhou is imbued with a charm unique to the south of the Yangtze River that has been fostered over many generations.

I spent 6 years working in Zhejiang Province and was personally involved in its development endeavor. So I am familiar with everything here, its land and its people. In China, there are many cities like Hangzhou which have gone through great changes and achieved tremendous development over the decades. Millions of ordinary Chinese families have changed their lives through hard work. When they are added up, these small changes have become a powerful force driving China's development and progress. What we see here in Hangzhou showcases what has been achieved in the great course of reform and opening up upon which China has embarked.

© People's Publishing House 2020
People's Daily, Department of Commentary,
Narrating China's Governance,
https://doi.org/10.1007/978-981-32-9178-2_9

- A New Starting Point for China's Development, A New Blueprint for Global Growth—Speech at the Opening Ceremony of the B20 Summit (September 3, 2016).

Commentary

"Scenic splendor southeast of River Blue, and capital of ancient Kingdom Wu, Qiantang is as flourishing as ever." Hangzhou is one of the six ancient capitals in ancient China. It was the capital of the state of Wuyue during the Five Dynasties and Ten Kingdoms period. Here, Liangzhu culture, Wuyue culture, Southern Song culture, and Ming–Qing culture have formed a complete series of cultural developments, which have not only left numerous places of interest but also nurtured many talents in literature and writing. Bai Juyi composed more than 3,600 poems during his lifetime, among which more than 200 are on the landscape of West Lake. He defended and dredged the lake and re-dredged the six wells, so that the civilians could live by the lake in peace and enjoy their work. This also established the physical feature of West Lake, which he described as follows: "facing the city while hugged from behind by mountains." Su Dongpo, who created the delicacy "Braised Dongpo Pork" and is known for the famous line, "West Lake may be compared to the Xi Shi (one of the renowned Four Beauties of ancient China), whether she is richly adorned or plainly dressed," capitalized upon swamps and turnip grass to build a long causeway crossing the lake from north to south. With six bridges and nine pavilions, the causeway was covered with peach, willow, and hibiscus trees, making West Lake a feast for the eyes. The history of Hangzhou is a history of a city that achieved distinction through West Lake and prospered due to the Beijing–Hangzhou Grand Canal. Well suited for sea transportation and inland navigation, Hangzhou has flourished in commerce since ancient times, and it developed into a megacity with a population of more than one million as early as the Southern Song Dynasty. Today, it has become a central city of the Yangtze River delta, serving as the economic center, cultural center, and science and education center of Zhejiang Province.

In 2002, Xi Jinping began to head the administration of Zhejiang Province. In the next 5 years, he developed an indissoluble bond with Hangzhou. It can be said that Xi Jinping is not only a witness of the changes in Hangzhou but a promoter of Hangzhou's great development. In 2003, shortly after he assumed the role of Party Secretary of Zhejiang Province, he led a special investigation in Hangzhou and urged the construction of a cultural province. After that, he published an article entitled *To Strengthen the Protection of West Lake Culture* in the special column "Fresh Ideas of Zhejiang" of *Zhejiang Daily* under the pen name "Zhexin". The article stated that "West Lake is immersed in historical stories and instinct with culture," and stressed that "Hangzhou should play a leading role and do better in protecting cultural relics, extending the city context and carrying forward the historical culture." After West Lake became open to the public free of charge, he made three suggestions to the management department of the lake. First, the public toilets by the lake should be open for free 24 × 7. Second, rubber tires should be installed at the bow of the pleasure boats to protect the bridge openings from being damaged by the passing boats. Third, the benches should be placed at certain intervals in the scenic areas. He considered that "Many lovers like strolling along West Lake. If the benches are set too close, they will feel uncomfortable." It is thus evident that Xi Jinping conducted a thorough investigation of Hangzhou.

"To cure a disease, one should treat its root causes; to fix a problem, one should target its source." While the world economy is entering a new era of "mediocrity", how can we reinvigorate the "lake"? At the Opening Ceremony of the B20 Summit, Xi exemplified China's great development with Hangzhou's success story. This not only inspired the world's confidence in the economy but also conveyed a message to the G20: "When added up, small changes will become a powerful force driving our development and progress," and only if we join hands, can we "ensure that growth and development [will] benefit all countries and peoples and the livelihood of all people."

If we were to say that the G20 Antalya Summit held in 2015 made an accurate assessment of the health of the world economy, then the B20 Hangzhou Summit in 2016 came up with an integrated prescription to address both the symptoms and the root causes. To this point, Xi proposed four key words: innovative, open, interconnected, and inclusive. The reason why this "Chinese Plan", rooted in China's reform and opening up practice, is able to boost confidence in the world economy and win a broad consensus in the international community is, as Xi has noted, "It is a pursuit not to establish China's own sphere of influence but to support the common development of all countries. It is meant to build not China's own backyard garden but a garden shared by all countries."

THE CHANGES IN LIANGJIAHE VILLAGE

Toward the end of the 1960s when I was in my teens, I was sent from Beijing to work as a farmer in the small village of Liangjiahe near Yan'an of Shaanxi Province, where I spent 7 years. At that time, the villagers and I lived in "earth caves" and slept on "earth beds". Life was very hard. There was no meat in our diet for months. I knew what the villagers wanted the most. Later I became the village's party secretary and began to lead the villagers in production. I understood their needs. One thing I wished most at the time was to make it possible for the villagers to have meat and have it often. However, it was very difficult for such a wish to come true in those years.

At the Spring Festival early this year, I returned to the village. I saw blacktop roads. Now living in houses with bricks and tiles, the villagers had Internet access. Elderly folks had basic old-age care, and all villagers had medical care coverage. Children were in school. Of course, meat was readily available. This made me keenly aware that the Chinese Dream is after all a dream of the people. We can fulfill the Chinese Dream only when we link it to our people's yearning for a better life.

– Speech at the Welcoming Dinner Hosted by Washington Local Governments and Friendly Organizations in the United States (September 22, 2015).

Commentary

At the foot of the mountains on the Northern Shaanxi Plateau, more than 60 km away from Yan'an, there is small village called Liangjiahe. At the beginning of 1969, the small village ushered in a special team—an educated youth team that included Xi Jinping, who was barely 16 years old at the time, and 14 other teenagers from Beijing Bayi High School. They came to Liangjiahe on foot, and this marked the start of Xi's 7 years of farming life.

Life was tough on the loessland. At that time, there was no electricity in the village, and Xi had to live with five other educated youths in an "earth cave" and sleep on an "earth bed". In the earth cave, he was bitten all over his body; thus, he had no other way to eliminate the fleas but to dust insecticide under the bed mat. At the very beginning, he was incapable of even the most basic farm work such as digging, growing corn, and cutting wheat, thus he followed and learned from the villagers. In those years, Xi performed all types of hard labor and barely rested—carrying manure, hauling a coal cart, farming, and building dykes. The villager Zhang Weipang recalled, "It was a rough time for Xi Jinping, as rough as we villagers lived."

Life was also full on the loessland. The farming life in Liangjiahe enhanced Xi's perseverance, making him "able to walk 5 km on the mountainous path with two dangling baskets filled with almost one hundred kilograms of wheat on a shoulder-pole," and it taught him various skills such as "making noodles, steaming dumplings, pickling cabbage." The village gave him a stage upon which to display his talents. Growing into a capable and hardworking young man in the eyes of the villagers of Liangjiahe, Xi was called "a tough boy" by the locals. By gaining their trust, he was elected Village Party Secretary. Reading from a newspaper that some villages in Sichuan Province were pioneering in gathering cooking gas, he immediately traveled to Sichuan at his own expense to learn from their experience. After returning to Liangjiahe, he led the villagers in building a methane tank for gathering cooking gas, the first in northern Shaanxi, helping the villagers solve the difficulties they faced in terms of cooking and lighting. In a bid to prevent erosion, he led the farmers to reinforce the riverbank in the slack season of winter. Every time, he took the initiative to stand barefoot in the icy water to break the ice and clear the dam foundation. In addition, he helped the village to find a mill and a tailor shop, and he organized a cooperative of blacksmiths, which improved the locals' lives.

After being recommended for enrollment at Tsinghua University in 1975, the villagers lined up to bid him farewell, many of whom wept at his parting. They even presented him with a framed certificate that read, "A Good Secretary for the Poor and Lower-middle Peasants," which conveyed their respect for him. On the eve of the Spring Festival in February 2015, Xi Jinping, as navigator of the 1.3 billion Chinese people, revisited Liangjiahe. On the occasion of the reunion with the villagers with whom he had lived and struggled, Xi said with emotion, "Although I left that year, I left my heart here."

As the president of a large country and standing in the middle of the world stage, Xi Jinping introduced China to the world without magnificent description or statistical figures but only through his own story—one between him and the most significant village in his life. Such thinking stems from Xi's constant "original aspiration". What happened in Liangjiahe was but a microcosm of the progress China has made.

Never forget why you started, and you can accomplish your mission. Seven years of toiling alongside the villagers allowed Xi to grow and to hold his faith more firmly. He once recalled in an article, "I arrived at the loessland as a 15-year-old teenager, who was slightly lost, and I left as a 22-year-old man with determined aspirations and self-confidence." Such transition was promoted by his constant original aspiration that gestated on the Northern Shaanxi Plateau: to serve the people, to be of one mind with the people, to bear hardships with the people, and to work together with the people. Liangjiahe is the place where he came to understand the words "the people", and Liangjiahe's villagers, for whom he has never stopped pining, are the people who enlightened him as to the meaning of those words.

A NIGHT SPEECH AT YINGTAI

To understand today's China and predict tomorrow's China, one has to know China's past and culture. Modern Chinese people's thinking and the Chinese government's strategy of national governance are steeped in traditional Chinese culture. The Chinese people have cherished national independence, unity, and dignity since ancient times. The Chinese government must comply with the people's will, firmly safeguard national sovereignty, security and territorial integrity, maintain ethnic solidarity and social stability, and unswervingly pursue the path of peaceful development. China and the US have different national conditions, history and culture, and development paths, and they are in different phases of development. The two countries should understand and respect each other and live in harmony by focusing on similarities and allowing divergences. It is inevitable for the two countries to have some divergences, yet this is not the mainstream of the bilateral relations. Both governments should serve as stabilizers and properly handle related divergences.

– Speech at a meeting with President Barack Obama at Zhongnanhai (November 11, 2014).

Commentary

In the evening in Zhongnanhai, the lake water rippled, and the tree shadows flickered. Xi Jinping greeted Obama in front of Yingtai, and the two heads of state shook hands warmly and exchanged greetings. On Yingtai Bridge, the two heads of state leaned on the railing overlooking the pavilions scattered around under glorious lights. Xi Jinping briefed Obama on the history of Yingtai, which has witnessed the vicissitudes of China for centuries. Xi Jinping said that knowing the modern history of China is of great importance to understanding contemporary Chinese people's ideals and paths of development.

Xi explained to Obama that Yingtai was built during the Ming Dynasty, and during the Qing Dynasty, it served as the emperor's business office and a place to escape the summer heat and host receptions. Yingtai witnessed many historic events. The Qing Emperor Kangxi made policies to pacify civil strife and recover Taiwan from the Ming loyalists. Emperor Guangxu, who launched the Hundred Days of Reform when the dynasty began to fall into decay, was imprisoned there by the Empress Dowager Cixi after his modernizing reform failed. Obama replied that China and the US shared that aspect of history—that reform nearly always encounters resistance and demands courage to push forward.

It was an unforgettable night. In the moonlight, the two heads of state strolled while chatting with great interest. The scheduled 90-min banquet lasted nearly 2 h, and the 30-min tea break lasted nearly 1 h. When Xi Jinping said, "Let's go to dinner. I do not want to have my guest chat with me in hunger," Obama said, "I would like to talk to you about a few more questions." The wonderful dialog made Peter, Obama's official photographer who sniffled all night due to the cold weather, reluctant to go indoors. Five hours passed by in a flash. The meeting in Yingtai did not end until after 11 pm due to the prolonged discussion. Just before parting, Obama summed up his feelings, saying, "Tonight, I have obtained an unprecedentedly comprehensive and in-depth understanding of the history and conception of governance of the CPC as well as your thoughts."

The talk at Yingtai was a continuation of the open-ended informal summit at the Annenberg Retreat in California. Why did Xi relay the history to Obama in the cold wind? Because only by learning about China's history from its suffering and fighting against aggression to becoming a rising nation on the way toward development, can one understand why China assiduously pursues the centenary dream of national rejuvenation. Only by gaining insight into the exploration, struggle, and decisions made by China to stand firmer and stronger among the world's nations can one understand why the Chinese people choose Marxism, choose the CPC, and choose the road of socialism with Chinese characteristics. Simply put, "Knowing the modern history of China is of great importance to understanding today's Chinese people's and their development path." The night talk at Yingtai focused on history, but the subject was not history itself. The aim was to discuss the present—to build a new model of major-country relations between China and the US. From "the retreat meeting" to "the talk at Yingtai" and then to "the autumn reunion in the White House", the presidents of China and the US are jointly writing a new chapter in the history of international relations through communication, dialog, and mutual trust.

APEC BLUE

These days, the first thing I do in the morning is to check the air quality in Beijing, hoping that the smog won't be too bad, so that our distinguished guests will be more comfortable while you're here. Fortunately, with the efforts of our people and the cooperation of the weather, the air quality in Beijing in the recent couple of days is much better than before. Well, this may be a premature conclusion, but I do hope and pray that the weather tomorrow will turn out just fine! The improved air quality, which is not easy to secure, is the result of the combined efforts of nearby provinces and cities and relevant government agencies. I want to say "thank you" to all those who have helped to make it a reality. And I want to thank the APEC meeting for prompting us to be even more determined to protect the environment. We will do a better job at protecting the environment in the future. Some people refer to the clear Beijing sky these days as "APEC blue" and say it is beautiful but temporary, and it will be gone soon after the APEC meeting. I hope and believe that, with persistent efforts, APEC blue will be here to stay.

– Toast at the Welcome Dinner of the 22nd APEC Economic Leaders' Meeting (November 10, 2014).

Commentary

Xi Jinping has coined many new phrases such as "where did the time go", "pretty strenuous," and "APEC blue". These popular phrases are like an array of hyperlinks; a click on any of them will produce a vivid story.

Notwithstanding the multiple rounds of attacks of smog in October 2014, Beijing's sky was blue in early November. The monitoring data showed that the air quality in Beijing was at an excellent level from November 1 to 12, except for the 4, when the air was slightly polluted. During that period, the APEC Economic Leaders' Meeting was held in Beijing. Thus, Chinese netizens coined the phrase "APEC blue". Although the phrase was somewhat one of ridicule, it embodied the people's expectation of the blue sky.

In fact, to ensure the APEC meeting's good air quality, the Chinese government implemented measures such as closing factories and exerting production restrictions on factories in North China and the surrounding areas, enforcing odd–even day vehicle prohibition in some cities, giving government workers in Beijing the week off, and conducting intensive supervision. In a sense, it was the special measures issued in the special period that turned the sky above Beijing blue. Some netizens questioned this: "Is it a bit formalistic to shut down the factories, turn off the boilers and give Beijing a week off?" However, Xi Jinping deliberated on the matter, "It is actually an attempt to promote collaborative governance by capitalizing on the opportunity derived from the APEC. Through joint remediation by multiple provinces and municipalities, we eventually reduced pollution emissions by more than 30%. This helped us accumulate ideas about the beneficial experience for both the adjustment of the industrial structure and the industrial layout in the future. These were pragmatic efforts that were done not only for the meeting."

Immediately after the APEC meeting, Xi traveled to Brisbane to attend the G20 Summit. On the plane, when the accompanying reporter referred to the popular phrase, "APEC blue", Xi offered a dialectical remark: "A bad thing could turn into a good thing." He added, "After we realized the harm of smog and reached a consensus, we made active efforts to eliminate smog. This process aroused and enhanced our awareness of environmental protection. Is it not a good thing?"

As Mr. Lu Xun said, "Only the one who dares to face the problem has the courage to think, to speak out, to carry out initiatives and to take the consequences." Xi Jinping's speaking of "APEC blue" of his own accord on such an important occasion as the APEC meeting incarnated his style of governance, "not to sidestep conflicts and not to conceal problems," and he even conveyed a response to the people's expectations and showed the world his resolution to lead the government to curb environmental pollution together with the people.

In early 2014, Xi Jinping especially took up smog elimination when he made an investigation into Beijing. He stated, "We should intensify efforts to control air pollution. The primary task of tackling smog pollution and improving air quality is to control PM2.5. We must take major measures from multiple perspectives. For example, we should reduce the use of coal, strictly control the growth of car ownership, adjust the industrial structure, strengthen environmental management, carry out inter-regional coordinated pollution prevention and control, and promote the control of environmental pollution by law. We should also focus on the critical fields, strictly carry out index assessment, strengthen supervision over environmental law enforcement and seriously conduct responsibility investigation."

GULING IN HIS HEART

In the spring of 1992, when I was working in Fuzhou city in Fujian province, I came across an article titled "My Guling" in a newspaper. It told a story about an American couple who tried but failed to revisit a place called Guling in China, which had a special place in their heart. Milton Gardner, the husband, was a Professor of Physics at the University of California. In 1901, his parents took him to China, and he had a happy childhood in Guling, Fuzhou, which left him with unforgettable memories. In 1911, the family returned to California. In the decades that followed, Milton Gardner longed to revisit his childhood home. However, he could not make it due to failing health. In the final days of his life, he kept uttering "Kuling, Kuling". His wife had no idea where this Kuling was, but still she went to China several times, hoping to find the place that meant so much to her late husband. However, her efforts were in vain until finally a Chinese student in the United States helped her locate Guling. After I read their story, I immediately contacted Mrs. Gardner through the relevant departments and invited her to visit Guling. I met her 4 months later in August 1992 and arranged for her to visit the place her husband had missed so much. There, she met nine childhood friends of Milton Gardner, all in their 90s, and she listened to them reminiscing about the past. It was a happy occasion. Mrs. Gardner was so excited that she finally fulfilled her husband's last wish. And she said that she would cherish this bond of friendship between her husband and the people of China because after seeing for herself the beautiful Guling and the warmth of the Chinese people, she now understood why her husband had been so deeply attached to China. I am sure there are many such touching stories between our two peoples. We should further strengthen our people-to-people exchanges and build even stronger public support for mutually beneficial China–US cooperation.

– Work Together for a Bright Future of China–US Cooperative Partnership—Speech at the Welcoming Luncheon Hosted by Friendly Organizations in the United States (February 15, 2012).

Commentary

Kuling, a place in Milton's heart, is a symbol of a longstanding friendship. However, half a world from each other, Guling and Muscatine came to have a connection in this speech. Having happened 20 years prior, the anecdote about Guling told by Xi Jinping is an epitome of the China–US friendship that is well established and vigorously developing. Through this touching story, Xi told the world that the engagement and support of the people are always the basis of friendship among nations.

Xi Jinping's expressed eager expectations for cultural and people-to-people exchanges and regional cooperation between China and the US. After Mrs. Gardiner's visit to Guling, Xi Jinping sent her a letter of congratulations, in which he said, "I believe, through the article titled "My Guling" by Mr. Zhong Han and published in the *People's Daily*, the touching story about your husband will widely spread in Fuzhou and even further. It will encourage more people to continue to make efforts to enhance the friendship between our two peoples." When Xi later visited the US for his trip to Muscatine in 2012, he told his old friends, "The development of China–US relations did relies on the enthusiastic engagement and vigorous support of the people of the two countries. And the advance of the mutual understanding and friendship between the two peoples will determine the future of our bilateral relations."

Epilogue: To Be a Good "Storyteller" of China's Stories

Lu Xinning

Some scholars believe that politics can be divided into sensational politics and rational politics. "Telling stories" can be employed as an approach to interpreting ideas and provoking thinking, regardless of whether they are shared in the context of diplomatic activities or literary works and speeches. This approach can even help effect audiences, draw them closer to the speaker, and eventually connect them with the speaker in terms of both mind and heart. This can be described as a combination of rationality and sensibility.

"Profound truth should be conveyed to audiences through stories to move them and persuade them." As we studied President Xi Jinping's series of important speeches, what became clear was that storytelling is helpful in "conveying truth". We can transform profound thoughts and abstract principles into colorful stories and vivid examples. Such transformation makes our expressions down-to-earth and literary, and they can widen an audiences' scope of vision and reveal the speaker's accomplishments in communication.

Because of this, we generated the idea of exploring the mysteries of the anecdotes and sayings of Xi Jinping. Designing the structure and layout of this book, Yang Zhenwu, the President of the *People's Daily*, assigned me to lead the Editorial Department to compile this book. He even wrote a preface to the book, in which he summarized and expounded upon Xi Jinping's method of telling stories and the significance of the method, and further reflected on China's means of reform and development and great-power diplomacy and the people's means of self-cultivation implied by his stories.

As "the first speaker" of China's stories, the stories Xi Jinping tells contain rich connotations, and he demonstrates excellent skill in telling them.

© People's Publishing House 2020
People's Daily, Department of Commentary,
Narrating China's Governance,
https://doi.org/10.1007/978-981-32-9178-2

In this book, we also provide "further reading" sections after each story for two purposes. The first is to enrich the story, to supplement the story with more detail, and provide a detailed description of the people and things in the story. The second is to return to the original context of the speech in which he told the story, including when and to whom he told it, so that the reader can comprehend the story on the basis of its context and background. Our aim is to help the reader obtain a more comprehensive, intuitive, and deepening understanding of "Narrating China's Governance".

Joseph Samuel Nye, a Professor from Harvard University, once said with emotion, "The leader of China is a master of storytelling." It can be said that storytelling is also an important soft power. Another reason why we interpret the stories told by Xi Jinping is that we expect to have more people become the "storytellers" of China's stories. In the age of the Internet, everyone is an "outlet of value," and in the age of the global village, everyone is a "business card for his nation." What is more, this great era and time of great change enable the Chinese people to have very rich possibilities and more colorful life experiences. Dreams and struggles, successes and setbacks, and laughter and tears are the themes of the most inspiring stories. As long as we acquire the skill of discovering and telling the stories of ourselves and those around us, we can show the world a real, intuitive, and vivid China.

"Moving and persuading the reader" is a task of commentators of the Party newspaper. Therefore, telling good stories and telling stories well are what the editors of this book should learn and pursue. With respect to this book, the "Further Reading" following each story was written by Zhang Tie, Fan Zhengwei, Cao Pengcheng, Li Zheng, Li Bin, and Chen Ling. They are all from the Editorial Department of the People's Daily. Li Chunsheng, Vice President of the *People's Daily* headed the editing and design of the book. We hope this book will enlighten the reader in terms of thought and expression, so they can find a "golden key" to enable soulful communication, connect with the audience emotionally, and be understood by both China and the rest of the world.

(By the Deputy Editor-in-chief of the *People's Daily*).